THE REMINISCENCES OF CAPTAIN GRONOW

MARQUIS OF WORCESTER. LADY JERSEY. CLANRONALD MACDONALD. LADY WORCESTER.

THE FIRST QUADRILLE AT ALMACK'S.

Gronow wrote his reminiscences in the early 1860s when he was an old man. They were hugely popular.

After leaving Eton he was commissioned in the First Guards (Grenadiers) in December 1812. He served in the Peninsula War and, in June 1815, he played truant from his regimental duties in London to fight at Quatre Bras and Waterloo. He was with the allied armies in Paris when the Bourbons were restored. Thereafter he lived the life of a dandy. "He committed the greatest follies without in the slightest disturbing the points of his shirt collar." As a raconteur he is superb, with vivid descriptions of balls and battles, of duellists, gamblers, dukes and opera singers. Above all, he was a connoisseur of the eccentric and erratic, and he lived in an age when this taste could be gratified to the full.

The R.S. Surtees Society's edition combines in a single volume Gronow's *"Anecdotes of the Camp, the Court and the Clubs at the Close of the Last War with France"* and *"Recollections and Anecdotes"*.

It is based on the limited edition of 1889 and contains 17 full-page colour plates, including Joseph Grego's remarkable aquatints of etchings from original and contemporary sources.

Price **£14.95,** packing and postage included. Write to The Hon. Mrs. Robert Pomeroy, Rockfield House, Nunney, nr. Frome, Somerset. Your cheque should be made payable to "The R.S. Surtees Society".

PLAIN or RINGLETS

Miss Rosa McDermott was on the make. She had two admirers. One was best pleased when her hair was dressed plain, the other preferred it in ringlets. So there were changes of style while Mamma made financial investigations—and there was an exciting moment when both Miss and Mamma had hopes of the Marquess of Marchhare.

The description of Brighton ("Roseberry Rocks") at the beginning of the railway age is most entertaining. (Surtees had been a frequent visitor since the 1820s and died there in 1864.) It includes a vivid account of a race meeting and the fleecing of a banker's foolish son.

There are three first rate hunting characters—Jock Haggish, probably drawn from the Duke of Buccleuch's huntsman Williamson, and Jovey Jessop and his Jug. Jovey Jessop was an excellent fellow and an excellent M.F.H. but he suffered from too much hospitality, mostly his own. He had a shock when he consulted a London specialist. So the Jug came to live with him to take the brunt of the drinking.

The R.S. Surtees Society's edition of *Plain or Ringlets?* which it is intended shall be available by the end of **March, 1986**, will reproduce in colour the 13 full-page hand-coloured plates from the first (1860) edition, printed from engravings on steel by **John Leech.** Sets of these plates will be available separately. The text will be a facsimile of the first edition, slightly enlarged, and will include 45 black and white illustrations, also by **John Leech.**

The cover will have the same pictorial stampings as the first edition. In size and format *Plain or Ringlets?* will be similar to the Society's earlier Surtees publications. **Molly Keane** has agreed to write an Introduction.

Pre-publication prices

For those who subscribe for *Plain or Ringlets?* **before 1st December, 1985:**

(*a*) **£10.75** for books which are collected and
(*b*) **£12.70** (including p. & p.) for books which are posted.

A list of those subscribing **before 1st December, 1985,** will be printed at the end of the book.

The post-publication price will be £14.95.

Subscribers collecting their books will be notified when they are available at J. A. Allen & Co., 1 Lower Grosvenor Place, Buckingham Palace Road, London S.W.1.

All cheques will be acknowledged. All pre-publication money will be kept in a separate *Ringlets* bank account and will be returned in the event of publication not going ahead.

Write to The Hon. Mrs. Robert Pomeroy, Rockfield House, Nunney, nr. Frome, Somerset. Your cheque should be made payable to "The R.S. Surtees Society".

BEAU BRUMMEL IN DEEP CONVERSATION WITH THE DUCHESS OF RUTLAND. COMTE DE St. ANTONIO. PRINCESS ESTERHAZY. SIR GEORGE WARRENDER. COUNT St. ALDICONDE.

SKETCH OF A BALL AT ALMACKS, 1815.

THE

Reminiscences and Recollections

OF

CAPTAIN GRONOW

BEING

"Celebrities of London and Paris"

and

"Last Recollections"

THE R.S. SURTEES SOCIETY

First published in this edition in 1985
by The R.S. Surtees Society
Rockfield House
Nunney
Nr. Frome, Somerset.

ISBN 0 9507697 9 7

Printed and bound in Great Britain by
Butler & Tanner Ltd, Frome and London

CONTENTS.

LIST OF ILLUSTRATIONS,

NEWLY ETCHED FROM ORIGINAL AND CONTEMPORARY DESIGNS BY JOSEPH GREGO.

VOLUME THE SECOND.

CAPTAIN GRONOW'S RECOLLECTIONS AND ANECDOTES.

ALMACK'S IN 1815.—The personages delineated in the frontispiece are well worthy of notice, both from the position they held in the fashionable world, and from their being represented with great truth and accuracy. On the left, the man with the red face, laughing at Brummell, is Charles, Marquis of Queensberry; the great George himself, the admirable Crichton of the age, comes next, in a *dégagé* attitude, with his fingers in his waistcoat pocket. His neckcloth is inimitable, and must have cost him much time and trouble to arrive at such perfection. He is talking earnestly to the charming Duchess of Rutland, who was a Howard, and mother to the present Duke. The tall man, in a black coat, who is preparing to waltz with Princess Esterhazy, so long ambassadress of Austria in London, is the Comte de St. Antonio, afterwards Duke of Canizzaro. He resided many years in England, was a very handsome man, and a great lady-killer, and married an English heiress, Miss Johnson. The stout gentleman waltzing with the Russian ambassadress, Countess, afterwards Princess Lieven, is Baron Neümann, at that time secretary to the Austrian embassy. He was afterwards minister at Florence, and married a daughter of the Duke of Beaufort's. We next behold, in a wonderful light green coat, black tights, and a crushed hat, the late Sir George Warrender, the famous epicure, whose name was pronounced by Sir Joseph Copley to be really Sir George Provender. The worthy Baronet is talking to the handsome Comte de St. Aldegonde, afterwards a general, and at this period aide-de-camp to Louis Philippe, then Duke of Orleans.

The original sketch was given to Brummell by the artist who executed it; and it was highly prized by the king of the dandies. It was purchased at the sale of his effects in Chapel Street by the person who gave it to me.

THE DUKE OF WELLINGTON AND THE CAVALRY. —About three weeks after the battle of Waterloo I received orders from the Horse Guards to join my battalion in London. Two of my brother-officers who had gone over to Paris, Tom Brooke and Hunter, the adjutant, who were to accompany me, requested me to return by way of Brussels, as they were very anxious to see the field of Waterloo. I complied with their request, and acted as their cicerone. On the following day we arrived in Brussels, and dined, a few days afterwards, with General Sir George Cooke, who had commanded our division, and lost an arm. He was still suffering from his wound, and was living at the hotel where supper had been ordered for the Emperor Napoleon, in anticipation of his certain triumph on the 18th.

Sir George observed to us that it was lucky for Lord Uxbridge that the field had been won by us; for had this not been the case, he would have got into an awkward scrape for having engaged the cavalry without orders from the Duke. From what Sir George seemed to think, it was evidently the Duke's intention to keep the cavalry in hand, and perfectly fresh, so that they might have charged the French squadrons when the latter had exhausted themselves in their attacks on our squares. To corroborate this opinion, he told us an anecdote of the war in Spain, which may be interesting, as showing how opposed the Duke was to the harum-scarum custom of our cavalry officers, who hurled their men at full gallop on the enemy, without supports, and without any actual plan or intimation beyond the ardour of a sportsman going at a five-barred gate.

He stated, when Sir Stapleton Cotton went out to take the command of the cavalry, at his first interview with Lord Wellington, his chief addressed him as follows:—"General Cotton, I am glad to see you in command of the cavalry; and I wish you to bear in mind that cavalry should be always held well in hand; that your men and horses should not be used up in wild and useless charges, but put forward when you are sure that their onset will have a decisive effect. Above all, remember that you had better not engage, as a general rule, unless you see an opportunity of attacking the French with a superior force. In Spain, the Germans, the 14th Light Dragoons, and perhaps the 12th, under Fred. Ponsonby, were the only regiments that knew their duty and did not get into scrapes of every description."

THE DUKE AT CARLTON HOUSE.—The Duke of Wellington dined frequently with the Prince Regent, who, when he had finished his iced punch and a bottle of sherry, began to be garrulous. The Regent would invariably talk about the battle of Waterloo, and speak of the way in which *he* had charged the French with the Household Brigade: upon one occasion he was so far gone that he had the temerity to tell the Duke he had completely bowled over the French cavalry commanded by Marshal Ney. This was too much for the Duke to swallow, and he said, "I have heard you, sir, say so before: but I did not witness this marvellous charge. Your Royal Highness must know that the French cavalry are the best in Europe."

At this same dinner Sir Watkyns William Wynn asked the illustrious Duke whether he had a good view of the battle of Waterloo, whereupon the Baronet got the following laconic reply, "I generally like to see what I am about."

THE DUKE AND THE AUTHOR.—As everything connected with the Duke of Wellington is received with pleasure by the public, and as what I am going to relate is well known to many of my contemporaries, who have often urged me to put it into print, I am encouraged to relate an anecdote in which I played a prominent part, and which, though it happened forty-five years ago, made so deep an impression on my mind that I can narrate the circumstances as correctly as if they had occurred yesterday.

After leaving the Guards in 1821, I spent some time in Paris, where several of my friends had established themselves, and we all pronounced it to be the most delighful city in the world. I remember Luttrell, at a dinner where several alliterative toasts were given, such as London and Liberty, Edinburgh and Education, giving as his toast, Paris and Pocket-money. That most agreeable of men was seldom wrong in anything that he said; and in those days, as we all possessed plenty of the second ingredient of his "sentiment," we passed a most agreeable time, and perhaps lived "not wisely but too well;" at all events we enjoyed ourselves immensely.

In the midst of this very pleasant existence, I happened to call, one morning, upon the Princess M***, who lived in the Rue Basse du Rempart. No sooner had we shaken hands than she began speaking of the Duke of Wellington, who had arrived for a few days to see the King, and who was then about to leave Paris. She asked me if I was aware that I was no favourite with his Grace, and that he had even spoken of me in no measured terms. I replied that I had not the honour of knowing the Duke personally, and that my position was too humble a one to attract his notice. "You are mistaken," said Madame de M * * *; "he has doubtless heard very unfavourable reports of your character, for he has warned young Paul Lieven to beware of forming any intimacy with a man addicted to gambling and the society of opera-dancers and actresses, as such an acquaintance might not only lead him astray now, but be very detrimental to his prospects in after-life."

After hearing this agreeable communication, I lost no time in calling on my intimate friend, Captain Hesse, a natural son of the Duke of York's, and who was at that time an officer in the 18th Hussars. I related to my *fidus Achates* what had been told me by the Princess, and asked his advice as to the line of conduct I ought to pursue.

Hesse, who was personally well known to the Duke, offered to call at the English Embassy, where his Grace was staying, and ask for some explanation of so unwarrantable an attack. Unluckily, the great man had left for London, with Lord Fitzroy Somerset, that very morning. Hesse and I, therefore, concocted a letter to the Duke, in which I entreated his Grace to tell me if the lady's report was correct, as it appeared to me incomprehensible that a person of his exalted station should have thus attacked the private character of a man totally unknown to him.

This letter was duly forwarded to London, but did not reach the Duke there; for on his arrival in town he had found an invitation from the Prince Regent to pass some days with him at the Pavilion at Brighton, where my letter was placed in his hands. His Grace, with that promptitude for which he was always so remarkable, replied to me in a letter of four pages. I regret that this document, upon which I always placed a high value, is no longer in my hands. I lent it to Count d'Orsay, who was anxious to have a copy of it, and notwithstanding that a strict search has been made, since his death, amongst the papers that he left behind him, in the possession of his sister, the Duchesse de Grammont, I have not been able to recover a document of so much value to me and to society: for it expresses the opinions of a man whose every thought was certain to be respected and well received.

The Duke's letter was complimentary to me individually, and gave a most decided denial of his having uttered any expression that could be considered derogatory to me. He had, he admitted, given some advice to young Count Lieven, but these counsels had no reference to any of his associates. He added that he could not have spoken in such terms of me, as he was totally unacquainted with either my habits or my tastes. To the lady he never could have mentioned my name, as he had not once been in her society during his short visit to Paris. He had never made any observations about the imprudence or follies of gamblers, for in fact some of the best friends he had in the world belonged to that category. He concluded a most dignified letter in his characteristic style, by saying that if I was not fully convinced of his not deserving the imputation that had been cast upon him of abusing me, he was perfectly ready to give me any satisfaction that I might think proper to demand.

I cannot call to mind, even at this distance of time, the noble conduct of the great Duke on this occasion without feeling deeply affected.

Throughout the whole of his eventful career, the Duke of Wellington always placed first and foremost, far above his military and social honours, his position as an English gentleman. How few in his Grace's exalted station would have condescended even to notice such a letter as mine, worded though it was in a most respectful manner, or have deigned to give so full and ample an explanation; and how few would, like the truly great man, have waived their high military rank in a discussion with an obscure subaltern, and declared themselves ready to give him redress *sur le champ*, if he still considered himself injured and aggrieved.

I am proud to think that the great Duke did not bear malice, or think any the worse of me for the explanation I had demanded. In the year 1824, I happened to be walking one morning in the Park, near Apsley House, with my friend Charles, commonly called Cornet Wortley. We had not been there long when we met the Duke, who called Wortley to him, and, after a short conversation, as I stood on one side, I heard him ask Wortley who I was, and on his answering, as I took off my hat the Duke smiled, touched his, and nodded to me most good-naturedly several times.

WELLINGTON'S FIRST CAMPAIGN.—The Duke of Wellington had in his early career lost a considerable sum of money at play, and had been on the point of selling his commission in Dublin, with the view of relieving himself from some debts of honour which he had incurred.

At a dinner party at Mr. Greenwood's, of that excellent firm, Cox & Greenwood, I met Sir Harry Calvert, then Adjutant-General, who accompanied the Duke of York as one of his staff in his disastrous campaign in Holland; and he told us the following anecdote:—Lord Camden, the Viceroy, had been applied to by Lord Mornington, the brother of Captain Wesley (so his name was then spelt), for a Commissionership of Customs, or anything else in the gift of the Lord-Lieutenant of Ireland, as it was the intention of the Captain to sell his commission to pay his debts. Lord Camden, in an interview with Captain Wesley, inquired whether he left the army in disgust, or what motive induced him to relinquish a service in which he was well qualified to distinguish himself. Captain Wesley explained everything that had occurred, upon which the Lord-Lieutenant expressed a wish to be of service to him. "What can I do for you? Point out any plan by which you can be extricated from your present difficulties." The answer was, "I have no alternative but to sell my commission; for I am poor, and unable to pay off my debts of honour." "Remain in the army," said Lord Camden, "and I will assist you in paying off your liabilities." "I should like to study my profession at Angers," replied the young soldier; "for the French are the great masters of the art of war." Lord Camden assented to the proposition, supplied him with the means of living in France, and paid his debts.

Captain Wellesley, availing himself of the generous assistance thus offered, spent a considerable time at the Military School at Angers, where he laboured with intense application, and laid the foundation of that military reputation which placed him above all competitors. It was this education that enabled him to gain his first laurels. On his return to England, he was ordered to join the Duke of York in Flanders, as Major of the 33d Regiment of Foot; and the Colonel and first Major being absent, the command of the regiment devolved upon him. The expedition landed near Furnes in the Netherlands, the crack regiments first; and these, directly they set foot on shore, advanced helter-skelter, fancying themselves on the high-road to Paris.

When the 33d disembarked, Major Wellesley, knowing French tactics, addressed himself to Captain Calvert, the Duke of York's aide-de-camp, pointing out the certainty of a speedy attack of the enemy's cavalry and artillery, and the great probability that every man who had advanced would be cut to pieces. He said, "Pray allow me to form squares of divisions upon the beach before it is too late." This was done, and almost immediately afterwards, Vandamme, with the whole of his cavalry, supported by artillery, came down, threatening to sweep everything before them. Our troops rapidly dispersing, luckily found the 33d in square, and were thus saved from annihilation. The Duke of York, observing this adroit and ready manœuvre on the part of the young Major, called him to his council, and gave him the command of the rear-guard. After continually fighting and retreating for several weeks, the army embarked for England.

The reputation thus gained led to Major Wellesley's appointment in India, where he displayed those abilities which marked him out as the only man to oppose, and finally to conquer, the greatest of modern generals.

The lesson the Duke of Wellington had learnt at the gambling-table, as a young man, was deeply impressed upon him: he never afterwards touched a card; and so firmly did he set his face against gambling, that, in Paris, none of his staff, from Lord Fitzroy Somerset down to Freemantle, was ever to be seen either at Frascati's or the Salon des Étrangers.

THE GUARDS AND THE UMBRELLAS.—During the action of the 10th of December 1813, commonly known as that of the Mayor's House, in the neighbourhood of Bayonne, the Grenadier Guards, under the command of Colonel Tynling, occupied an unfinished redoubt on the right of the high-road. The Duke of Wellington happened to pass with Freemantle and Lord A. Hill, on his return to headquarters, having satisfied himself that the fighting was merely a feint on the part of Soult. His Grace on looking around saw, to his surprise, a great many umbrellas, with which the officers protected themselves from the rain that was then falling. Arthur Hill came galloping up to us saying, "Lord Wellington does not approve of the use of umbrellas during the enemy's firing, and will not allow 'the gentlemen's sons' * to make themselves ridiculous in the eyes of the army." Colonel Tynling, a few days afterwards, received a wigging from Lord Wellington for suffering his officers to carry umbrellas in the face of the enemy; his lordship observing, "The guards may in uniform, when on duty at St. James's, carry them if they please; but in the field it is not only ridiculous but unmilitary."

COLONEL FREEMANTLE AND THE DUKE'S QUARTERS.—When the British army was in full retreat from Burgos, Colonel Freemantle was sent by Lord Wellington to look out for comfortable quarters for himself and his staff. Freemantle, after galloping over many miles of desolate country, could only discover a hut. Accordingly, a good fire was prepared for the Commander of the Forces, and every preparation made for his reception. After Freemantle had

* "They are worthy the name given them by the army, that of gentlemen's sons."

communicated with his lordship, he lost no time in returning, when, to his surprise, he found the hut occupied by an officer of the line, who, standing with his back turned to the blazing fire, was whistling "for want of thought." The aide-de-camp politely told the officer that the hut had been secured for Lord Wellington, and therefore begged he would retire. The officer flatly refused, saying he would not give it up to Lord Wellington, or to Old Nick himself. "Well, then, I must use force: the provost-marshal shall be sent for, whose prisoner you will be until a court-martial shall sit for disobedience of orders." The officer surrendered at discretion, and was never more seen at headquarters.

This anecdote was told to Brummell at White's Club by Freemantle on his return to England, when the Beau exclaimed, "If I had been in your place, Freemantle, I should have rung the bell, and desired the servants to kick the fellow down-stairs."

A Word for Brown Bess.—When the British army invested Bayonne, it fell to my lot to be on outpost duty, and I then and there saw a long shot fired from one of our old muskets which showed that Brown Bess, though not equalling our modern weapons, had yet some good solid merits of her own, and when held straight was not to be despised even at a long range. Several shots had been fired from the French pickets, when Captain Grant of the 1st Foot Guards, being the senior officer on duty, came to me to inquire the cause of the firing, and desired me to make my way to the front and endeavour to ascertain what had occurred. Having arrived near the ravine which separated us from the French, I stumbled upon an advanced sentry, a German, who was coolly smoking his pipe. I asked him whether the shots that had been heard came from his neighbourhood, upon which he replied in broken English, "Yes, zir, that feelow you see yonder has fired nine times at mine target" (meaning his body), "but has missed. I hopes you, Capitaine, will let me have one shot at him." The distance between the French picket and ours could not have been less than 400 yards; so, without giving myself time to think, I said, "Yes, you can have one shot at him." He levelled his musket, fired, and killed his man; whereupon a sergeant and two or three French soldiers who had seen him fall, ran down to the front and removed the body.

A STRANGE RENCONTRE.—On the 10th of November 1813, while the light companies of the Coldstream and 3d Guards were skirmishing in front of Irun, the present Sir Wyndham Anstruther, then an officer in the Coldstream Guards, was severely wounded by a musket-ball just below the knee, and had he not received the most unceasing attention from the surgeon, Mr. Rose, he would in all probability have lost his leg. When the army commanded by the Duke of Wellington advanced, in the early part of the spring of 1814, Mr. Rose recommended Mr. Anstruther to return to England on sick leave; and he was placed, on his arrival, under the care of the celebrated surgeon, Sir Everard Home, by whose skill he completely recovered, but was not able to join the British army before it had reached Paris after the battle of Waterloo. Mr. Anstruther remained several months in Paris, and in the early part of 1816, after dining one day with Mr. Boulton, an old friend, who had hired a country-house at St. Maur, two leagues beyond Vincennes, was returning to town in a small carriage upon two wheels, called a *coucou*, commonly used in those days, and which travelled at the rate of about five miles an hour. Having placed himself on the front seat outside with the driver, after a time they got into conversation, and thinking, from his appearance, that he looked like an old soldier, Mr. Anstruther inquired whether he had served; to which the coachman answered in the affirmative, mentioning the number of his regiment and the battles in which he had taken part; and he added that he was afraid he had killed an English officer in front of Irun, on the banks of the Bidassoa. Mr. Anstruther naturally felt surprised at what he had heard, knowing that he was the only officer hit at the time and place specified, so he questioned the driver as to the nature of the ground, and his reasons for being so sure of having killed the officer. The man at once said that about three o'clock on the 10th of November, he and a few comrades ran down from Irun into a small clump of brushwood about half-way between the town and the hedges lined by the English; that they had not been there long before they wounded one of the Englishmen, and that an officer sprang forward to the assistance of the wounded soldier, when he, the coachman, fired and hit the officer, who fell, to all appearance, mortally wounded. The driver was perfectly astonished when informed that the English officer he thought he had killed was still alive and sitting by his side. The old soldier even shed (or pretended to shed) tears of joy; and after a minute examination of dates and details, Mr. Anstruther presented his quondam enemy with a couple of napoleons to drink his health. This he did, after placing his carriage in the yard of the village inn, and to some purpose, for he got very drunk, to the amusement of the villagers, to whom he recounted his story, and who carried him in triumph upon their shoulders, crying, "*Vive l'officier anglais!*"

English and French Soldiers on the Boulevards.—In 1815, during the period when the English Guards were doing garrison-duty in Paris, the usual rendezvous of the soldiers was on the Boulevard du Temple, where Punch and Judy performed, to the great amusement of our brave comrades. It was also the custom at the same period for the discharged officers of the Army of the Loire to congregate there; and I remember witnessing the following incident:—During the performance of Punch, a diminutive, humpbacked man made himself very noisy and troublesome to those in front of him. Two officers, wearing the Cross of the Legion of Honour, were much annoyed at this, and requested the dwarf to keep quiet, and to leave off annoying them. The diminutive gentleman replied by abusing them, and calling them *sacrés Bonapartistes*, an epithet of a disagreeable kind at that period, for it was not safe to be known by that denomination. The taller of the two officers, not relishing the impertinence of the dwarf, took him off the ground, placed him upon his shoulders, and walked up to M. Guignol, saying, "Take back your Punchinello; he has lost himself (*il s'est égaré entre nos jambes*)." Our soldiers, who witnessed this practical joke and well-deserved lesson, gave the French officer three cheers. This mark of sympathy from an enemy had its desired effect, for it produced a good feeling ever after, and we became on excellent terms with our former brave antagonists, whom the fortune of war had deprived of their rank and pay, and who were much to be pitied under the species of ostracism to which they were condemned.

"DATE OBOLUM BELISARIO." — The Marquis d'Aligre, the richest and most avaricious man in France, and supposed to be worth three or four millions of money, was once seen entering a church during a charity sermon. He was accosted by a great lady of the Faubourg St. Germain, who, holding a bag for charitable contributions, begged him to give her something for the poor. The Marquis did not appear to understand the request, but the lady returned to the charge; upon which the Marquis declined giving anything, stating that he had no money. The lady then placed the bag full of money under the nose of the Marquis, saying, "Help yourself, Monsieur d'Aligre, for this bag contains money for the poor; and as you say you are penniless, pray help yourself." Upon which the old miser, for once heartily ashamed of himself, pulled out of his pocket a purse full of gold, and threw it into the bag.

"HATS OFF."—At a party at the Vicomtesse de Noailles's soon after the Allied Armies had entered Paris, and at which I was present, some of the ladies expressed their surprise that Englishmen of high birth did not take off their hats when bowed to, as was the custom in France and other countries. Dupuytren, the celebrated surgeon, happened to join the party, when some one observed that perhaps the Doctor could solve the riddle, and explain the real cause of such apparent rudeness on the part of the English. Dupuytren, in his coarse and blunt manner, said, "The *teigne*, or scald-head, is a very common disease in Europe; it is therefore more than probable that those foreigners who keep their hats on in the presence of ladies are afflicted with that loathsome complaint." Lady Stafford, afterwards Duchess of Sutherland, who had been quietly sitting on one of the sofas, and whose presence had escaped the notice of Dupuytren, rose, and, in a dignified manner, said, "Doctor, that horrible disease is unknown in my country. My countrymen take off their hats to royalty, to ladies, and to none besides." Whereupon Dupuytren rejoined, "Surely, my lady, there is no law in England which precludes a well-bred gentleman from taking off his hat to his equals, and more especially to females." Lady Stafford retorted with spirit, "You can ridicule my countrymen if you think fit, Doctor; but with all their faults and apparent rudeness, they have never been guilty of cutting off the heads of beautiful and innocent women, as you have done in France." This severe retort on the part of her ladyship was considered by all present as quite uncalled for; but the Vicomtesse apologised to her friends by saying that Lady Stafford should be pardoned, for she lived in Paris during the Revolution as ambassadress from England, and was a great favourite and friend of Queen Marie-Antoinette. She conveyed to the poor

Queen when in prison many little comforts and necessaries; and when the embassy had left Paris, and Marie-Antoinette, after unheard-of barbarities, was guillotined, Lady Stafford regarded her execution as the most atrocious murder, and vowed the utmost detestation and abhorrence, not only of the ruffians who by their bloody deeds dishonoured France, but of the whole French nation.

Hatred of the Prussians by the French Peasantry.—During the memorable retreat of Napoleon from the Rhine to Fontainebleau, the Allies amounted to five times the number of the French. Though greatly outnumbered, yet there was unity of will and of purpose in the councils of Napoleon and his generals, which Schwartzenberg and Blucher failed to infuse into their troops. Wanting neither in alacrity nor in vigour when the glory of his country was concerned, Napoleon, with his handful of men, made supernatural efforts; taking advantage of every good position that presented itself, and attacking the enemy upon several points on the same day.

Upon one occasion he had completely divided the Allies by his comprehensive and well-arranged operations. Napoleon, to effect this gigantic manœuvre, took the bull by its horns, and accordingly fought the battle of Château-Thierry. In this sanguinary battle the French army succeeded in taking from the Prussians all their cannon and ammunition, and several thousand prisoners. After the battle, General Belliard, who commanded the advanced posts, naturally took possession of the town of Château-Thierry; and on entering the principal street with his staff, beheld a most shocking and horrible spectacle. The Prussians had committed every sort of cruelty during the period they occupied Château-Thierry prior to the battle, and the inhabitants of that place were driven to such a pitch of exasperation, that when the battle turned in favour of the French, the people acted in a most barbarous and cruel manner towards every Prussian, whether wounded or not, who fell into their hands.

The first thing which General Belliard saw in entering the town was a group of infuriated women, their hands bathed in blood, brandishing the knives with which they were busily employed in killing the wounded soldiers. The General and his staff had great difficulty in putting a stop to this horrid scene. The women, more like furies than human beings, addressed the General, saying they had undergone horrible treatment from the Germans, who had not only pillaged them of everything they possessed, but had violated all the women, both young and old, and had killed their husbands in cold blood. "Yes, General," cried one of those furies, "I have begun this butchery, and I will end it!" and in his presence she plunged her knife into the heart of a poor prisoner.

Severe Discipline in the Russian Army. — When we were quartered in Paris in 1815, a strange circumstance occurred. It became our duty to provide the guard for the Emperor of Russia, and a dinner was provided for us similar to that which is given at St. James's. Prior to dinner being served, our Adjutant informed the Colonel that there were four Russian general officers in our custody. It naturally struck us that something very horrible had occurred to have caused the disgrace of men of such high rank. It fell to the lot of Captain Vernon, son of the late Archbishop of York, to call upon those unfortunate officers to invite them to dinner — an invitation which they cheerfully accepted. During the first course, curiosity seized the gallant captain; for, in proposing the health of one of our prisoners, he begged the Russian would inform us of the cause of their disgrace. The reply was, the Emperor was not satisfied with the manner in which their men had marched past at the review; whereupon Vernon filled his glass up to the brim, and drank, "Confusion to all tyrants, and—*Vive Napoleon!*" The Russian generals appeared thunderstruck, and observed, that if they drank the toast proposed it would cost them their heads.

Nothing more was heard of the Russian generals until two days after, when we (the officers of the guard), were summoned before the Duke of Wellington, to explain what it all meant. The Duke having heard us, said he hoped that for the future we would abstain from alluding to Bonaparte, for as Louis XVIII. had been proclaimed the King of France, any allusion to the fallen hero would be both impolitic and mischievous; adding that he would make a point of presenting himself at the Emperor of Russia's hotel, and explaining the occurrence.

THE EMPEROR ALEXANDER IN PARIS.—The Emperor Alexander of Russia was fond of telling an anecdote of a circumstance which occurred to himself and the King of Prussia whilst in Paris, in 1815. They had lounged together to the Palais Royal, which in those days was surrounded by a number of narrow streets and alleys, and in returning to the Tuileries, they found that they were in a labyrinth, from which it was difficult to extricate themselves. The Emperor, after a time, accosted a well-dressed man who wore the cross of St. Louis, and asked the nearest route to the Tuileries. The answer was, "I am going there myself, and will readily accompany you. Will you do me the honour of informing me whom I am conducting?" The Czar replied, "I am the Emperor of Russia." The gentleman received the information with an incredulous smile. "And who is your companion?" said he. "This is the King of Prussia. But whom am I to thank for this politeness?" The Parisian, thinking that he would be a match for this waggish stranger, replied, "Oh, I am the Emperor of China." Little further conversation passed between them, the Frenchman apparently declining to be further hoaxed. On their arrival at the gate of the Tuileries, however, the *générale* was beat, the soldiers saluted, and hats were taken off, to the amazement of the *soi-disant* monarch of the Celestial Empire, who was now convinced that his companions had higher claims to a throne than he possessed. When the two great personages turned round to thank their "guide, philosopher, and friend," they found that he also had assumed an incognito, and had disappeared.

A Fire-Eater Cowed.—A singular incident occurred at the Café Français in 1816, at the corner of the Rue Laffitte. A celebrated duellist entered and began insulting all the persons who were seated at dinner; he boasted of his courage, and declared his determination to kill a certain M. de F***. A gentleman present, disgusted at such braggart insolence, quietly walked up to this fire-eater, and addressed him thus: "As you are such a dangerous customer, perhaps you will accommodate me, by being punctual at the entrance of the Bois de Boulogne, near the Porte Maillot, at mid-day to-morrow: earlier I cannot get there, but depend upon my arriving in due time with swords and pistols." The duellist began to demur, saying he did not know what right a stranger had to take up the cudgels of M. de F***; to which the gentleman replied, "I have done so because I am anxious to rid society of a dangerous fellow like yourself, and would recommend you before you go to bed to make your will. I will undertake to order your coffin and pay your funeral expenses." He then gave the waiter a note of a thousand francs, with the injunction that his orders should be executed before eleven the following day. This had the desired effect of intimidating the bully, who left Paris the following day, and never more was heard of or seen in public.

An Insult Rightly Redressed.—Soon after the restoration of the Bourbons, several duels took place for the most frivolous causes. Duels were fought in the daytime, and even by night. The officers of the Swiss Guards were constantly measuring swords with the officers of the old Garde Impériale. Upon one occasion a Frenchman, determined to insult a Swiss officer, who, in the uniform of his regiment, was quietly taking his ice at Tortoni's, addressed him thus: "I would not serve my country for the sake of money, as you do. We Frenchmen think only of honour." To which the other promptly retorted, "You are right; for we both of us serve for what we do not possess." A duel was the consequence; they fought with swords under a lamp in the Rue Taitbout, and the Frenchman was run through the body; but luckily the wound, though dangerous, did not prove fatal.

A Duel between Two Old Friends.—General A. de Girardin, some forty years back, had a serious quarrel with one of his old friends, the Marquis de Briancourt, about a lady. A duel was the consequence. Pistols were chosen; but, prior to exchanging shots, de Girardin's second went (as was the custom) and felt the right side of his friend's antagonist, but found nothing there to indicate the existence of padding, &c. Accordingly, after measurement of the ground, pistols were handed to the combatants. The Marquis changed his pistol from his right into his left hand; both parties fired, and the Marquis fell. The seconds flew to the aid of the wounded man, but, to their astonishment, on opening his waistcoat several sheets of thick paper were found folded over the region of the heart. Notwithstanding this device, the blow from the bullet created a sore on the left side, which was never effectually cured. The Marquis died shortly afterwards.

A Duel between Two Officers in the Life Guards about the Year 1821.—A lamentable duel took place in Paris during the Restoration between two officers of the Life Guards, Captain Walsh and Lieutenant Pellew, about a lady. The latter gentleman was shot through the head. It is quite enough to state that Captain Walsh was justified in the steps he had taken, for he had received the greatest injury that one man could inflict on another. Though this unfortunate duel took place above forty years back, I well remember it, for I refused to be the Lieutenant's second, because he had behaved so ill. The impression it made was very great, and the general feeling was in favour of the injured husband.

Fayot, the Champion of the Legitimists.—Fayot fought more duels than any man in France. His aim with a pistol was certain; but he was not cruel, and he usually wounded his adversary either in the leg or arm. He was likewise a good swordsman. General Fournier was afraid of Fayot, and only once measured swords with him; while the latter had a horror of Fournier for having killed so many young men belonging to good families. In his rencontre with Fayot, the General was severely wounded in the hand, and ever after Fayot hunted his antagonist from one end of France to the other, determined to put an end to the "assassin," as he was called; but the Revolution of 1830 came, and all was chaos.

Fayot's father was guillotined in the south of France in 1793. His mother, after the severe loss she had sustained in the death of her husband, whom she adored, brought up her son at Avignon, telling him, as he grew up to be a man, to take

JOHN BULL AND HIS FAMILY AT AN ICE CAFÉ. THE OCCUPATION.

every opportunity of avenging the death of his father. Upon the restoration of the Bourbons, Fayot came to Paris, where, by his singular manners and dress, he laid himself open to remark and ridicule. In the daytime he was usually dressed in a green coat, white waistcoat and neckcloth, leather pantaloons, and Hessian boots, with his hat on one side. He visited London in 1814, where he bought a tilbury and horse, which he brought to Paris, and in this gig he paraded every day up and down the Boulevards, from the Rue Laffitte to the Place de la Madeleine. His evenings were generally passed either at Tortoni's or Silve's, the respective rendezvous of the Bonapartists and Bourbons. In one or other of these *cafés* Fayot was sure to be found. He publicly gave out that he was ready to measure swords with any one who dared to insinuate anything against the royal family,—a threat sure to bring upon him serious rencontres; but nothing intimidated him. It was reported at the time, and generally believed, that he had, in the short period of two years, fought thirty duels without having been seriously wounded.

Upon one occasion Fayot repaired to the Théâtre Français to see *Germanicus;* party spirit then ran high, and any allusion complimentary to the fallen Emperor was received by the Bonapartists with applause. Fayot loudly hissed, and a great uproar arose, when Fayot entered the breach by proclaiming himself the champion of Legitimacy. The consequence was that cards flew about the pit; Fayot carefully picked them up, and placed them in his hat. After the play had terminated he repaired to Tortoni's, where he wrote his address upon several pieces of paper, which he distributed all over the Boulevards, stating that he was to be found every morning between the hours of eleven and twelve at the well in the Bois de Boulogne, near Auteuil. Strange to say, after all this row at the theatre, only one antagonist was forthcoming. On the second day, at the hour appointed, a gentlemen arrived with his seconds, who found Fayot in his tilbury, ready for the fight. The name of his antagonist was a Monsieur Harispe, the son of the distinguished Basque General. Pistols were chosen, and at the first discharge Fayot shot his adversary in the knee; then, taking off his hat, he left the ground and proceeded to Paris in his tilbury to breakfast at Tortoni's, where a great many persons had congregated to know the result of this terrible duel.

The Revolution of 1830 drove Fayot away from Paris, and he retired to his native Avignon, where he lived much respected by the principal inhabitants of that quaint town. In passing through Avignon some twelve years back I called upon him, and found him much altered, but still dressed in his original costume,—the green coat, white neckcloth, &c.

The Gardes du Corps.—I knew several of those gentlemen who had succeeded in getting into the companies of the Gardes du Corps—St. Arnaud, Fouquainville, Odoard, Warrelles, St. Roman, Fromasson, and, though last, not least, Warren, an Irishman by birth, but whose father had married a French lady. Warren stood six feet four inches in height, and was an extremely powerful man. He was always in hot water with his comrades, and had fought duels with several of them, and his face and body showed marks of sabre cuts; indeed, fighting and drinking were his delights. I never saw a man so violent; when he had finished his bottle of champagne and a few glasses of brandy he became quite outrageous. He usually breakfasted, when off duty, at Tortoni's upon beefsteaks and broiled kidneys; and any one to whom he bore a grudge who entered the room at that moment was sure to be roughly handled.

It happened that Monsieur * * *, a distinguished painter, had returned to Paris from England, where he had played a shameful and disgusting part. The painter had been employed by the celebrated Mr. Hope of Duchess Street to paint the portrait of his wife, Mrs. Hope, afterwards Lady Beresford. When the painting was finished, Mr. Hope objected to pay for it, stating that it was a daub. The enraged painter, determined to be revenged, took the portrait home with him, and in a few days returned it with the addition of a beast representing Mr. Hope, in the presence of his beautiful wife. A trial was the consequence, and the painter was cast in damages. After this untoward event, London proved too hot for the Frenchman, and he returned to Paris, where his imprudence in speaking in no measured terms of the English got him into a scrape which cost him his life.

The painter (unluckily for him) arrived at Tortoni's to breakfast at the moment when Warren was in one of his dangerous fits, and attempted to appease Warren by going up to him and begging him to be more tranquil. This sort of impertinence Warren could not brook, and exclaiming, "You are the blackguard who laughs at the English," he seized hold of the artist, carried him as if he had been a bundle of straw, and held him out of the window. By the interference of those gentlemen present and the crowd below in the street, Warren was persuaded to carry back the terrified painter into the room. A duel was the consequence, in which the combatants were to fight with pistols until one of them was killed: Warren won the first toss, he levelled and fired, and his adversary fell mortally wounded. This duel was much talked of, but no one lamented the result of the duel; for the painter was overbearing, and generally disliked by his countrymen as well as by foreigners.

I can scarcely look back to those days of duelling without shuddering. If you looked at a man it was enough; for without having given the slightest offence, cards were exchanged, and the odds were that you stood a good chance of being shot, or run through the body, or maimed for life.

The late Marshal Castellane.—Marshal Castellane, a member of a distinguished family, entered the army under Napoleon when First Consul, and was employed during the Russian war. His political feelings were always in favour of Legitimacy, and therefore, on the return of the Bourbons, he gladly retained his rank. The following circumstance, which occurred when he was colonel of a crack regiment of hussars, explains the cause of his so rapidly obtaining the rank of general in the royal service:—

A ball was about to be given at the Tuileries, to which the Duchesse de Berri graciously invited the officers of Colonel Castellane's regiment. He, however, resolved that they should not be present, and meeting some opposition to his will, he determined to carry his point by placing them under arrest. The Duchesse de Berri, finding that her assembly would thus lose some of its most brilliant guests, went to the King, and requested the royal interference. His Majesty observed to her Royal Highness that Castellane was a great martinet, but that it would be dangerous to interfere with his command; "however, when he comes to the Tuileries send him to me." The Colonel, on making his appearance at the palace, was ushered into the royal presence; and the King thus addressed him, "General Castellane, I am happy to see you." "I beg your Majesty's pardon," replied the gallant officer, "I have no claim to the title by which you have done me the honour to notice me: I am Colonel Castellane." "Sir," said the monarch, "it gives me great pleasure to be the first to announce your promotion: your commission is already made out. I am certain you will serve me as faithfully and honourably in a higher grade as you have done when your military rank was not so great."

The General was, of course, highly gratified; so also was the Lieutenant-colonel of his regiment, upon whom, by this advancement, the command necessarily devolved. The first step of the new Colonel was of course to remove the officers from the disagreeable position in which Colonel Castellane had placed them; and they had the gratification of attending the ball at the Tuileries, where, of course, the Duchesse de Berri gave them a welcome reception.

General Castellane showed himself a gallant soldier, and a determined opponent of mob-rule. Although he did not abandon the service of his country when it was under a republican government, he always boldly proclaimed his preference for Legitimacy. When some tumultuous assemblages took place at Rouen, he dispersed them by military force; and upon some of the functionaries of the day observing that he ought to have waited for orders from the government, he unhesitatingly replied, "Had any of the ministers themselves disturbed the public quiet whilst the district is under my command, I should show them that I know my duty better than they know theirs." He had afterwards the command at Lyons, where he evinced on every occasion firmness and decision. A telegraphic despatch from a private hand announced the death of the Emperor; and he was advised to proclaim Henri the Fifth. A subsequent telegram summoned him to Paris, where he attended the Emperor, who said to him, "Why, General, I learnt that you were a stanch Bourbonist, and that I could place no dependence upon your support." The General answered, "Sire, it is true I have always advocated the cause of Legitimacy; but I have seen that the country submits to your rule and is pleased with it. I have therefore taken the oath of allegiance to you as my sovereign; and I can give my assurance that as long as your Majesty lives you will have no soldier more devoted to your service than I am, and shall remain." The General was shortly after elevated to the rank of Marshal in the imperial service, and faithfully and steadily carried out his principles of adhesion to the imperial government.

He died not long since, greatly esteemed by his brethren in arms, and much deplored at Lyons, where he had for some time held the command.

There he spent a large sum in constructing a magnificent mausoleum, in which his body now lies. His funeral was gorgeous, as is usual with Marshals of the Empire.

The Comte de Castellane, a near relation, was a very eccentric character, but a great favourite in Paris, where he gave large parties. He fitted up a private theatre, where amateur performances by some of the most fashionable persons collected together the *beau monde.* His loss was severely felt last year by a large number of persons, to whom he was in the constant habit of extending a splendid hospitality.

THE LATE GENERAL GABRIEL.—Whatever might have been General Gabriel's abilities as a field-officer, as a soldier his bravery was unquestionable. He was the son of a clergyman, and was so handsome that he received the cognomen of "The Angel Gabriel." On entering the army he had to make his way in the service by the force of merit and good fortune alone. Instances of his dashing and headlong courage in the Peninsula caught the eye of one of our celebrated general officers, the Honourable Sir William Stewart, who commanded the division commonly known by the name of "The Fighting Division," and he placed Gabriel upon his staff. Upon one occasion, in the Pyrenees, Sir William was not a little surprised to find that his aide-de-camp was *non est inventus;* and upon asking his nephew, Lord Charles Churchill, what had become of him, he was answered thus—"Oh, Gabriel having heard the roaring of cannon to our right, has galloped off to enjoy the fun." Sir William Stewart, addressing his staff, said, "Well, then, we cannot do better than follow him;" and off they went. On reaching the pass of Roncesvalles, to their astonishment they saw Gabriel, at the head of a few stragglers whom he had picked up on the way, charge a bridge which the enemy were crossing, and completely rout them. Sir William Stewart was so delighted with this act of daring bravery, that he recommended his young aide-de-camp for promotion, which the Duke of Wellington ratified in one of his earliest despatches to the Duke of York.

Admiral la Susse.—Admiral Baron de la Susse, well known in the best society of London and Paris, was a great favourite of Louis Philippe's. He carried his Majesty to Portsmouth in a French steam-frigate on the occasion of his last visit to our gracious Queen. During the Admiral's stay at Portsmouth, Lord Adolphus Fitzclarence was instructed by the Admiralty to attend upon the French Admiral, and to show him the dockyard and fortifications. After visiting everything worth seeing, Admiral de la Susse said he was much surprised that our principal port was so badly fortified; adding that an enemy, with a few ships and ten thousand infantry, could easily destroy the fortifications and burn the arsenal. Soon after, the Duke of Wellington happened to meet Lord Adolphus, who mentioned the particulars of the conversation he had had with the French Admiral; upon which the Duke observed, that if a war were to break out between us and France, and the French fleet were permitted to cross the Channel, Portsmouth would stand but a bad chance. "But the Channel," added his Grace, "is a nasty ditch to cross, and to bring over ten thousand men at one given point; and if the enemy brought fewer, they would fail, and in all probability be taken prisoners."

Admiral de la Susse, in his younger days, was celebrated as a man of fashion. He was rather good-looking, with a neat figure, and was very popular in society. He was in his youth a very good waltzer, and prided himself upon that accomplishment; but being unfortunately extremely short-sighted, he consequently got himself frequently into scrapes. At a ball given by a lady in the Faubourg St. Honoré, La Susse, in a turn of the waltz, accidentally, and without the slightest intention of insulting any one, came into violent contact with a looker-on, who, in a German accent, exclaimed aloud, "*Quand on est si maladroit, on ne doit pas valser*." Cards were exchanged, and on the following morning the parties met in the Bois de Boulogne. La Susse's adversary won the toss, and took his aim with great coolness, but luckily without effect. La Susse then fired, when the German fell. The seconds hastened to render every assistance in their power; but judge of their astonishment when, instead of finding the German mortally wounded, as they expected, they only found a bullet indented against a well-padded cuirass. La Susse, after looking attentively with his glass in his eye at what was passing, desired his antagonist to rise, as he would have another shot at him; upon which the cuirassed hero rose, and received a well-merited and well-applied kick, without making the slightest resistance, and then walked off the ground as if he had accomplished some wonderful achievement. This extraordinary duel took place in 1816, and was the subject of much conversation for a length of time in the fashionable circles in Paris.

At the commencement of the Crimean war, the Admiral was named commander-in-chief of the French fleet; and when off the Piræus, had gone on shore to pass a few days up the country with some friends, when unexpected orders came for the different vessels under his command to weigh anchor, and to proceed to a new destination immediately. The Admiral, bent on his amusements, was not to be found for three days; and on this becoming known to the Emperor, he was immediately superseded, and Admiral Parseval-Deschênes named in his place. Poor La Susse never recovered from this dreadful blow, and considered himself ever after as a disgraced and dishonoured man. He lingered on for a few months, and may be said to have died of a broken heart.

Marshal Lobau.—The famous General Mouton, the bravest of the brave, was created Count of Lobau for his heroic conduct in the desperate attack upon the island of that name at the battle of Wagram. His commanding figure and stentorian voice many persons now living may remember, when, as a marshal of France under Louis Philippe, he commanded the National Guard. He was a most excellent man in all the relations of life, but of very parsimonious habits. One of his old comrades related to me the following anecdote of him:—

General Mouton, who was a great favourite with

the Emperor Napoleon, was visiting his illustrious chief one morning at the Tuileries, when his Majesty, happening to look out of the window, beheld in the courtyard a very shabby-looking vehicle. "Is that your carriage, Mouton?" asked the Emperor. "Yes, sire." "It is not fitting that one of my bravest generals should go about in a hackney coach." "Sire, I am not a Crœsus, and can't afford a better." The next day Mouton received a cheque on the Bank of France for 300,000 francs (£12,000). About a fortnight afterwards, General Mouton again paid a visit to the Tuileries in the same hackney coach. On looking out, the Emperor's countenance clouded over, and he looked greatly displeased as he recognised the obnoxious vehicle. "Did you not receive an order for 300,000 francs?" he inquired of the general. "Yes, sire," replied Mouton, "and I am truly grateful for the gift; but if your Majesty insists upon my spending it, I would rather return the money."

MONTROND.—At an evening party at Lady Granville's, at the Embassy in Paris, the whist table was placed in the throne-room. The card party consisted of the ambassador, J. Rothschild, Lamarc, and Montrond. They were playing high points, or stakes, when two ladies approached the table, and in a suppliant manner begged the gentlemen would aid them by giving a small pittance for some poor persons who deserved their charity. Montrond, annoyed at this demand, said, "*Que voulez-vous, mesdames?*" "*Monsieur, nous faisons la quête pour les filles repenties.*" "*Très bien, très bien, madame, si elles sont repenties je ne donne rien, ab-*

solument rien; mais pour les femmes qui ne sont pas repenties j'irai moi-même leur porter de l'argent."

Chateaubriand.—This great man passed many years of his life in absolute poverty and distress in London. He was even obliged to wash his own linen. After the restoration of the Bourbons, Louis XVIII. named Chateaubriand his ambassador in England, and during this period his great delight was to enumerate the many shifts he had employed to keep body and soul together; but what delighted him more than all was to revisit the banks of the Thames, near Chelsea, where he formerly washed his shirts and stockings.

Parson Ambrose.—During the winter of 1816, I had the honour to receive a general invitation to the Sunday *soirées* of the Duchess of Orleans, the mother of Louis Philippe. Upon one occasion I remember seeing two celebrated ladies there, Madame de Staël and Madame Recamier. There were many English present also. Among the most remarkable was a gentleman known by the appellation of "Parson Ambrose," a natural son of Lord de Blaquiere's. He was good-looking, and dressed like a gentleman of the old *régime.* He wore black silk breeches, with buckles both to his knees and shoes, and the frills to his shirt were of the finest Malines lace. Sir Charles Stewart, upon entering the saloon, beckoned to the parson, who said, "Well, Sir Charles, I am in a bad state." "What is the matter with you?" "I have a complaint in the chest, your Excellency." "What doctor have you consulted?" "Lafitte," replied the parson. "I never heard of him except as a banker. Well, what has he done for you?" "Nothing." Sir Charles, now discovering the meaning of the "*chest* complaint," said, in his good-natured way, "Come to the Embassy to-morrow morning, and I will see what can be done to cure your complaint." The parson accordingly went, and found the ambassador at breakfast with the Duke of Wellington. After talking over olden times, when the Duke was merely Captain Wellesley, and lived on intimate terms with the parson in Dublin, his grace kindly presented Ambrose with a hundred guineas, to take him back to England for change of air; which, he trusted, would contribute to the restoration of his health.

CAPTAIN WILDING. — After our *corps d'armée*, under the command of Sir John Hope, had crossed the Adour, we were ordered to advance as close as possible under the walls of the town. Accordingly, after suffering considerable loss, we succeeded in investing the town and fortress. The enemy, not contented with firing from the batteries, actually brought a nine-pounder on to the high-road, half-way from their stronghold. This gun did us great injury, and I was witness to a very gallant act of some of the infantry of the German Legion, which effectually stopped any further loss. Captain Wilding, who commanded a company of Hanoverians, suddenly dashed out of a burial-ground to the left of the road, rushed upon the gunners, bayoneted them, and brought the gun in triumph into our lines, amidst the loud cheers of our soldiers. In this gallant exploit Captain Wilding was badly wounded in the leg, and was obliged to return to

England for his recovery; but prior to his removal he had the satisfaction to see, in general orders, the approval, by the commander-in-chief, of his gallant bearing in the capture of the gun. Captain Wilding was a Hanoverian, and brother of Prince Butera, to part of whose vast estates in Sicily he succeeded, and is now known by the title of Prince Radali, which was bestowed upon him by the old King of Naples.

The Church Militant.—I was acquainted, during the Peninsular war, with one of the army chaplains, the Rev. Mr. Frith, who was attached to the Fifth Division. He considered it part of his duty to attend the troops into action, and would frequently expose himself, with them, to the hottest fire. He showed the greatest courage and devotion, and rescued many wounded soldiers on several occasions, performing these, and many other gallant actions, as a matter of course and without any idea of display; for although a man of such remarkable bravery, he was of a quiet and gentle demeanour.

I remember on one occasion being present when a party of staff officers were trying to find a ford for the passage of a deep and rapid stream by a part of the army; most of the horses refused the water, when the reverend gentleman pushed forward, saying, "I daresay my nag will take it," and he was in a few minutes over on the other side and back again. Mr. Frith went by the name of "the fighting parson" in his division, and was an admirable and excellent specimen of the Church militant.

Louis XVIII.—Louis XVIII. was famous for his repartees. His Majesty being very infirm, could only show himself to his people in a carriage; he could not mount a horse, and had great difficulty in walking a few steps. He was very fond of having all the news of Paris, and had numerous visitors during the day, who related to him everything that happened. An ambassador of long standing, the Bailli de Ferrette, used to be a frequent attendant at the Tuileries, and upon one occasion the King said to the Bailli, "What news have you for me to-day?" "None worth communicating to your Majesty," said M. de Ferrette, "unless it is that the people in Paris are beginning to murmur because their King is not able to ride and review his soldiers as other sovereigns have done from time immemorial." His Majesty replied, "Oh, I suppose they want a monarch who can ride well. Perhaps I had better abdicate in favour of Franconi."

THE BRIDGE OF JENA SAVED.—When Blucher was meditating the destruction of the bridge of Jena by blowing it up with powder, one of the old generals of the Empire proceeded to the Tuileries, saw the King, and mentioned what the Prussians intended doing. Louis, enraged, cried out, "What vandalism! I will place myself on the bridge and be blown up with it, rather than so fine a monument should be destroyed." The King then sent the Duc de Guiche to mention to the Duke of Wellington what had been communicated to him, upon which our illustrious chief ordered his horse, and galloping off to the Guards' bivouacs in the Bois de Boulogne, gave directions to Sir P. Maitland to drive the Prussians off the bridge at the point of the bayonet, *coûte que coûte.* The

Guards, on approaching the bridge, found the Prussian engineers hard at work undermining; but on discovering we were bent on mischief, and that our firelocks were loaded with ball cartridge,—only five minutes being given them to remove all their pick-axes and other implements,—they quietly marched off, to the great mortification of the officer in command, and to the disgust of Marshal Blucher, who never forgave Wellington for thwarting his purpose.

Louis XVIII. and Sosthènes de la Rochefoucauld.—A few days after the King's arrival in Paris in 1814, Sosthènes de la Rochefoucauld collected together a mob in the Place Vendôme, with the intention of hurling from its pedestal the statue of the Emperor, endeavouring at the same time to pull down the pillar, which all the world has seen and admired. Hundreds of ropes were held by the mob, who pulled away with all their might for several hours; but, night coming on, they were obliged to desist from their fruitless attempts. The King, having been told of this outrageous conduct, sent for Rochefoucauld and asked him whether he had acted in the manner reported of him. The Duke pleaded guilty, upon which the King said—"You are playing the enemy's game; it is by such means I shall be made unpopular. For the future, bear in mind that Louis XVIII. is King of France, and not King of the Vandals."

The Duc de Grammont.—The Duc de Grammont, better known as the Duc de Guiche, was the type and model of the real French gentleman and *grand seigneur* of the olden time. He was the handsomest man at the court of the elder branch of the Bourbons; and during the Empire, when in exile, had served in the English army. I knew him well in Spain, in 1813, when a captain in the 10th Hussars, and subsequently at Bordeaux, in 1814, when he accompanied the Duc d'Angoulême, and having then left our service, was arrayed in a French uniform as aide-de-camp to the Dauphin. He spoke English perfectly, was quiet in manner, and a most chivalrous, high-minded, and honourable man. His complexion was very dark, with crisp black hair curling close to his small, well-shaped head. His features were regular and somewhat aquiline, his eyes large, dark, and beautiful; and his manner, voice, and smile were considered by the fair sex to be perfectly irresistible.

He served with distinction as a general officer in the Spanish campaign of 1823, and was specially attached to the person of the Dauphin, whom he was obliged to keep in great order. As is often the case with princes, the Dauphin, or Duc d'Angoulême, as he was sometimes called, would frequently emancipate himself, and take liberties with those around him, if permitted to do so. Once, when driving with the Duc de Guiche, the Prince, in his somewhat ape-like manner, pinched his companion. A few moments afterwards, the Duke returned the caress with interest, to the great surprise of the Dauphin, who started and turned angrily round, to meet the winning, placid smile of his friend and mentor.

The Duke was universally beloved and regretted; and I should instance him as being, perhaps, the most perfect gentleman I ever met with in any country.

The Montmorencies.—At this time, when a lawsuit is about to take place in France respecting the right of a grandson, in the female line, of the late Duke to assume the title of Duke of Montmorency, it may not be uninteresting to call to mind how illustrious a family is about to become extinct in the male line.

The Montmorencies bore the title of first Christian Barons and Premiers Barons of France, and have been rendered illustrious by no less than ten constables, and innumerable marshals, generals, cardinals, archbishops, and governors of princes. Their alliances by marriage with the royal family have been frequent; and for ten consecutive centuries, the heads of this great house have shone forth as the most eminent personages in French history, and have held the highest and most important offices in the state.

I remember the late Gaston de Montmorency, Prince de Robecq, a most gallant, amiable, and accomplished man, in whom all the hopes of the family were centred, but who died in the prime of life, a few years after the Revolution of 1830. He used to say that he would never marry, for that the present age was not worthy to possess Montmorencies, now that the age of chivalry was gone, and his country had fallen into the hands of Louis Philippe and the *épiciers* of the Rue St. Denis. He kept his promise; and at the present moment, the only male representatives of this illustrious race are the two Princes of Montmorency-Luxembourg, both aged men, who have no male descendants.

The name was always a popular one with the French people. The Montmorencies, though proud and haughty to their equals, were kind, generous, and charitable to their inferiors, and were celebrated for the magnificence of their establishments. Even in the days of "liberty, equality, and fraternity," and at periods of revolutionary excesses, the name of Montmorency has always inspired a certain respect; even the fiercest Republicans have felt a sort of pride when the name of this ancient and illustrious race has been pronounced before them.

In England, and strange to say, in Africa, there are still supposed to be living descendants of the earlier chiefs of this family. The ancient Irish sept of Macmorris, or Morris, who have taken the name of Montmorency within the last fifty years, and possess the Irish titles of Mountmorris and Frankfort, claim descent—and, I believe, on well-grounded evidence—from Hervé de Montmorency, in the eleventh century. They have, however, in taking the name, committed a great error in assuming the motto of *Dieu ayde*, which was not the *devise* of their supposed ancestor, but adopted for the first time by one of the Constables of France, a Montmorency who lived several hundred years afterwards.

With regard to Africa, it is well known to all French officers who have been quartered at Oran, that there is in the neighbourhood of that town an Arab tribe which bears the name of "Momoransi," and which is very proud of the family; and the tradition is, that they are the descendants of an illustrious French leader in the first Crusade.

Curiously enough, the Irish and Arab offshoots of the family must have separated from the parent stem at about the same time, and have been fourth or fifth in descent from "Bouchard;" for by that not very harmonious name the patriarch of the Montmorencies was first known. But I much fear that the female ancestress of these Arab chiefs must have gone astray with the pious crusader, and that they are only illegitimate descendants of the Montmorencies; for in all the old chronicles of the time there is not a single instance of a Christian knight having intermarried with an infidel.

This calls to my recollection a story I have heard of a Duke of Montmorency in the reign of Louis XV., who was married to a lady of ancient family and great beauty; but, like many nobles of that time, he was not quite a model of what husbands ought to be, and lived a very riotous and improper life. He even went so far as to appear in public with the celebrated dancer, Mademoiselle Guimard, about whom all the young men of the day were raving. One night, on the Duchess entering her box at the opera with several friends, she beheld, to her horror and amazement, the Duke, her husband, seated at the back of the pit box in which the charming dancer displayed her charms. Whatever might be done in private, in those days a certain decorum was preserved in public, and the appearance of the Duke in Guimard's box was an outrage which the Duchess could not endure. She sent one of the gentlemen who were with her to request her husband's immediate presence, and thus addressed the astonished culprit: "I have always been a devoted and faithful wife; but let me warn you in time. If you ever again commit such an outrage, remember this, that you cannot make Montmorencies without me, and I *can* make them without your assistance." The Duke's pride and fear were roused by this very broad hint; and it is said that he, from that time, reformed, and became ever after *le modèle des pères et des époux.*

OUVRARD, THE FINANCIER. — Before the French Revolution, the largest fortunes in France were possessed by the farmers of the revenue, or *fermiers-généraux.* Their profits were enormous, and their probity was very doubtful. It is related that one evening at Ferney, when the company were telling stories of robbers, they asked their host, Voltaire, for one on the same subject. The great man, taking up his flat candlestick, when about to retire, began, "There was once upon a time a *fermier-général*—I have forgotten the rest."

The prodigality, magnificence, and ostentation of these Crœsuses were the subject of every play and every satire; and when the bloody tribunals of 1793 ruled over France, their fortunes were confiscated, and very few of the *fermiers-généraux* escaped the fate which many of them had well deserved.

At that unhappy period, just before the fall of Robespierre, the funds fell to 7, and shortly after his execution and the establishment of the Directory, they rose to 40. By such fluctuations many large fortunes were made by speculators and army contractors; they were protected by the very corrupt chief of the Directory, Barras, and realised enormous sums. The most prominent among the latter was Ouvrard, a man sprung from a very humble origin, but of very great financial capacity. During his long career of success, which lasted from the latter part of the last century till 1830, he made and spent millions of money. He was ruined by making large sales on the funds, under the expectation that the government of Louis Philippe could not stand. He was born in 1770, and his first operation, which consisted in buying up all the paper made in Poitou and Angoumois and retailing it at immense profit to the Paris booksellers, laid the foundation of his fortune. He soon afterwards made a contract for provisioning the Spanish fleet, which had joined the French squadron in 1797, and made a net profit of £600,000. In 1800, he was supposed to possess a fortune of a million and a half of English money. Soon after, he had the contract for supplying the French army in the campaign which closed with the battle of Marengo. His prosperity continued for many years; and, in 1812, the Government owed him, for enormous advances made by him, nearly three millions of English money. He was *munitionnaire-général* for the Waterloo campaign; and, in 1823, contracted to supply the Duc d'Angoulême with everything necessary for the entry of the French army into Spain in 1823, but the non-fulfilment of his contract entailed heavy losses upon him, and in 1830 he was completely ruined.

No man was more reckless in his expenditure, or more magnificent in his manner of living, than Ouvrard. At the time of the Directory, the *fêtes* given by him at Le Raincy were the theme of the whole of Parisian society of that time. At his splendid villa near Rueil, during the Empire, he was in the habit of giving suppers to all the *corps de ballet* of the opera twice a week; and he used to send several carriages, splendidly equipped, to bear away the principal female performers when the performance was over. There an enormous white marble bath, as large as an ordinary-sized saloon, was prepared for such of the ladies as, in the summer, chose to bathe on their arrival. Then a splendid supper was laid out, of which the fair bathers, and many of the pleasure-seekers of the day, partook; and, besides every luxury of the culinary art, prepared by the best cooks in Paris, each lady received a donation of fifty louis, and the one fortunate enough to attract the especial notice of the wealthy host, a large sum of money.

Mademoiselle Georges, the celebrated tragedian of that day, cost him (as he was fond of relating) two millions one hundred thousand francs for a single visit. He had invited her to sup with him at his villa, but the very day she was to come, a note informed him that she was compelled to give up the pleasure of supping with him, as the Emperor Napoleon had given her a rendezvous for the same hour, which she dared not refuse. Ouvrard was furious at this *contretemps*, and (as he said when I heard him tell the story) he could not bear to yield the *pas* to "*le petit Bonaparte*," whom he had known as a young captain of artillery, too happy to be invited to his house in the days of the Directory. This feeling, and his pride of wealth, got the better of his prudence, and he sent to Mademoiselle Georges to insist upon her coming to Rueil, adding, as a postscript, that she would find a hundred thousand francs *sous les plis de sa serviette* at supper. This last argument was irresistible, the lady sent an excuse to the Emperor, pleading a sudden indisposition, and was borne rapidly in one of Ouvrard's carriages to his country residence.

The following day the great financier received a summons forthwith to appear at the Tuileries, and was ushered into the Emperor's presence. After walking once or twice up and down the room, the great man turned sharply round on his unwilling guest, and, with his eagle glance riveted on Ouvrard's face, sternly demanded, "Monsieur, how much did you make by your contract for the army at the beginning of the year?" The capitalist knew it was in vain to equivocate, and replied, "Four millions of francs, sire." "Then, sir, you made too much; so pay immediately two millions into the Treasury."

Ouvrard passed several years in prison for a considerable debt owed by him to Séguin, another army contractor; but he lived magnificently even when in prison, and his creditor, strange to say, used frequently to go and dine with him there. I saw Ouvrard shortly before his death, which took place in 1846.

MADAME DE STAËL.—I frequently met the famous Madame de Staël in Paris during the years 1815 and 1816. She was constantly at Madame Crauford's, in the Rue d'Anjou St. Honoré, and at Lady Oxford's, in the Rue de Clichy. She was very kind and affable to all the English, and delighted to find herself once more in sight and smell of the *ruisseau* de la Rue du Bac, which she once said she preferred to all the romantic scenery of Switzerland and Italy. She was a large, masculine-looking woman, rather coarse, and with a thoracic development worthy of a wet nurse. She had very fine arms, which she took every opportunity of displaying, and dark, flashing eyes, beaming with wit and genius.

Her career was a chequered one, and her history is a romance. The only child of the Minister Necker, in troublous times she married the Swedish ambassador at Paris, the Baron de Staël, in 1786. Full of great and noble sentiments, she took up the cause of the unfortunate Louis XVI. and his Queen with generous ardour. She arranged a plan of escape for the King in 1792, and did not fear to present to the revolutionary tribunal, in 1793, a petition in favour of Marie-Antoinette. She remained in Paris during the Directory; and it was under her influence and protection that Talleyrand obtained office in 1796. She was always opposed to Napoleon, and was exiled by him from Paris in 1802. She returned, however, and her presence was tolerated till the appearance of her book *De l'Allemagne*, the sentiments and allusions of which were decidedly hostile to the imperial despotism which then oppressed nearly the whole of Europe. The book was seized by the Emperor's police, and Madame de Staël was again exiled, and did not return till 1815 to Paris, where she died in 1817, aged fifty-one.

Admirable as her writings were, her conversation surpassed them. She was "well up" on every subject—"*nihil quod tetigit non ornavit.*" Her *salons* were filled with all the most celebrated persons of her time. The statesmen, men of science, poets, lawyers, soldiers, and divines, who crowded to hear her, were astounded at her eloquence and erudition. Disdain and contempt for her personal charms or mental powers was one of the causes of the hatred she had vowed to the first Napoleon; and, unequal as a contest between the greatest sovereign of the age and a woman would at first sight appear, there is no doubt that, by her writings and her sarcastic sayings, which were echoed from one end of Europe to the other, she did him much injury.

Talleyrand, when he married Madame Grant, a beautiful but illiterate idiot, said he did so to repose himself after the eternally learned and eloquent discourses of Madame de Staël, with whom he had been very intimate. On one occasion, alluding to her masculine intellect and appearance, while she was holding forth at great length, he said, "*Elle est homme à parler jusqu'à demain matin.*" At another time, when he was with her in a boat, and she was talking of courage and devotion, qualities in which the *ci-devant* bishop was notoriously deficient, she put the question, "What would you do if I were to fall into the water?" Looking at her from head to foot, he answered, "Ah, madam, you must be such a good swimmer" ("*vous savez si bien nager*").

A pretty saying of Madame de Staël's is cited, which showed her good taste and good feeling. A person in a large company, in beholding her and Madame Récamier,—the most beautiful woman in France, and who prided herself not so much on her personal appearance as on her intellectual gifts,—said, "Here is wit" (pointing to Madame de Staël) "and beauty" (pointing to Madame Récamier).

Madame de Staël answered, "This is the first time I was ever praised for my beauty."

The person in England who was the great object of Madame de Staël's admiration, and in the praise of whom she was never weary, was Sir James Mackintosh, one of the greatest men of the age, and certainly the best read man of the day. She also lived on most intimate terms with the celebrated orator and publicist, Benjamin Constant; but her *liaison* was supposed to be a Platonic one: indeed, she was secretly married, in 1810, to M. de Rocca, a young officer of hussars, who was wounded in Spain, and who wrote a very interesting account of the Peninsular war.

Madame de Staël was perhaps at times a little overpowering, and totally deficient in those "brilliant flashes of silence" which Sydney Smith once jokingly recommended to Macaulay. In fact, as a Scotchman once said of Johnson, she was "a robust genius, born to grapple with whole libraries, and a tremendous conversationist."

A story is told of the Duke of Marlborough, great-grandfather of the present Duke, which always amused me. The Duke had been for some time a confirmed hypochondriac, and dreaded anything that could in any way ruffle the tranquil monotony of his existence. It is said that he remained for three years without pronouncing a single word, and was entering the fourth year of his silence, when he was told one morning that Madame la Baronne de Staël, the authoress of *Corinne*, was on the point of arriving to pay him a visit. The Duke immediately recovered his speech, and roared out, "Take me away—take me away!" to the utter astonishment of the circle around him, who all declared that nothing but the terror of this literary visitation could have put an end to this long and obstinate monomania.

A Feminine Foible.—During the first Empire, the great ladies of the Faubourg St. Germain (like ladies of all times) were very shy of divulging their ages. The Duchess of S * * *, once beautiful and replete with wit, was congratulating herself on her youthful looks, and pretending that she was born at least twenty years later than she really was, when her daughter, more beautiful than her mother, endeavoured to put a stop to her exaggerations by crying aloud, " O mamma, do leave at least nine months between our ages ! "

Mademoiselle le Normand.—One of the most extraordinary persons of my younger days was the celebrated fortune-teller, Mademoiselle le Normand. Her original residence was in the Rue de Tournon, but at the time of which I write she lived in the Rue des St. Pères. During the Restoration, the practice of the "black art" was strictly forbidden by the police, and it was almost like entering a besieged citadel to make one's way into her *sanctum sanctorum.*

I was first admitted into a good-sized drawing-room, plainly but comfortably furnished, with books and newspapers lying about, as one sees them at a dentist's. Two or three ladies were already there, who, from their quiet dress and the haste with which they drew down their veils or got up and looked out of the window, evidently belonged to the upper ten thousand. Each person was summoned by an attendant to the sibyl's boudoir, and remained a considerable time, disappearing by some other exit without returning to the waiting-room. At last I was summoned by the elderly servant to the mysterious chamber, which opened by secret panels in the walls, to prevent any unpleasant surprises by the police. I confess that it was not without a slight feeling of trepidation that I entered the small square room, lighted from above, where sat Mademoiselle le Normand in all her glory.

It was impossible for imagination to conceive a more hideous being. She looked like a monstrous toad, bloated and venomous. She had one wall-eye, but the other was a piercer. She wore a fur cap upon her head, from beneath which she glared out upon her horrified visitors. The walls of the room were covered with huge bats, nailed by their wings to the ceiling, stuffed owls, cabalistic signs, skeletons—in short, everything that was likely to impress a weak or superstitious mind. This malignant-looking Hecate had spread out before her several packs of cards, with all kinds of strange figures and ciphers depicted on them. Her first question, uttered in a deep voice, was whether you would have the *grand* or *petit jeu*, which was merely a matter of form. She then inquired your age, and what was the colour and the animal you preferred. Then came, in an authoritative voice, the word "*Coupez*," repeated at intervals, till the requisite number of cards from the various packs were selected and placed in rows side by side. No further questions were asked, and no attempt was made to discover who or what you were, or to watch upon your countenance the effect of the revelations. She neither prophesied smooth things to you nor tried to excite your fears, but seemed really to believe in her own power. She informed me that I was *un militaire*, that I should be twice married and have several children, and foretold many other events which have also come to pass, though I did not at the time believe one word of the sibyl's prediction.

Mademoiselle le Normand was born in 1768, and was already celebrated as a fortune-teller so early as 1790. She is said to have predicted to the unfortunate Princesse de Lamballe her miserable death at the hands of the infuriated populace. She is also reported to have been frequently visited and consulted by Robespierre and St. Just; to have reported his downfall to Danton, at that time the idol of the people; to have warned the famous General Hoche of his approaching death by poison; to have foretold to Bernadotte a northern throne, and to Moreau exile and an untimely grave.

The Empress Josephine, who, like most creoles, was very superstitious, used frequently to send for Mademoiselle le Normand to the Tuileries, and put great faith in her predictions; which she always asserted in after years had constantly been verified. But, unfortunately for the sibyl, she did not content herself with telling Josephine's fortune, but actually ventured to predict a future replete with malignant influences to the Emperor himself. This rash conduct entailed upon her great misfortunes and a long imprisonment; but she survived all her troubles, and died as late as 1843, having long before given up fortune-telling, by which she had amassed a large sum of money.

An Ominous Fall.—I remember Count d'Orsay telling me that on the day previous to the appearance of the celebrated *ordonnances*, or decrees of July 27, 1830, which caused the Revolution and drove Charles X. from the throne, his sister, the Duchesse de G * * *, niece by marriage to Prince Polignac, and a violent Royalist, was seated at the piano, playing and singing with triumphant vigour, "*La victoire est à nous*," when suddenly the music-stool gave way, and the beautiful Duchess lay sprawling on the floor. D'Orsay, who was a Liberal, assured her, laughingly, that this fall in the midst of her Legitimist song was *de très mauvais augure*, and a bad prognostic for the success of the party to which she belonged. He did not at the time believe his own prophecy, so firmly did the Bourbons appear to be established; but before the end of the month Charles X. had left France, and was followed by the fair Duchess and her husband, the most faithful friends and adherents of the fallen monarch, and as true to him in adversity as when he shone forth as one of the most powerful sovereigns of Europe.

Louis Philippe and Marshal Soult. — Louis Philippe's cunning was proverbial, and he showed great talent and ingenuity in managing his ministers; but he had great difficulties to encounter. The most *exigeant* of all his officials was the celebrated Marshal Soult, who was perpetually asking the King for some place or appointment for one or other of his friends or relations, to the disgust of Louis Philippe. Upon one occasion, when all the ministers had assembled in the royal closet, the

King, observing that the Marshal appeared displeased, inquired, "What is the matter, Marshal?" "Oh, nothing, sire; except that I intend giving into your Majesty's hands my resignation." This untoward and unexpected announcement alarmed the rest of the ministers, who, one and all, intimated that in such case they also must tender their resignations. The King, not alarmed in the slightest degree, requested the Marshal would follow him into his private room, and begged the rest of the ministers to remain until his return. The interview lasted a considerable time, and the King, fearing that he had kept the ministers too long waiting, and that their patience was exhausted, popped his head into the council-room, crying out, "A little more patience, gentlemen. All will be well; for the Marshal and myself have already shed tears." The truth became known the following day; at all events it was generally whispered that Soult had frightened the King out of a promise that all places of emolument and advancement in the army should centre in him, which promise was religiously adhered to until Soult left the Ministry of War.

Decamps and the Duke of Orleans.—Some twenty years back, or thereabout, I was breakfasting with my late lamented friend, Lord H. Seymour, when Decamps, the celebrated painter, was announced. During breakfast Decamps told us the following anecdote, which, he said, had occurred the day before:—A gentleman called at his lodging, on the third storey, and asked the porter if M. Decamps was at home, and being answered in the affirmative, the visitor was about to ascend the staircase when the porter called after him, and said, "As you are about to visit the artist, perhaps you will have no objection to carry with you his trousers, which I have just mended." "By all means," replied the stranger; "I shall be happy to render you this little service." Arriving at the door, the visitor rang the bell, and Decamps, on opening the door, to his utter amazement, recognised the Duke of Orleans, who laughingly presented to him the trousers he had received from the porter. This little anecdote is one out of many I could relate to illustrate the truly amiable character and unaffected simplicity of the lamented heir of Louis Philippe's throne.

Fashion in Paris.—It has been said of the French that they are constant only in their fickleness, worshipping one day what they execrate the next, and throwing down with their own hands from its pedestal the idol they themselves had set up a few weeks before. But there is one deity to whom they have never proved faithless; at whose shrine they bow with the same devotion to-day as they did centuries ago, whose fiat is law, and whose dictates none dare resist. This capricious, exacting, ever-changing goddess is Fashion.

I remember once expressing my admiration for a very handsome, charming lady, in the presence of a Parisian "man-milliner of modern days." During all my encomiums the Gaul preserved a stern silence. "Do you not admire Lady X * * *?" I asked, rather provoked by his disdainful looks. "She has purple gloves—*c'est une femme jugée*," he replied, with a look of supreme contempt, which was truly amusing to behold. Though it is now the fashion in

Paris to imitate the fast generation of perfidious Albion in many articles of dress, such as looped-up petticoats, wideawake hats, nets for the hair, and Balmoral boots, in former days no English lady who had not been brought up at the feet of some female Parisian Gamaliel, could be supposed by any possibility to know anything about *la toilette.*

Many years ago I was asked one day to dine with the late Lord Pembroke, to meet Lord C * * *, and a goodly array of French *élégants.* Even after this lapse of years I can still smile at the recollection of the anxiety with which these gentlemen —among whom, by the bye, was the handsome Henri de Noailles, afterwards Duc de Mouchy—awaited the arrival of the celebrated London dandy. At length the great man was announced; for, true to London rule, he came last, and long after the hour fixed for dinner. There was no one more agreeable or cleverer than Lord C * * *, and no one, at the time of which I write, was more the fashion in London; but to appreciate him one required to be accustomed to his peculiar appearance and rather eccentric manner. Short of stature, and rather inclined to be obese, even at five-and-twenty, he wore a coat very much thrown open, a variety of splendid jewels adorning a transparent cambric shirt elaborately embroidered, and (oh, tell it not in Gath!) an exceedingly short, rose-coloured waistcoat, just covering his ample chest, and cutting his somewhat square-built torso exactly in two. Add to this, very long, straight, straw-coloured hair, which he had the habit of throwing continually back, or, by a rapid gesture, bringing forward to fall over his wild but very expressive eyes, and his *tout ensemble* appeared, to French notions, very strange indeed: the Parisian exquisites could hardly believe that they saw before them the Lovelace, the *fleur des pois* of English society, of whom they had heard so much.

Those who, like myself, are old enough to recollect the beautiful Lady Blessington in her brightest days, can remember that she always wore a peculiar costume, chosen with artistic taste to suit exactly her style of beauty. The cap she was in the habit of wearing has been drawn in Chalon's portrait of her, well known from the print in the *Keepsake*, and in all the shop windows of the day. It was "a mob-cap" behind, drawn in a straight line over the forehead, where, after a slight fulness on each temple, giving it a little the appearance of wings, it was drawn down close over the cheeks, and fastened under the chin. Nothing could have been more cunningly devised to show off the fine brow and beautifully-shaped oval face of the deviser, or to conceal the too great width of the cheeks, and a premature development of double chin. Lady Blessington had also a style of dress suitable to her figure, which was full, but then not "of o'er-grown bulk." She always wore white in the morning, a thick muslin dress, embroidered in front and lined with some bright colour, and a large silk bonnet and cloak to match. This was her costume in London, but, on her arrival in Paris, two or three French ladies got hold of her, declared she was *horriblement fagotée*, and insisted on having her dressed in quite a different style by a fashionable *modiste;* they managed so completely to transform her that, in the opinion of myself and all who had seen her in

England, her defects were brought out, and all her beauty disappeared. But, nevertheless, in her new and unbecoming attire, she was pronounced *charmante* by a jury of fashionable dames, and forced, *nolens volens*, to take an eternal farewell to the lovely and becoming costumes of her youth.

Fashion has such a wonderful power over the French mind, that it can actually transform the body so as to suit the exigency of the moment. In former days, we old fellows may remember that the French type of womankind was *une petite femme mignonne et brune*. In the whole of society, thirty or forty years ago, one could scarcely have numbered more than half-a-dozen tall women. They were looked upon as anomalies, and saluted not unfrequently with such very uncomplimentary appellations as "*chameaux*," "*gens darmes*," "*asperges*," &c., &c. Now that it is the fashion to be tall and commanding, one sees dozens of gigantic women every day that one goes out, with heels inside as well as outside their boots; perhaps even stilts under those long sweeping petticoats. I know not how the change has been effected, but there it is.

Frenchwomen used to have dark hair; blondes were not generally admired, and tried by every possible means to darken their hair; but now, since the Empress has made fair hair *à la mode*, all the women must be blondes, and what with gold powder and light wigs they do succeed. As to complexions, a dark one is now unknown; roses and lilies abound on every cheek: even some young men of fashion have not disdained the use of cosmetics, but have come out from the hands of the *coiffeur* romantically pale or delicately tinted.

Fashion is very capricious, and it does not suffice to sit in high places in order to govern *la mode.* With the exception of the Duke of Orleans, so prematurely cut off in the flower of his youth, not one of Louis Philippe's family, male or female, ever exercised the smallest influence over this capricious goddess. There were young and handsome princesses, always well and tastefully dressed, but they were pronounced *rococo;* and no one ever dreamt of wearing any particular bonnet or cloak, because the beautiful Duchesse de Nemours, or the graceful Princesse de Joinville had appeared in a similar one.

It is not because the Empress Eugénie is the wife of Napoleon III. that she sets the fashion, even to those who don't go to court, and who turn up their noses at her *entourage.* She is considerably older and certainly not handsomer than was the Duchesse de Nemours, when she left France to die in exile; but she has the *chic,* if I may use such a word, that the Orleans princesses did not possess; and the quietest dowager, before she ventures to adopt a *coiffure,* as well as the gayest lady of the *demi-monde,* will cast a look to see what the Empress wears. Strange to say, the supreme good taste and elegance which reign in her Majesty's *toilettes* were by no means conspicuous in her younger days; for, as Mademoiselle Montijo, she was voted beautiful and charming, but very ill-dressed.

The style of French cookery has also changed as completely as the style of dress, at the dictates of

Fashion. Modern attire and modern cookery are alike over ornamented. Thirty years ago, simplicity in dress, especially in the morning, was the right thing: if by any extraordinary chance a Parisian lady of rank condescended to take a walk (a rare occurrence), she could only be remarked by the extreme plainness and neatness of her attire; and any article of dress that could in anywise resemble what might be worn by the *lorette* of that day was studiously shunned. To be taken for anything of a lower grade than what she was, and spoken to by an unknown person, would have been looked on as an insult so great that the humiliating incident would never have been breathed to mortal ear; but now-a-days it is considered only a good joke. How astonished and horror-struck would be the great ladies of the Restoration, if they could rise from their graves and behold their granddaughters emulating the *demi-monde* in their dress, language, and manners; *affichant* their *liaisons* in the sight of the sun; walking into their lovers' houses unveiled, undisguised, or riding with them publicly, and having their carriages called under their own names at the restaurants, or small theatres, where they have been *tête-à-tête!*

The dignified, artful, proud, but perhaps not more virtuous, grandmother would have been unutterably disgusted, not so much at the immorality as at the bad taste displayed in such arrangements; which then existed just as much as now, but were supposed to be unknown. Great was the amusement of the clever and charming Lady G * * *, at one of her small receptions thirty years ago, at seeing the celebrated statesman, Comte M * * *, saluting in the most respectful and distant manner, and with all the formal politeness of *la vieille cour*, the Comtesse de C * * *, with whom it was supposed that he had long been on terms of more than friendly intimacy, and whom he had probably left but a few hours before. The lady, without even extending the "shake hands" now so much in vogue, returned the salutation by an equally reserved and dignified courtesy; and a minute after this formal greeting, Lady G * * * overheard the elderly minister, in a voice full of enthusiastic admiration, address the middle-aged lady thus, "*Pauline, tu as quinze ans!*"

I am sorry to say that *esclandres*, or scandals which made a noise in the world, were supposed to be perpetrated by my countrywomen alone. Comte Alfred de Maussion, a very dark, handsome man, who was a great Lovelace, especially amongst the English ladies some forty years ago, used to say, "Those charming Englishwomen are really *très compromettantes*. They are not happy if they do not run away from their stupid, good-natured husbands, who only ask to be permitted to shut their eyes and see nothing."

Certainly in these modern times the order of things is reversed. Frenchmen need not take the trouble of publishing their successes with their own countrywomen; their victims are only too happy to relate them: indeed, modern French husbands would consider their wives very *rococo* and *provinciales*, if they had not at least one *cicisbeo* to follow in their train. *Le mari trompé* exists now only in the drama or novel. His eyes are wide open; no one tries to deceive him; and he is perfectly satisfied.

Literary Salons in France.—One of the most agreeable *salons* in Paris was held by the late Madame Emile de Girardin, the Mrs. Norton of France. Like our own gifted countrywoman, she was endowed not only with poetic genius, but likewise with great conversational wit and much personal beauty.

She was a tall, good-looking woman, with the aspect of a Muse, or rather of what one fancies a Muse ought to be. She had an abundance of beautiful fair hair, large blue eyes, an aquiline nose, and very fine teeth, and bore a striking resemblance to the pictures of Marie-Antoinette. She was also somewhat like the beautiful Duchesse de Guiche (mother of the French ambassador at Vienna); but it was remarked that she looked like the case in which Madame de Guiche had been laid, being of coarser build, and with larger features; though in intellectual gifts Madame de Girardin was considerably the other lady's superior.

She had many great and estimable qualities. Her mind and heart, like her outward frame, were on a large and grand scale. She was above all the littlenesses that too often disfigure women's characters. She was (a rare thing in a woman) an enthusiastic admirer of beauty even in her own sex, and took pleasure in drawing round her the women most distinguished for their personal or mental qualities. She possessed a peculiar knack of making her guests appear to the best advantage, drawing them out, and placing them in the little circle where they would be sure to shine and be appreciated; for she felt that she could afford to subdue the light of her brilliant wit, and allow the little glowworms around her to twinkle to their own satisfaction.

PARISIAN SOCIETY. CHAUSSÉE D'ANTIN, 1826.

You were sure to meet in the *salon* of Madame E. de Girardin all the celebrities of the day, whether fashionable, literary, or political—Lamartine, Balzac, Dumas, Frederic Soulié, Emile Souvestre, Theophile Gautier, with the Dukes and Counts of the Faubourg St. Germain, Orleanist deputies, and the handsome Englishwomen who used to gladden Parisian eyes and win Parisian hearts.

Every one felt at ease,—the women looked their best, the men made themselves agreeable, and the charming hostess seemed happy in the enjoyment of those around her.

Any one who wishes in some degree to appreciate the brilliant and vivacious wit of Madame E. de Girardin may obtain some idea of it by reading the charming *Lettres Parisiennes*, published under the pseudonyme of Vicomtesse de Launay; though (admirable as they are) they give only a dim reflection of that true *esprit français*, which Madame de Girardin possessed in its highest perfection, and the great charm of which lies in quick repartees and the *à propos* of the moment.

In addition to her great gifts as a prose writer, she was also a poetess of the highest order; and her *pièces de théâtre* enjoyed the greatest popularity, and met with well-deserved success.

Though in reality far superior to her husband, both in cleverness and judgment, she had a high and even exaggerated opinion of his merits as a politician. In the darkest days of that melancholy experiment yclept the *République française* of 1848, an intimate friend was sitting one morning in Madame de Girardin's boudoir. They were lamenting over the miserable state of things which had succeeded the era of constitutional liberty. After discussing the dangers and difficulties of the moment, Madame de Girardin added, with a grave expression of countenance, and a deeper intonation of voice, "Happily, there is one above who can restore order and tranquillity to the country; and he alone can save us." The visitor, somewhat astonished at what he thought a pious observation coming from a lady of rather Voltairian principles, muttered out something about Providence, and good coming out of evil. "That's not the question," said Madame de Girardin; "I am not talking about Providence, but of my husband, who is at this moment overhead, and engaged in writing an article for the *Presse*, which will appear to-morrow, and set everything to rights."

Madame de Girardin and her sister, Madame O'Donnell, a very clever and agreeable, but less good-natured woman, both inherited their great gifts from their mother, Madame Sophie Gay, the celebrated authoress of *Les Malheurs d'un Amant Heureux*, and other novels, much appreciated some thirty or forty years ago.

Salons like that of the gifted Madame Emile de Girardin are extremely rare now-a-days, owing greatly to the unlimited extension of what is called society; and also, perhaps, in some measure, to the strong line of demarcation drawn by political animosity. The thirst for noisy active pleasure has well-nigh destroyed the charming little *coteries* of the olden time, where men did not think it beneath them to be well-bred and amiable, where they consented to speak of other things besides their horses and mistresses, and where women were not satisfied with being pretty and well-dressed, but aimed also at being thought clever and agreeable.

One of the pleasantest of these *salons* was that of the Comtesse Merlin. In a different way, that lady was almost as remarkable a person as Madame Emile de Girardin. She was a Spanish Creole by birth; and though even when I made her acquaintance, some thirty years ago, she was what our English novelists call "somewhat *embonpoint*," her beauty was still of the very highest order. Her face was one which, once beheld, could never be forgotten; the perfect oval of the contour, the small regular features, fine brow, and dark flashing eyes were in perfect harmony. Though she had the Spanish defect of a too long *corsage*, and a somewhat thick waist, yet her bust and arms were faultless.

And she was not only surpassingly beautiful, but possessed a voice equal to those of any of the first-rate singers who have appeared upon the stage. She could sing with Malibran, Grisi, Rubini, and Tamburini, without appearing out of place. In her later years what once had been so great a charm became the terror of her friends; for she did not feel her declining powers, and her voice, which had become uncertain, and even hoarse, sounded in her own ears as mellow and enchanting as ever. She was one of those who will not grow old. As she approached sixty, her gowns became more *décolletées*, and her bravuras more frequent. She used to have all her grey hairs plucked out; so that at last, as was wittily observed, instead of being *coiffée en cheveux*, she was *coiffée en tête*.

But perhaps these illusions as to her appearance and perpetual youth enabled Madame Merlin up to the end of her life to remain the same kind, generous-hearted, agreeable woman she had been in her young days, when all the world was at her feet. She still thought herself far superior to the young beauties who had succeeded her; and no doubt even the sere and yellow leaf of her autumnal time was more attractive than the spring of many younger ones around her.

She had less wit and more genuine good-nature than Madame de Girardin. She might have a moment of violent anger, but bore no malice; and she had too much reliance on the variety of her attractions to fear any rivalry. As the *étudiant* says in the well-known print of Gavarni, "*C'était là une riche nature de femme et si bon enfant.*"

Madame Merlin gave charming concerts, followed by very agreeable suppers. Her house was a sort of neutral ground, where the ministers of the Orleans dynasty met the leaders of the Legitimist party, and the most celebrated writers of the day; where Duchesses sat down with singers, and all aristocratic pretensions were laid aside. Madame Merlin, among her many good qualities, had one which is rare and admirable, and is the stamp of a truly noble nature. She was thoroughly independent. The poor wayworn musician who formed one of a chorus met with as civil and kind a reception as the Duke or Count just arrived from the Faubourg St. Germain. There was the kind, beaming, southern smile of recognition for the second-rate artiste, when met in some great house where he or she was kept at arm's length. There was in her no respect of persons for their rank or position, no cringing to the debasing laws of social etiquette. She possessed what is much rarer than we all imagine,—a truly kind heart; and she reaped her reward, for though Madame Merlin had not always a great regard for appearances, no one had the courage to fling a stone at the generous-minded, warm-hearted woman.

Sir John Elley.—I have alluded in my former volume to the extraordinary personal bravery of General Sir John Elley on the field of Waterloo, and his series of hand-to-hand encounters with the French cavalry on that great day. It is perhaps not generally known that this most distinguished officer commenced his career as a private in the Blues. He afterwards commanded that celebrated regiment, for which he always had a great liking; and on a lengthened tour he once made through Europe, after the war, although a major-general, he always wore the uniform of the Royal Horse Guards.

When he arrived at Vienna, he was invited to dine at a full-dress dinner at the British Ambassador's on the occasion of King George IV.'s birthday. He was covered with orders, bestowed by the different sovereigns of Europe in 1815; and amongst these gorgeous ribands and crosses the modest Waterloo medal appeared. Sir John happened to sit next to a French Secretary of the Embassy, who criticised the English decoration, and said, "Surely, General, that is a very poor sort of order the Government have given you and the other brave officers of the English army. It cannot have cost them five francs." "True," replied Sir John, making a low bow, "it has not cost our country more than five francs; but it cost yours a Napoleon."

An English Dandy in Paris.—During the days of Georges III. and IV., a number of gentlemen, remarkable for their eccentricities of dress and manners, were the lions of the day both in London and Paris. For example, we had such men as Brummell, Pierpoint, John Mills, Meyler, Bradshaw, and others, who seemed to think that the principal object of their existence ought to be that of obtaining notoriety by their dress. In addition to this class, we had a series of fops about town, who were yet more extravagant in their dress and manners.

I well remember Captain T * * *, in Paris, immediately after the war. He lived in a magnificent style, having taken no less than two different hotels, which naturally created a good deal of gossip in the fashionable world. His carriages and horses were English, and considered the most perfect things of the day. But the most remarkable feature of his eccentricities was the Captain's dress: he wore trousers capacious enough for a Turk; his coat, which he always designed himself, was remarkable for its wide, bagged sleeves, and an ingenious mode of making the collar a sort of receptacle for a voluminous quantity of shirt frill; indeed, the shirt collar appeared to descend from his ears all the way down his back, so that you might suppose he was looking out of a black chimney-pot.

Nature had bestowed upon him handsome features, and a profusion of hair, which he had curled and arranged in such an eccentric style that the snaky locks appeared to be always desiring to escape from his head, and were only detained on his cranium by a tight-fitting little hat, suitable for a boy about fourteen. He wore a pair of golden spurs, with rowels of the circumference of a small dessert-plate. Thus he strutted about the streets of Paris, inviting the smiles of those who knew him, and the positive laughter of strangers to whom he was unknown. When Mike Fitzgerald met him for the first time, after the end of the war, he said, "Well, T * * *, I am happy to find you have won your spurs: made of doubloons, I suppose."

Peace to his ashes! He died in the flower of his age, much regretted by a large circle of friends; and his death was mourned by nearly all the best families of the Faubourg St. Germain, with whom he had lived on the most intimate and friendly terms for a quarter of a century.

SHERIDAN AND THE ELECTORS OF STAFFORD.—In my last volume I have spoken of my return as member of Parliament for Stafford. Many circumstances have been brought to my mind lately with regard to Sheridan, who had been one of my predecessors, by my witnessing a wild drama that has been brought on the French stage, under the title of *L'Homme de Rien*, which purports to be a biography of that distinguished man. Those who have seen how Mrs. Siddons, Edmund Kean, and Dean Swift have been rendered ridiculous by the incredible ignorance of dramatic authors in France about everything English, and of every circumstance of the lives of those they purport to represent, would not be surprised at the liberties they have taken with the great orator, wit, and dramatist.

I heard from some very old men amongst my constituents the singular history of the canvass of Sheridan for this immaculate borough. His reputation had already reached the town, but the defects which unfortunately also rendered him conspicuous were then unknown. He was reported to possess, besides, unbounded influence with the Government, and to have the entire management of Drury Lane Theatre. His voters, being fully convinced that they ought to receive a *quid pro quo* for their "most sweet voices," every one had a favour to ask. One had a son who had great dramatic talent, another was an admirable scene-painter, others had cousins and nephews who would make excellent door-keepers, lamp-lighters, check-takers, or box-openers; there were tailors, *coiffeurs*, and decorators, who could dress with inimitable effect the *dramatis personæ.* Sheridan listened with his usual bland smile to every request, and complied with them all; each individual being furnished with a letter to the stage-manager of Drury Lane, they all started off for the metropolis, full of eager expectation. On their arrival they were favourably received, and each person obtained the situation that he had desired. When letters from London announcing the fulfilment of Sheridan's promises reached the hungry constituents of Stafford, a fresh batch of aspirants for office posted off, and all were equally successful; the consequence was that, on the day of election, the favourite was returned with every demonstration of admiration and confidence.

Scarcely, however, had the member of Parliament left the town than innumerable reproaches were heaped upon his head; it was found that upon application for the payment of the salaries due to the different persons employed there was no money in the treasury. On Saturday night the receipts were carefully handed over to Sheridan, who carelessly spent the money; so that the whole of the humbler *employés* received nothing, whilst the higher order of actors contrived to dun and worry the thoughtless and extravagant *entrepreneur* out of a portion of their salaries.

Great was the indignation excited amongst Sheridan's constituents on finding that they had placed their political interests in the hands of such a man, and a deputation of three persons was despatched to London to remonstrate with him. They went at a fixed hour to the residence of the great man where they found a large crowd of his creditors assembled, many of them apparently bent on saying some very disagreeable truths. After waiting for some time, the folding-doors were thrown open, and out stepped the delinquent, in the first style of fashion. Looking around him with a fascinating smile, he addressed a few words to each of his would-be tormentors in succession; each one in his turn was delighted, and quite incapable of making unpleasant observations. They saw before them the man whose speech they had just read in the *Times* and *Courier*, which had proclaimed him in their leading articles the first orator of the age; and they had seen in the *Morning Post* a paragraph describing the irresistible wit which had convulsed Brookes's with laughter, and which concluded by pronouncing the honourable member an ornament to British society.

On this occasion, Sheridan soon observed that the deputation from Stafford was an angry one; so he walked quietly up to each individual, and put some questions to him relating to his domestic concerns. He had not forgotten anybody or any circumstance. He asked one of his constituents if Mrs. Grundy's preserves and jams, which she was making when last he saw her, had proved of first-rate quality; whether Miss Grundy the elder continued to charm the world with playing Steibelt's "Storm" on the piano; if Miss Grundy the younger still took lessons from Mr. Town in velvet-painting; and whether Dr. Squill had successfully vaccinated Master Tommy. To each the great man had something to say which seemed calculated to soothe the irritation of the hearer, and to prevent him from uttering a word of blame. Each man saw before him the most fascinating individual in the kingdom fixing upon him his dark flashing eye, and addressing him in persuasive accents, with the blandest smile. Sheridan moved through the admiring circle with graceful step, no one venturing to stop him; and as he reached the door he turned round, made an enchanting bow, and having entered his carriage, kissed his hand gracefully to his surrounding friends, and loudly told the coachman to drive to Carlton House. Away he went in a carriage for which the coachmaker had received no money, driven by a coachman and footman whose wages had not been paid for months, but who were still so pleased with their master that they were willing to wait, and in fact rather starve in his service, than live in the family of the richest nobleman upon the fat of the land.

Upon the dissolution of Parliament, Sheridan went down to Stafford; but he found circumstances completely changed; he could not obtain the promise of a single vote from his old friends. In consequence of his continued excesses, he had lost much of the charm of outward appearance that had won him friends at an earlier period, and nothing remained of his once expressive face but the remarkable brilliancy of his eyes; his cheeks were bloated, his nose was of a fiery red, and his general aspect bespoke the self-indulgence of the reckless man. His appearance on the hustings was the signal for a volley of opprobrious terms. One man in the crowd bawled out, "We won't send you to Parliament, for your nose will set the House of Commons on fire;" another had some doggerel rhymes to recite about

"The Whigs' banners are blue;
Your nose and your cheeks are red,
From port-wine and brandy too,
And there's *sherry* in your head."

In vain did the once-admired orator attempt to gain a hearing; he was driven away amid the derision of the crowd, and never again was enabled to show his face in Stafford.

It has been said that his first election cost him £2500; but this has been strenuously denied. An anecdote, however, was in circulation, and had reached his biographer, Thomas Moore, to the effect that a deputation from Stafford had waited upon Sheridan, requiring that he should give a vote contrary to his own views, and that his answer was a decided negative, expressed in these words, "Gentlemen, I bought you, and I assure you that I shall sell you whenever it suits my convenience."

Many of the follies and extravagances that marked the life of this gifted but reckless personage must be attributed to the times in which he existed.

Drinking was the fashion of the day. The Prince, Mr. Pitt, Dundas, the Lord Chancellor Eldon, and many others, who gave the tone to society, would, if they now appeared at an evening party, "as was their custom of an afternoon," be pronounced fit for nothing but bed. A three-bottle man was not an unusual guest at a fashionable table; and the night was invariably spent in drinking bad port-wine to an enormous extent.

SHERIDAN AT DRURY-LANE THEATRE.—However, many of the tricks played by Sheridan were quite unjustifiable. A very old man, and who had suffered severely by his confidence in the great orator, was pointed out to me. On a Friday evening, after the second price had been received, the treasurer of Drury-Lane Theatre came to Sheridan with a wofully long face, and told him that there was not money enough to pay even the subordinates on the following day; and that unless a certain sum could be found he was persuaded that the house could not open on Monday. Sheridan suggested several plans for raising the wind, but all were declared by Mr. Dunn to be useless. Sheridan gazed round at the thinly-peopled boxes, and at length called to one of the porters in waiting, "Do you see that stout, good-tempered-looking man seated next a comely lady in the third box from the stage, in a front row? Immediately the play is over, go to him; have a couple of wax candles carried by a boy who can make graceful bows; open the box door, and in a voice loud enough to be heard by every one, say, 'Sir, Mr. Sheridan requests the honour of a private interview with you in his own room.' Let every one on the way treat him with the greatest civility; and, Mr. Dunn, will you have the kindness to see that a bottle of the best port and a couple of wine glasses are placed on the table in my study."

The orders were duly obeyed. The gentleman was ushered into the presence of Sheridan with honours almost approaching those shown to royalty, and was received by him with the most cordial marks of friendship and regard. "I am always so happy to see any one from Stafford. I was glad you called at my house for an order to this theatre, where I hope you will come when you please; you will find your name on the free list. I think I remember you told me you always came twice a year to London." "Yes," was the reply; "January and July, to receive my dividends." "You have come for that purpose now," continued Sheridan. "Oh, yes; and I went to the Bank of England and got my six hundred pounds." "Ah," said the manager, "you are in Consols, whilst I, alas, am Reduced, and can get nothing till April, when, you know, the interest is paid; and till then I shall be in great distress." "Oh," said his constituent, "let that not make you uneasy; if you give me the power of attorney to receive the money for you when it is due, I can let you have three hundred pounds, which I shall not want till then." "Only a real friend," said Sheridan, shaking his dupe by the hand with warmth, "could have made such a proposition. I accept it thankfully." And the three hundred pounds were immediately transferred from the pocket-book of the unwary man of Stafford into that of the penniless manager of the theatre.

April arrived, a power of attorney was one

morning handed over for signature to Sheridan, whose only reply was, "I never spoke of Consols *in* Reduced, I only spoke of my consols being reduced; unhappy is the man who does not comprehend the weight of prepositions." The Stafford man, burning with indignation, rushed up to London, and found his cajoler calmly seated in his room at Drury Lane. Sheridan, apparently not at all disconcerted, with outstretched hand and benignant smile welcomed his victim, whose rage was at first uncontrollable; but his attack was met by the manager with an acknowledgment that, in a moment of urgent necessity, he had been compelled to throw himself on the generosity of a man whom he had heard from every one was a model of worth, and whose acquaintance would be acceptable in the highest quarters. "But excuse me, my dear sir," he added; "I am now commanded to go to the Prince of Wales, to whom I shall narrate your noble conduct. My carriage is waiting, and I can take you to Carlton House." The eye of the provincial sparkled with delight. Was it possible that he meant to take him to the Prince of Wales? It sounded something like it. He shook Sheridan by the hand, saying, "I forgive you, my dear friend; never mention the debt again." "I will take care never to do so," said the manager. The carriage came round to the door, the two friends entered it, and when they arrived at Carlton House, Sheridan got out, and closing the door, told the coachman to drive the gentleman to his hotel. The Stafford man, with a last hope, naïvely said, "I thought I also was going into Carlton House." "Another mistake of yours," replied Sheridan. The worthy constituent returned that night to Stafford; and in future his vote was given against Sheridan.

SHELLEY'S FIGHT AT ETON.—In the year 1809 an incident occurred at Eton which caused no small sensation and merriment throughout the school. It was announced one morning that Shelley, the future poet, had actually accepted wager of battle from Sir Thomas Styles. Whether he had received an insult, and that vast disparity in size gave him confidence, or that, over-full of the warlike descriptions of Homer's heroes, he was fired to imitate their exploits against some one or other, remains a secret. Meet, however, they did, after twelve, in the playing-fields. The usual preliminaries were arranged—a ring was formed, seconds and bottle-holders were all in readiness, and the combatants stood face to face. The tall, lank figure of the poet towered above the diminutive, thick-set little Baronet, by nearly a head and shoulders. In the first round no mischief was done; Sir Thomas seemed to be feeling his way, being naturally desirous of ascertaining what his gigantic adversary was made of; and Shelley, though brandishing his long arms, had evidently no idea of their use in a pugilistic point of view. After a certain amount of sparring without effect, the combatants were invited by their seconds to take breath. The Baronet did not hesitate to accept the offer to sit upon the knee of his second; but Shelley disdainfully declined to rest, and, calculating upon finishing the fight by a single blow, stalked round the ring, looking defiance at his little adversary.

Time was called, and the battle was renewed in earnest. The Baronet, somewhat cautious, planted his first blow upon the chest of Shelley, who did not appear to relish it. However, though not a proficient in the art of self-defence, he nevertheless went in, and knocked the little Baronet off his legs, who lay sprawling upon the grass more dead than alive. Shelley's confidence increased; he stalked round the ring as before, and spouted one of the defiant addresses usual with Homer's heroes when about to commence a single combat; the young poet, being a first-rate classical scholar, actually delivered the speech in the original Greek, to the no small amusement of the boys. In the third and last round, Styles went to work like a first-rate artist, and, after several slighter blows, delivered what is called in the prize-ring "a heavy slogger" on Shelley's bread-basket; this seemed positively to electrify the bard, for, I blush to say, he broke through the ring, and took to his heels with a speed that defied pursuit. His seconds, backers, and all who had witnessed the fight, joined in full cry after him, but he outran them all, and got safe to the house of his tutor, Mr. Bethel.

This incident naturally excited much merriment at Eton at the time, and Shelley never more, during his stay at college, ventured to enter the pugilistic arena, but passed his leisure hours in making various experiments in chemistry and natural science. He even went so far as to employ a travelling tinker to assist him in making a miniature steam-engine, which burst, and very nearly blew the bard and the Bethel family into the air.

EPIGRAM BY CANNING. — When Tomlyn, the Bishop of Winchester, died, every effort was made

PLAY AT CROCKFORD'S CLUB. 1843 COUNT D'ORSAY CALLING A MAIN.

by Pelham to succeed to the bishopric. The following epigram was written by Canning:—

"Says Priggish Pelham, 'May I beg a hint on
The shortest road from Exeter to Winton?' *
Says Bloomfield,† 'Sure you cannot fail to light on
The shortest road through *Hertford* ‡ and through Brighton.'"

Mr. Canning and Lord Lyndhurst. — When George Canning succeeded Lord Liverpool as Premier, he was at a loss to find a Chancellor. He had quarrelled with Copley (Lord Lyndhurst) a few nights before, for having, in a violent speech, inveighed against the Catholics in no measured terms: Canning had even accused him of having learnt by heart a pamphlet, published the day before, by the Bishop of Exeter against the Catholics. Nevertheless, Canning, when forming his ministry, wrote the following laconic note to Copley: — "*Non obstante Philpotto,* will you be my Chancellor?" The bait took, and Copley the same day became Chancellor, and forty-eight hours after was gazetted Lord Lyndhurst.

Crockford's Club.—I have alluded, in my first volume, to the high play which took place at White's and Brookes's in the olden time, and at Wattier's in the days of Brummell and the dandies. Charles Fox, George Selwyn, Lord Carlisle, Fitzpatrick, Horace Walpole, the Duke of Queensberry, and others, lost whole fortunes at faro, macao, and hazard; almost the only winners, indeed, of that

* Winton, the old name of Winchester.

† Sir B. Bloomfield, afterwards Lord Bloomfield, a great favourite of the Prince Regent's.

‡ The Marchioness.

generation were General Scott, father-in-law of Canning, the Duke of Portland, and Lord Robert Spencer: Lord Robert, indeed, bought the beautiful estate of Woolbidding, in Sussex, with the proceeds of his gains by keeping the bank at Brookes's.

But, in the reign of George IV., a new star rose upon the horizon in the person of Mr. William Crockford; and the old-fashioned games of faro, macao, and lansquenet gave place to the all-devouring thirst for the game of hazard. Crockey, when still a young man, had relinquished the peaceful trade of a fishmonger for a share in a "hell," where, with his partner Gye, he managed to win, after a sitting of twenty-four hours, the enormous sum of one hundred thousand pounds from Lords Thanet and Granville, Mr. Ball Hughes, and two other gentlemen whose names I do not now remember. With this capital added to his former gains, he built the well-known palace in St. James's Street, where a club was established and play organised on a scale of magnificence and liberality hitherto unknown in Europe.

One may safely say, without exaggeration, that Crockford won the whole of the ready money of the then existing generation. As is often the case at Lords' Cricket-ground, the great match of the gentlemen of England against the professional players was won by the latter. It was a very hollow thing, and in a few years twelve hundred thousand pounds were swept away by the fortunate fishmonger. He did not, however, die worth more than a sixth part of this vast sum; the difference being swallowed up in various unlucky speculations.

No one can describe the splendour and excitement of the early days of Crockey. A supper of the most exquisite kind, prepared by the famous Ude, and accompanied by the best wines in the world, together with every luxury of the season, was furnished gratis. The members of the club included all the celebrities of England, from the Duke of Wellington to the youngest Ensign of the Guards; and at the gay and festive board, which was constantly replenished from midnight to early dawn, the most brilliant sallies of wit, the most agreeable conversation, the most interesting anecdotes, interspersed with grave political discussions and acute logical reasoning on every conceivable subject, proceeded from the soldiers, scholars, statesmen, poets, and men of pleasure, who, when the "house was up" and balls and parties at an end, delighted to finish their evening with a little supper and a good deal of hazard at old Crockey's. The tone of the club was excellent. A most gentlemanlike feeling prevailed, and none of the rudeness, familiarity, and ill-breeding which disgrace some of the minor clubs of the present day, would have been tolerated for a moment.

Though not many years have elapsed since the time of which I write, the supper table had a very different appearance from what it would present did the club now exist. Beards were completely unknown, and the rare mustachios were only worn by officers of the Household Brigade or hussar regiments. Stiff white neckcloths, blue coats and brass buttons, rather short-waisted white waistcoats, and tremendously embroidered shirt-fronts with gorgeous studs of great value, were considered the right thing. A late deservedly popular Colonel in the Guards used to give Storr & Mortimer £25 a year to furnish him with a new set of studs every Saturday night during the London season.

The great foreign diplomatists, Prince Talleyrand, Count Pozzo di Borgo, General Alava, the Duke of Palmella, Prince Esterhazy, the French, Russian, Spanish, Portuguese, and Austrian ambassadors, and all persons of distinction and eminence who arrived in England, belonged to Crockford's as a matter of course; but many rued the day when they became members of that fascinating but dangerous coterie. The great Duke himself, always rather a friend of the dandies, did not disdain to appear now and then at this charming club; whilst the late Lord Raglan, Lord Anglesey, Sir Hussey Vivian, and many more of our Peninsula and Waterloo heroes, were constant visitors. The two great novelists of the day, who have since become great statesmen, Disraeli and Bulwer Lytton, displayed at that brilliant supper-table the one his sable, the other his auburn curls; there Horace Twiss made proof of an appetite, and Edward Montague of a thirst, which astonished all beholders; whilst the bitter jests of Sir Joseph Copley, Colonel Armstrong, and John Wilson Croker, and the brilliant wit of Alvanley, were the delight of all present, and their *bons mots* were the next day retailed all over England.

In the play-room might be heard the clear ringing voice of that agreeable reprobate, Tom Duncombe, as he cheerfully called "Seven," and the powerful hand of the vigorous Sefton in throwing for a ten. There might be noted the scientific dribbling of a four by "King" Allen, the tremendous backing of nines and fives by Ball Hughes and Auriol, the enormous stakes played for by Lords Lichfield and Chesterfield, George Payne, Sir St. Vincent Cotton, D'Orsay, and George Anson, and, above all, the gentlemanly bearing and calm and unmoved demeanour, under losses or gains, of all the men of that generation.

The old fishmonger himself, seated snug and sly at his desk in the corner of the room, watchful as the dragon that guarded the golden apples of the Hesperides, would only give credit to sure and approved signatures. Who that ever entered that dangerous little room can ever forget the large green table with the croupiers, Page, Darking, and Bacon, with their suave manners, sleek appearance, stiff white neckcloths, and the almost miraculous quickness and dexterity with which they swept away the money of the unfortunate punters when the fatal cry of "Deuce ace," "Aces," or "Sixes out," was heard in answer to the caster's bold cry of "Seven," or "Nine," or "Five's the main."

O noctes cœnæque deûm! but the brightest medal has its reverse, and after all the wit and gaiety and excitement of the night, how disagreeable the waking up, and how very unpleasant the sight of the little card, with its numerous figures marked down on the debtor side in the fine bold hand of Mr. Page. Alas, poor Crockey's! shorn of its former glory, has become a sort of refuge for the destitute, a cheap dining-house. How are the mighty fallen! Irish buckeens, spring captains, "welchers" from Newmarket, and suspicious-looking foreigners, may be seen swaggering, after dinner, through the marble halls and up that gorgeous staircase where once the chivalry of England loved to congregate; and those who remember Crockford's in all its glory, cast, as they pass, a look of unavailing regret at its dingy walls, with many a sigh to the memory of the pleasant days they passed there, and the gay companions and noble gentlemen who have long since gone to their last home.

"KING" ALLEN.—The late Viscount Allen, commonly called "King" Allen, was a well-known character in London for many years. He was a tall, stout, and pompous-looking personage, remarkably well got up, with an invariably new-looking hat and well-polished boots. His only exercise and usual walk was from White's to Crockford's, and from Crockford's to White's.

Who in this ponderous old man would have recognised the gallant youth who, as Ensign in the Guards, led on the men with incredible energy and activity across the ravine at Talavera; where, if the great Duke had not sent the 48th Regiment to their assistance, very little more would have been heard of "King" Allen and his merry men? But one of the most famous dandies of the day was not fated thus to perish; and he was preserved for thirty years after the great battle, to swagger down Bond Street or lounge on the sunny side of Pall Mall, to become an *arbiter elegantiarum* amongst the tailors, and a Mæcenas at the opera and play.

To render the "King" perfectly happy, one little item was wanting—money. His estates, if he ever had any, had long passed from him, and he had much difficulty in making the two ends meet. When, for economy's sake, he was obliged to retire for a short time to Dublin, he had a very large door in Merrion Square, with an almost equally large brass plate, on which his name was engraved in letters of vast size; but it was very much doubted whether there was any house behind it. He was a great diner out; and one spiteful old lady, whom he had irritated by some uncivil remarks, told him that his title was as good as board wages to him.

Strange to say, this *mauvais sujet* was a great friend of the late Sir Robert Peel, when Chief Secretary for Ireland; and on one occasion, when they were proceeding in an open carriage to dine with a friend a few miles from Dublin, in passing through a village, they had the misfortune to drive over the oldest inhabitant, an ancient beldam, who was generally stationed on the bridge. A large mob gathered round the carriage; and as Peel and the Tory Government were very unpopular at the period to which I refer, the mob began to grow abusive, and cast very threatening and ominous looks at the occupants of the barouche; when the "King," with a coolness and self-possession worthy of Brummell, rose up, displaying an acre of white waistcoat, and called out, "Now, postboy, go on, and don't drive over any more old women." The mob, awe-struck by "King" Allen's majestic deportment, retired, and "the industrious and idle apprentices" went on their way rejoicing.

The "King" was not a very good-natured person; and as he had a strong inclination to, and some talent for, sarcasm, he made himself many enemies. To give an idea of his "style." When the statue of George III. was erected in front of Ransom's bank-ing-house, Mr. Williams, one of the partners, commonly known by the name of "Swell Bill," petitioned the "Woods and Forests" to remove that work of art, as it collected a crowd of little boys, who were peculiarly facetious on the subject of the pigtail of that obstinate but domestic monarch, and otherwise obstructed business. Lord Allen, meeting Williams at White's, said, "I should have thought the erection of the statue rather an advantage to you, because, while you are standing idle at your own shop door, it would prevent you seeing the crowds hurrying to the respectable establishment of Messrs Coutts & Co., close by in the Strand."

The "King" did not possess much wit, but no one could say more disagreeable things at the most disagreeable moment. I remember his setting down the late Lady N * * *, daughter-in-law of a celebrated legal functionary of that name, in rather an amusing manner. She was a vulgar Irish grazier's daughter, extremely plain, and clipped the King's English in a vain attempt to conceal a mellifluous King's County brogue. After passing many years in Rutland Square, Dublin, she suddenly found herself a Countess, with a large income. Her first step after this accession of dignity and fortune was to start for London, where she affected to have passed her life. On meeting Lord Allen soon after her arrival, she extended one finger of her little fat hand, and in a drawling, affected tone of voice said, "My L*a*rd Alleen, how long have you been in London?" "Forty years, ma'am," growled out the "King."

Lord Allen greatly resembled in later life an ancient grey parrot, both in the aquiline outline of his features, and his peculiar mode of walking, with one foot crossed over the other in a slow and wary manner. He was a regular Cockney, and very seldom left London ; but on one occasion, when he had gone down with Alvanley to Dover for the sake of his health, and complained to his facetious friend that he could get no sleep, Alvanley ordered a coach to drive up and down in front of the inn windows all night, and made the boots call out, in imitation of the London watchmen of that day, "Half-past two, and a stormy night." The well-known rumble of the wheels, and the dulcet tones of the boots, had the desired effect; the "King" passed excellent nights, and was soon able to return to his little house in South Street with renewed health and spirits.

Lord Allen was at last obliged to leave London, after coming to an understanding with his creditors; and after passing some time at Cadiz, died at Gibraltar in 1843, when his title became extinct.

Ball Hughes.—I was at Eton with my late friend Ball Hughes, whose recent death was so much lamented in Paris. He was known at Eton by the name of Ball only; but the year before he came of age, he took the additional name of Hughes, his uncle, Admiral Hughes, having left him the fortune he had amassed during his command of the fleet on the Indian seas, and which was supposed to be not less than forty thousand a year. But Hughes entered the army early in life, his uncle having bought him a commission in the 7th Hussars, and made him a handsome allowance. He was a great imitator of the Colonel of his regiment, the Earl of Uxbridge, afterwards Marquis of Anglesea, whom he took as a model for his coats, hats, and boots; indeed, everything that his noble commander said or did was law to him. Hughes was a remarkably handsome man, and made a considerable figure in the best society; his manners were excellent; he was a thoroughly amiable, agreeable fellow, and universally popular.

When he came into his fortune, he was considered a great match by all the women in London. He fell desperately in love with Lady Jane Paget, the daughter of his Colonel, and the marriage-settlements were all arranged; but, unluckily for the disappointed lover, Lady Jane, at the last moment, gave a most decided negative, and the match was broken off. Ball was not long disconsolate, but looking around him, fixed his attention upon the lovely Miss Floyd, who afterwards married Sir Robert Peel; finding his attentions unacceptable in that quarter, he proposed to Lady Caroline Churchill, afterwards Lady Caroline Pennant, but here he was refused. This, however, did not prevent him from being considered an eligible match by a great many mothers, who diligently sought his society. He was courted, followed, and admired by every one who had daughters to dispose of; but, unfortunately for him, the young ladies, having heard of his numerous disappointments, were not ready to unite their fate with a man whose rejected addresses were so well known. "The Golden Ball," as he was called, continued, nevertheless, to make his appearance everywhere. He was devoted to female society; no dinner, ball, pic-nic, or party, was complete unless the popular millionaire formed one of the social circle.

Ball Hughes's first step, on entering into possession of his fortune, was to employ Mr. Wyatt the architect to furnish a mansion for him in Brook Street. No expense was spared to make it as near perfection as possible. Wyatt had *carte-blanche*, and bought for him buhl furniture, rich hangings, statues, bronzes, and works of art to an extent that made an inroad even upon his wealth.

A beautiful Spanish *danseuse*, named Mercandotti, arrived about this time in London, in the midst of the gay season of 1822, under the immediate patronage of Lord Fife. She was then only fifteen years of age, and by some she was believed to be his daughter, by others only his *protégée*. At Barcelona she was considered inimitable; at Madrid she gained great applause; in Seville she acquired immense reputation; and by the time the lovely girl reached London, great curiosity was excited to see the new candidate for public favour at the King's Theatre, where she was engaged for the season at £800. The new *débutante* met with complete success, and was pronounced divine. All the dandies who had the *entrée* behind the scenes surrounded her and paid her homage, and more than one scion of the fashionable world offered to surrender his liberty for life to the fascinating dancer. Ebers, then manager of the theatre, was pestered from morning to night by young men of fashion anxious to obtain an introduction to Mademoiselle Mercandotti, but they were invariably referred by the *impresario* to Lord Fife.

One night, March 8, 1823, the house was enormously crowded by an audience eager to see the favourite in the then popular ballet by Auber,

"Alfred;" when, just before the curtain drew up, the manager came forward and expressed his regret that Mademoiselle Mercandotti had disappeared, and that he had been unable to discover where she had gone. Knowing ones, however, guessed that she had been carried off by the "Golden Ball," whose advances had been very favourably received, and who had evidently made a strong impression upon the damsel; and a few days after, the *Morning Post* announced that a marriage had taken place between a young man of large fortune and one of the most remarkable dancers of the age. The persons present at the marriage were the mother of the bride, Mr. Ebers, and Lord Fife. The honeymoon was passed at Oatlands, which the happy bridegroom had shortly before purchased from the Duke of York.

Ainsworth wrote the following epigram on this event:—

> "The fair damsel is gone; and no wonder at all
> That, bred to the dance, she is gone to a Ball."

Ball Hughes died at St. Germains two years ago. His fortune had dwindled down to a fourth of its original amount, for he was perhaps the greatest gambler of his day. His love of play was such, that at one period of his life he would rather play at pitch and toss than be without his favourite excitement. He told me that at one time he had lost considerable sums at battledore and shuttlecock. On one occasion, immediately after dinner, he and the eccentric Lord Petersham commenced playing with these toys, and continued hard at work during the whole of the night; next morning he was found by his valet lying on the ground, fast asleep, but ready for any other species of speculation. His pur-

PREMIÈRES DANSEUSES AND THEIR ADMIRERS_ THE GREEN ROOM OF THE OPERA HOUSE (KINGS THEATRE) 1822.

EARL OF FIFE. BALL HUGHES. MDLLE. MERCANDOTTI. MDLLE. NOBLET. PRINCE V. ESTERHAZY. MDLLE. HULLIN. LORD PETERSHAM

chase of Oatlands, which at the time was considered a foolish one, proved a very good speculation; for it was sold, for building villas, for so large a sum, that Hughes, whose fortune had dwindled to a mere pittance, became in his latter days very well off again; and though he lived in retirement, kept a large establishment, and was in the enjoyment of every luxury.

Scrope Davies. — The name of Scrope Davies is now but little known, except in connection with Brummell's exit from the fashionable world of London, and from his being occasionally mentioned by Lord Byron and by Moore; yet few men were better received in society, or more the fashion than he once was. He was educated at Eton, and from thence he migrated in due time to King's College, Cambridge, of which he became a fellow; there he formed those acquaintances that at a later period served as an introduction into that world of which he soon became a distinguished ornament. His manners and appearance were of the true Brummell type: there was nothing showy in his exterior. He was quiet and reserved in ordinary company, but he was the life and soul of those who relished learning and wit; being a ripe scholar, and well read, he was always ready with an apt quotation.

As was the case with many of the foremost men of that day, the greater number of his hours were passed at the gambling-table, where for a length of time he was eminently successful; for he was a first-rate calculator. He seldom played against individuals; he preferred going to the regular establishments. But on one occasion he had, by a remarkable run of good luck, completely ruined a young man who had just reached his majority and come into the possession of a considerable fortune. The poor youth sank down upon a sofa in abject misery, when he reflected that he was a beggar; for he was on the point of marriage. Scrope Davies, touched by his despair, entered into conversation with him, and ended by giving him back the whole of his losses, upon a solemn promise that he never would play again. The only thing that Scrope retained of his winnings was one of the little carriages of that day, called a dormeuse, from its being fitted up with a bed, for he said, "When I travel in it I shall sleep the better for having acted rightly." The youth kept his promise; but when his benefactor wanted money, he forgot that he owed all he possessed to Scrope's generosity, and refused to assist him.

For a long time Scrope Davies was a lucky player; but the time arrived when Fortune deserted her old favourite; and, shortly after the Dandy dynasty was overthrown, he found himself unable to mingle with the rich, the giddy, and the gay. With the wreck of his fortune, and indeed but little to live upon beyond the amount of his own Cambridge fellowship, he sought repose in Paris, and there, indulging in literary leisure, bade the world farewell. He had but few intimates, and those only whom he had formerly known in his days of affluence.

He was a great admirer of Moore, and when some one said the poet had incurred reproach for writing "Little's" Poems, Scrope said the Roman poet had best expressed himself on that subject: "*Ubi plura nitent, non ego paucis offendar maculis;*" which he thus translated, "Moore shines so brightly that I cannot find fault with Little's vagaries." He also said, *Ne plus ultra*—nothing is better than Moore. Somebody observing that Moore was a true Irish name, but it was nothing without the addition of O, "Oh," replied Scrope, "I always thought that O'thello, Moor of Venice, was an Irishman, from the blunders that he made." He remarked, on one occasion, "You can find in Shakespeare an apt expression for everything that this earth affords." Somebody asked, "Where does Shakespeare ever allude to the treadmill?" "Oh," answered Scrope, "you will find in *King Lear* the words, 'Down, down, thou climbing sorrow!'" "Not an exact quotation," retorted one who was present. "Yes," said Scrope; "but the old king was in a rage when he expressed himself."

Scrope Davies bore with perfect resignation the loss of the wealth he had once possessed; and though his annual income was very limited, he made no complaint of poverty. He daily sat himself down on a bench in the garden of the Tuileries, where he received those whose acquaintance he desired, and then returned to his study, where he wrote notes upon the men of his day, which have unfortunately disappeared: that they existed there can be no doubt, as he occasionally read extracts from his diary to those in whom he placed confidence. Ball Hughes was about the last of his visitors. Scrope found the former gay young man very much improved in mind by adversity, and was wont to say, "He is no longer 'Golden Ball;' but since the gilt is off, he rolls on much more smoothly than he did." Having heard that Brummell had obtained a consulship when Lord Melbourne came into office,

Scrope went over to London and had an interview with the noble Lord; but he told his friends, "Lamb looked so sheepish when I was ushered into his presence, that I asked him for nothing; indeed, there were so many nibbling at his grass, that I felt I ought not to jump over the fence into the meadow upon which such animals were feeding."

THOMAS MOORE.—During my residence in Paris, several distinguished men took up their abode for a time, and were universally well received. Thomas Moore stayed for a considerable length of time, and his diary, admirably edited by Lord John Russell, shows most minutely how his hours were spent, and the people with whom he mingled. He was a favourite guest everywhere, but he was attracted only where a good *cuisine* would satisfy the taste of the *gourmet*. He realised (at least in Paris) Sir Edward Lytton Bulwer's admirable conception of Lord Guloseton, in his ever favourite novel, *Pelham*. When Moore had received an invitation to dinner from an untried Amphitryon, previous to returning an answer he cross-examined all who visited him. Had his friend an established kitchen, with a *chef* of his own? or did he depend upon a neighbouring *restaurateur?* Did the *chef* deserve the name of an *artiste?* Were the wines of a choice quality? Did they come direct from wine-growing countries? or were they likely to be the product of some Parisian wine-doctor? All these questions were asked with a serious earnestness that exhibited the great poet's exquisite taste in the pleasures of the table. It must, however, be added, that he was equally anxious that the invited should be intellectual or distinguished persons; and one stipulation in accepting the invitation was that English should be the language of the table: nothing seemed to annoy him more thoroughly than to find that, for the sake of a single individual, French should be the order of the day.

Whatever might be his peculiarities and his demands, however, they were amply repaid by the brilliancy of his conversation and the charm of his manners. He would now and then, when entirely at his ease with well-known friends, give an imitation of the great Irish orator Curran, which those who had known the original pronounced to be perfect, while those who had never seen him were delighted with the wit and humour that were introduced; but it was when the dinner was ended, the drawing-room reached, and a few of his much loved countrywomen were present, that the charm of Moore's society was felt. Almost without an invitation he would unaffectedly sit down to the pianoforte and warble forth some of those enchanting melodies which he has given to a grateful nation, accompanying himself with exquisite taste; his voice was rich in tone, and the expression he threw into his own words, combined with his beaming face and genial manner, elicited the admiration of all. Those who have heard him sing "Those Evening Bells," and "Oft in the Stilly Night," will carry a recollection of one of the most agreeable moments of their lives. He fully deserved the cognomen of "Anacreon," by which he was much known in Parisian society. The French are accustomed to Christian names of Greek origin; they have Achilles, Hector, and I have known several Nestors and one Epaminondas: indeed, it is their not unfrequent custom to drop the surname.

Many men are distinguished entirely by the prenomen; and as "Anacreon" Moore had been the sobriquet of the illustrious Irish lyric poet, from the time of his translation of the classic bard, he was soon christened "Anacreon," and as such generally known.

I remember once visiting M. Sommarivas's collection, and on mounting the staircase, the domestic whispered into my ear that "Monsieur Anacréon" was in one of the saloons; as that name had not then reached my ears, I asked him who was "Monsieur Anacréon;" the man looked at me with something like astonishment at the question, and after a short pause said, "It is your great English Béranger that is looking at our collection." On entering the saloon my mind was enlightened by recognising the bard of Erin, who, with animated looks and lively gestures, was pointing out the beauties of an antique statue; he wore the earnest and intellectual expression which distinguished him when delighting his friends with a barcarolle, or one of his sweetest melodies. Moore always heard with infinite pleasure any compliment paid to his wife; indeed, one of his most remarkable characteristics was his intense fondness for her; he was in fact the most uxorious of mortals, and though he could smile on any pretty woman, all his affections were centred in his charming "Bessy."

Francis Hare. — Francis Hare, sarcastically nicknamed "The Silent Hare," from his extreme loquacity, was remarkable for his leanness, his appetite, and his conversational powers. He could not only speak every European language, but all the various *patois* of each tongue, with a rapid and effervescent utterance that reminded one of the rushing of some alpine torrent, or Pyreneean *Gave* battling with the impediments that obstruct its course. His memory was as surprising as his loquacity; he could repeat whole pages from almost any book that was mentioned in his presence, and "come down" with effect on any unlucky wight who had made an incorrect quotation from some rare or obsolete volume, which might have been supposed to be unknown to all present.

One day, in a country house, his friends had made a bet that they would catch him napping, and start a subject on which he could have nothing to say. With this view they read up an article in an encyclopædia of that time, on Chinese music. At dinner one of the conspirators introduced the subject, a second took it up, and a third exhausted the knowledge they had gained by reading the learned essay. To their intense astonishment, Hare, in his excited, spluttering manner, took up the topic, contradicted all the statements that had been made, proved that they were all in the wrong, and concluded by saying, "I see, my good fellows, where you have taken your impressions about the harmony of the Celestial Empire. You have found them in an article in such an encyclopædia, which I myself wrote ten years ago; but since then I have studied the subject and conversed with well-informed travellers, and I have arrived at conclusions diametrically opposed to those I held when I wrote the article." *

Hare was very fond of practical jokes and mystifications of all sorts. While passing a winter at

* This anecdote is also told of Professor Whewell, the Master of Trinity.

Pisa, he amused himself (rather sacrilegiously, I must admit), one day that he was visiting the baptistry, by entering a confessional. In this quiet old town the priests have a good deal of rustic simplicity about them, and doubtless Hare would never have attempted the same joke either at Florence or Rome, where tales of deadly crimes are too common to astonish the confessor.

Hare, having selected a round-faced, innocent-looking priest as his victim, went up to the confessional, knelt down with a look of penitential sorrow, and poured forth in the purest Tuscan the most hideous tale of guilt that ever reached a good father's ear: robbery, blasphemy, sacrilege, rape, and murder were owned to in quick and horrifying succession; till at last the fat priest's placid countenance wore an expression of frantic terror, and opening the other door of the confessional, without cap or breviary, he rushed from the place, and tore down the street, never stopping till he had reached his own dwelling.

In mentioning the name of Hare, I am reminded of a circumstance which occurred to him during the Hundred Days. The English, including our embassy, were so frightened at the unexpected return of the Emperor, that they fled from France as if Old Nick had made his appearance. Hare, on the contrary, remained, and at the first levee held by Napoleon, he made his appearance at the Tuileries, where he was presented to his Majesty.

Napoleon addressed him in the following words:—"Well, sir, what has kept you in Paris, when your countrymen have all left?" "To see the greatest man in Europe, sir." "Ah, it is, then, your opinion, having seen and conversed with me, that I am not that wild beast I am represented to be by your ministers and the members of your Houses of Parliament." "Oh no, sir, it cannot be the opinion of the English ministers; but I blush when I call to mind the manner in which your name has been traduced by our garrulous members of both Houses."

This little episode, and the remarks said to have been made by Hare, reached London in an incredibly short time, when our newspapers attacked him in no measured terms, stating that he was a traitor to his country, and ought to be prosecuted forthwith. But Hare could afford to laugh at their abuse and threats; and on his return to England after the fall of Napoleon, used often to relate with pleasure, and not without some emotion, the conversation he had held with the great French Emperor.

THEODORE HOOK.—I remember being present at a dinner in London, when a very severe and saturnine Scotch Presbyterian was abusing Sunday newspapers, and concluded a violent tirade by saying, "I am determined to set my face against them." "So am I," said Theodore Hook, "every Sunday morning." He was well known at that time to be the editor of the *John Bull* weekly journal.

COSWAY THE PAINTER.—The miniature painter Cosway enjoyed the reputation of drawing the long bow to a remarkable extent. He was once relating, in my presence, to a large party of incredulous listeners, the story of a boy who had fallen from the top of a church steeple without sustaining any material injury. When he had come to a conclusion, there were a few murmurs, expressive of doubt as to the possibility of such a miraculous preservation, when Cosway, looking round on the company with a glance of solemn defiance, exclaimed, "I was that boy!"

Martin Hawke.—The Hon. Martin Hawke was a remarkable character, of a somewhat original and eccentric turn of mind. He lived many years abroad, and was the principal person who introduced, and rendered popular on the Continent, horse-racing, cricket, and other manly sports. He was well known in Paris, Tours, and Boulogne. He was an excellent horseman, a first-rate pugilist, a capital shot, was passionately fond of field sports, and had a great aversion to anything in the shape of poaching. He had several very serious encounters in France with some very rough customers, whom he found shooting on the manors he had hired; and nothing but his great strength and courage prevented him from falling a sacrifice to their vengeance. Upon one occasion he discovered, to his great joy, a net, which had been set near a wood the night before, and was full of woodcocks. He placed them in his greatcoat pocket, and, arriving at the market-place at Boulogne, where several of his friends had congregated, he addressed them thus:—"Gentlemen, I will show you a strange sight—some live woodcocks." His friends laughed, and rallied him for endeavouring to impose upon their credulity. In an instant out flew, from his greatcoat pocket, several woodcocks. Brooke Richmond, who squinted a little, asked Martin for one of the cocks, upon which

Martin replied, "My good fellow, they have all flown away—except the one in your eye."

When in Paris some forty years back, Hawke received, through Sir C. Stewart, our ambassador, an invitation to accompany the Duc de Berri on a shooting excursion in the forest of St. Germain. Prior to the chase, Alexandre de Girardin, the *grand veneur*, or huntsman, informed the gentlemen who were invited that it was not etiquette for them to fire before his Royal Highness had discharged his gun. As bad luck would have it, Hawke, in the ardour of the moment, had completely forgotten the hint given him; for on the first cock-pheasant getting up, Hawke, who was rather quicker than the royal sportsman, knocked it over close to the feet of the Duke, who in a great rage cried out, in English, "Who the devil are you, sir, who have disobeyed my orders?" Martin, rather ashamed, mentioned his name. The Duke replied, "A droll name yours is, Mr. 'Hock;'" upon which Martin, nothing abashed, said, "Oh, sir, your Royal Highness must be acquainted with it already, for my grandfather Admiral Hawke's name was well known in the French navy." The Duc de Berri took this retort very good-humouredly, and said, "Well, well, Mr. Hawke, you are a plain-spoken sort of fellow; I like your frankness and spirit, and therefore hope, the next time I have a shooting party at St. Germain, you will accompany me again." Alas! the following night the good-natured Prince, on entering the opera, was assassinated by Louvel.

Lord Normanby.—The first time I ever saw Lord Normanby was in 1816, during a morning visit at the Right Hon. George Tierney's, in Stratton Street. He was then a remarkably pleasing and good-looking young man; and I remember a circumstance which may account for his entering political life as a Liberal.

His father, Lord Mulgrave, was a high Tory, had long been a member of the administration of Pitt and his successors, and at the time of which I speak was Master-General of the Ordnance. On the occasion to which I refer, Lord Normanby, in the course of conversation, informed those present that his father had in a most unceremonious manner been dismissed from his high post to make way for the Duke of Wellington. He denounced, in the bitterest terms, the conduct of the Government towards so old a public servant as his father, and swore he never would forgive them.

He shortly afterwards entered Parliament as an advanced Liberal, always voted with the Whigs; and when they came into office in 1830, he was appointed Governor of Jamaica. On his return thence to England, he filled the post of Lord-Lieutenant of Ireland, under very difficult circumstances, and at a period of great importance, with general applause. His pleasing and conciliating manners made him a general favourite; and the Vice-Regal Court during his stay was a very brilliant one. He afterwards became Secretary of State; and in 1847, ambassador at Paris. He conducted himself with considerable tact, and showed a certain amount of ability during the latter part of the reign of Louis Philippe. On the establishment of the Republic, he had the good sense to keep quiet, and to remain on good terms with the poets, wood-merchants, and journalists who successively held office. But I do not think he conducted his relations with the present Emperor in a very adroit manner. He misjudged the Prince's capacity and character, and assumed rather a protecting tone with him; and when the *coup d'état* took place, he did not believe that Lord Palmerston would, with his usual decision and foresight, recognise Louis Napoleon as Emperor, immediately the choice of the French nation became known. Lord Normanby afterwards engaged in intrigues against his chief at the Foreign Office, and the latter period of his embassy was not a very satisfactory one, either to himself or to his admirers.

On his resignation, and after an attack of paralysis, he was appointed minister to Florence. This post was given him in lieu of a retiring pension, and because the climate suited him; and Lord Normanby, with his palazzo in town and the Villa Normanby near Fiesole, recalled to his old friends the pleasant days they had spent with him thirty years before, when he resided there as a private gentleman before his accession to office, and when his theatricals were the delight of all who visited Italy.

On the accession of the Tories to power, Lord Normanby and Lord Howden, our envoy to Madrid, were, with an unparalleled want of courtesy, immediately informed by a telegraphic despatch that her Majesty had no longer any occasion for their services. The insulting nature of this dismissal at the hands of Lord Malmesbury had no effect upon the fixed determination of Lord Normanby to leave his old friends the Whigs. It is supposed that the immense success of the paternal governments of Naples, Florence, Parma, Lucca, and Modena, in making their people happy and contented, must have produced this change in Lord Normanby's opinions; for, immediately on his return to England, he became a most violent Tory; and in his frequent speeches in the House of Lords arraigned and attacked on all occasions the foreign policy of the Whigs, and that with a blind and almost rabid violence, and a degree of bitterness and ill-nature, which astonished and disgusted his old friends.

Let us hope that this extraordinary change both in the opinions and feelings of so generally popular and amiable a man was the effect of disease, and attributable to the severe attack of illness from which he had suffered for several years before his death. He was *the* man of all others who should *not* have left the Liberal party. He was the spoiled child of the Whigs, and had received from them every great appointment and every distinction it was in their power to give. Besides the high offices I have before enumerated, he was made a Marquis, a Grand Cross of the Bath, and a Knight of the Garter.

I remember, *à propos* of this, that when Lord Melbourne was minister, Edward Ellice and the Premier were looking one morning from the windows of the First Lord's residence in Downing Street into St. James's Park, and saw Lord Normanby approaching. On Mr. Ellice inquiring what he could be coming for, Lord Melbourne said, in his off-hand manner, "I don't know what the devil the fellow can want, unless he comes to ask for a second garter for his other leg." In fact, the commonest gratitude should have made Lord Normanby pause before he took the fatal step which sullied the close of his political career.

Let me turn from this last lamentable error, and remember only his many good and amiable qualities. He was certainly one of the most courteous and agreeable of our ministers and diplomatists. There was no hauteur or reserve in his manner, and yet a natural dignity which prevented all undue familiarity. He was a fluent and ready speaker, and wrote with ease and elegance. When in Dublin he was much beloved by all around him, for he was a thoroughly good-natured man; and because this expression has been often misunderstood and supposed to mean weak or silly, let us not despise this rare and precious gift, much oftener bestowed on men of intellect than on fools. Till his illness, Lord Normanby was never heard to say an unkind thing of any one; and though in the latter years of his life he carried this amiable quality too far, when he took the part of the ex-King of Naples, the Duke of Modena, the Pope, and the brigands and assassins of Antonelli and Merode, yet this kindness in the days of his prosperity had a winning charm, because it was genuine, and sprang from a really good heart.

Had Lord Normanby not taken to politics and become a Viceroy and Secretary of State, he would have achieved great success as a literary man. His two novels, *Matilda*, and *Yes and No*, were worthy to be placed on a par with the best of their day; and had he been obliged to earn his bread, he might have been a Bulwer or a Kemble. For, besides his literary acquirements, he had a remarkable talent for acting; and his theatre at Florence, some forty years ago, might have vied with many of the best establishments in London or Paris. Lord Normanby had a thousand good and amiable qualities; and those who knew him will long remember with regret his pleasant conversation, his genial smile, and kind, open-hearted manner.

A MOTHER IN ISRAEL.—Old Madame Rothschild, mother of the mighty capitalists, attained the age of ninety-eight; her wit, which was remarkable, and her intellectual faculties, which were of no common order, were preserved to the end. In her last illness, when surrounded by her family, her physician being present, she said in a suppliant tone to the latter, "Dear doctor, try to do something for me." "Madame, what can I do? I can't make you young again." "No, doctor, I don't want to be young again, but I want to continue to grow old."

EQUIPAGES IN LONDON AND PARIS—THE FOUR-IN-HAND CLUB.—When lately in London, on driving through the parks, I was struck with the inferiority of the equipages, to those which I remember fifty years ago. Paris now quite equals London in external display; indeed, the horses are, generally speaking, even superior. The Emperor, whose long residence in England gave him an opportunity of forming an idea of the care and attention necessary to produce a fine breed of horses, has been indefatigable in selecting a stud; and being ably seconded by General Fleury, introduced into France a love of sport which seemed almost peculiar to England.

I look back upon the time when the most magnificent parade of horses and carriages attracted attention in London, and when the famous Four-in-hand Club was the theme of general admiration. The spectacle of a grand turn-out of the members of that distinguished body was one of the glories of the days of the Regent. There was a perfection in the minutest detail that made a well-appointed four-in-hand appear like a choice work of art. The symmetry of the horses, the arrangement of the harness, the plain but well-appointed carriage, the good taste of the liveries, the healthy, sturdy appearance of the coachmen and grooms, formed altogether one of those remarkable spectacles that make a lasting impression upon the memory.

The list of the members will show that some of the most distinguished scions of the aristocracy were the persons who vied with each other in producing this effect. The original club embraced, I believe, the following leading members:—Lord Sefton, Lord Barrymore, Colonel Berkeley, afterwards Earl Fitzhardinge, Mr. Akers, Sir Bellingham Graham, Sir Henry Peyton, Mr. Clutterbuck, Mr. Cholmondely of Vale Royal, Sir John Lade, Mr. Lewis, Sir H. Mainwaring, Tom Richards, Mr. Fenwick, Lord Worcester, Mr. Rowles, and the Hon. Major Forrester. They assembled in George Street, Hanover Square, and drove in regular order to Salt Hill, to the well-known house, named the Windmill, kept by Botham, where a sumptuous dinner awaited them; after which they returned to London, in high spirits, and not unfrequently somewhat overcome by the quantity of sound port wine, for which that inn was celebrated.

The driving was never of such a character as to

cause any accident; it was steady, and well regulated; one of the rules of the club being that no coach should pass another, and that the pace should never exceed a trot.

This club lasted in full vigour for upwards of twenty years, when it was broken up, in consequence of the death of many of the members, and the advanced age of several others. The love of coaching still existed amongst many distinguished leaders of fashion, and at a meeting held at the house of Lord Chesterfield, in Stanhope Street, it was determined to revive, in its former splendour, this national institution, which has served as an encouragement to the breeding of the finest cattle in the universe. Amongst my papers I found a list of the original members of this club, which met at Richmond on Saturday, June 2, 1838, and passed a series of resolutions, that formed the basis of the regulations which were observed during its existence.

The Earl of Sefton was one of the leaders of the former club; he drove splendid bay horses, and was acknowledged to be a man of considerable taste. This noble Lord, with a frame somewhat deformed, was a capital horseman, and was seen daily in the parks, accompanied by his two daughters; one of whom had some pretensions to beauty, and married a son of the Whig member for Marlow, Pascoe Grenfell, a proprietor of copper works at Swansea. Lord Sefton was amongst the most conspicuous lovers of the gastronomic art, and had secured Ude, the well-known *chef de cuisine* of Louis XVI. The noble Lord prided himself upon the invention of a famous *plat*, composed of the soft roe of the mackerel, which was served up in the form of *petits pâtés*.

Towards the end of his life, Lord Sefton became an *habitué* of Crockford's, and it was supposed that he left behind him there no less a sum than two hundred thousand pounds. After the death of the noble Lord, the fishmonger presented to his eldest son, who succeeded to the title, an acceptance of the late Lord's, to the tune of forty thousand pounds; and Lord Sefton, notwithstanding the uncertainty that attended a claim so abruptly made, felt it his duty to discharge the debt which he was led to believe had been incurred by his father.

The Marquis of Worcester, a spirited, dashing, handsome young man, was much admired by the fair sex, and led a life of great gaiety. His father, the Duke of Beaufort, receiving some hints that this promising youth was in danger of becoming the victim of a siren who had almost extorted from him a promise of marriage, the Marquis was sent to join the Duke of Wellington, became his aide-de-camp, and upon every occasion showed that he was worthy the race of John of Gaunt, from which he sprang.

The lady in question (Harriet Wilson) was one of the most notorious *traviatas* of the day, had written her memoirs, and become the scandal of the metropolis; one of her sisters had married a peer of the realm, and another a famous harpist of very doubtful character, who had been one of the most licentious men of the day, and afterwards carried off the wife of a distinguished English composer.

Upon the return of the Marquis from the army, he devoted his time to the sports of the field, his father's hunting establishments, both in Gloucestershire and Oxfordshire, being the admiration of every lover of the chase. He married Miss Fitzroy, daughter of General and Lady Anne Fitzroy. Lady Anne, a sister of the Duke of Wellington, on the death of the General, became the wife of Sir Culling Smith. After the death of his beautiful wife, the Marquis of Worcester married her half-sister, from whom sprang the present Duke of Beaufort, who retains his ancestors' love of sport, and has lately made such a sensation in France by the splendid retinue he brought with him on the occasion of his visiting that country for the purpose of wolf-hunting. His late father was a universal favourite; a dandy of the first water, and very much beloved by all classes with whom he came in contact.

In the days of which I speak there were amateur coachmen, who drove with unflinching regularity, and in all weathers, the public stage-coaches, and delighted in the opportunity of assimilating themselves with professional Jehus. Some young men, heirs of large landed proprietors, mounted the box, handled the ribbons, and bowled along the high-road; they touched their hats to their passengers, and some among them did not disdain even the tip of a shilling or half-crown, with which it was the custom to remunerate the coachmen. Many persons liked travelling to Brighton in "The Age," which was tooled along by Sir Vincent Cotton, whilst others preferred Charley Tyrrwhit. On the Holyhead, Oxford, and the Bath and Bristol roads, Lord Harborough, Lord Clonmel, Sir Thomas Mostyn, Sir Charles Bamfylde, Sir Felix Agar, Sir Henry Parnell, Sir Bellingham Graham, Mr. Clutterbuck, Sir John Lade, and other members of the Four-in-hand Club, were seen, either driving the coach or sitting cheek by jowl with the coachman, talking about horses and matters relating to "life upon the road." One of the members of the Four-in-hand Club, Mr. Akers, was so determined to be looked upon as a regular coachman, that he had his front teeth so filed that a division between them might enable him to expel his spittle in the true fashion of some of the most knowing stage-coach drivers.

Lord Onslow devoted his time to his stud, and being the master of four of the finest black horses in England, was always conspicuous in the parks; but he was too eccentric to obtain the suffrages of any of the Four-in-hand Club, for his carriage was painted black, and the whole turn-out had more the appearance of belonging to an undertaker. Mrs. Humphrey, at whose shop in St. James's Street were exhibited all the best caricatures of the day, had a capital one in her window, in which the noble Lord was depicted driving his mournful equipage; and the following lines at the bottom were read with great glee by those who had seen the original:—

"What can Tommy Onslow do?
He can drive a curricle and two.
Can Tommy Onslow do nothing more?
Yes, he can drive a phaeton and four."

There was an individual once familiar in the dandy circle, whose turn-out made always a sensation from its excessive elegance; his name was Richards, but he acquired the cognomen of "Tom Pipes" from the following circumstance. Having run through an enormous fortune, he was compelled to borrow money at an exorbitant interest, and a well-known tobacconist in Oxford Street lent him large sums on the condition that Richards should take one-half of the amount in tobacco pipes, and other such commodities, and the needy man was always inviting his friends to take off his hands a portion of this stock in trade. He, of course, like all other borrowers upon post-obit bonds, became completely ruined, and one kind friend obtained for him what in those days was a refuge of the destitute—a consulship. It was to Nantes he went; but his pecuniary difficulties hung about him, and he got into scrapes, and lost his appointment.

Richards had one redeeming point; he was a learned naturalist, and spent his little all in the purchase of animals. He got into trouble about a rare snake which he petted. Travelling in the Bath mail, he had placed the reptile in a basket under his feet; it crawled out and glided up the petticoat of a lady, who, suddenly waked up with an unusual sensation, pressed her hand upon the visitor, and irritated the snake, which gave her a severe bite.

Kate North.—In the days when "Skittles," "Anonyma," and other notorious descendants of the Laises and Phrynes of old, are topics of conversation and newspaper comment, I may be permitted to "point a moral and adorn a tale," by relating a remarkable episode in the life and adventures of the beautiful and once celebrated Kate North.

Kate was the daughter of a discharged sergeant of the Guards, who had the appointment of suttler at Chatham. Her mother dying after a long illness,

Kate, though young, worked hard early and late, and managed her father's house for a length of time; and the entire garrison, from the commanding officer to the private soldier, were loud in their praise of this incomparable young girl, whose marvellous beauty was the theme of conversation.

Among the officers at Chatham there happened to be a young ensign, extremely good-looking, upon whom Kate's beauty made a strong impression; he succeeded in captivating the affections of the charming and innocent girl, and at last seduced her. The regiment to which the ensign belonged having received marching orders, Kate determined to follow her seducer, and she marched with the soldiers to London. The secret of her seduction was not long before it got known and reached the ears of the Commander-in-Chief, the Duke of York; who, being informed that the poor girl was in a state of destitution, sent an aide-de-camp to discover her retreat, which proved to be an unfurnished room in the worst part of Spitalfields. The aide-de-camp told her his errand, but at the same time bound her to secrecy.

Early robbed of her virtue, abandoned by her betrayer, and an utter stranger in London, she reproached herself with her sin, and in a paroxysm of remorse and despair, the wretched girl determined to poison herself. She had purchased some laudanum, and was on the point of swallowing it, when a gentle rap at the door was heard outside. She opened the door, and in walked the Duke of York. His Royal Highness was struck with her beauty, modest deportment, and the frankness with which she answered all his questions, and, on his taking leave, said that he would send her a few necessaries to make her comfortable; upon which the poor girl fell upon her knees, and, in a voice almost inarticulate with emotion, thanked her benefactor.

When the Duke again called, she expressed her gratitude for all she had received, but hinted to her royal visitor that her earnest desire was to live an honourable life. The Duke was astounded, but said nothing in reply. He was simply dressed in a plain riding costume, and was, without exception, one of the finest men England could boast of. He stood above six feet; was rather stout, but well proportioned; his chest broad, and his frame muscular; his face bore the stamp of authority, and every feature was handsome; his brow was full and prominent, the eye greyish, beaming with benevolence; and a noble forehead, with premature grey hairs, though the Prince was hardly in the vale of years, completed the picture which presented itself to the unhappy Kate. The poor girl, overawed by the royal presence, attempted to leave the room, but was prevented. Her thoughts were how to avoid the danger which she felt was awaiting her, if the Royal Duke should persist in his assiduities.

His Royal Highness, not knowing the girl's feelings, paid her frequent visits, and each succeeding day became more and more enamoured of her; though upon all occasions she evinced a desire to avoid his presence. The thoughts of her seducer, and the degrading situation in which she stood, contrasting with the benevolence, and apparent affection of the Royal Duke, overwhelmed her. She wept bitterly, and flung herself upon her bed in an agony of distress. Her first resolution was to tell the Duke that she could not bring herself to consent to his proposals; but scarcely was the resolution formed, when the royal visitor again made his appearance. He promised never to desert her; and at length, overcome by his kindness and his importunities, she exclaimed, "If you really love me, Duke, I consent to be yours." The Duke was made happy; a house, carriages, &c., were supplied to the fair Kate, who lived with him many years. As she had a love for reading, and a desire for knowledge, masters were engaged for her; and by dint of perseverance, and applying herself to study, she was enabled to dissipate that weight of sorrow which would have otherwise hastened her death.

One summer morning a friend of the Duke of York's called and told her that his Royal Highness would be under the necessity of giving up his connection with her, for he had promised the King, his father, that if his debts were paid, he would never more see the object of his affection. Poor Kate's heart was full; she could not reply to the messenger, but bursting into tears, hid her face, and flew out of the room. The sting which had been inflicted was more than she could bear, and she was seized with brain fever; but with much care and quiet, in course of time, the poor creature recovered her health and composure of mind.

There was no woman so much admired in London at the time as Kate North; her bewitching manners, the charm and grace of her conversation, brought to her pretty house in Green Street innumerable admirers. Among those anxious to woo her, a noble Scotch lord was most assiduous in his attentions, and he at length succeeded in prevailing upon her to accept the offer of his protection; she lived with him several years, and bore him a daughter, who is now the wife of a baronet and the mother of a numerous family. But the canker in Kate's mind was all this while corroding her life. She visited Paris for change of air and scene; but there her senses left her: she became raving mad, and died in a foreign land, without a friend to close her eyes.

Sally Brooke.—There was a celebrated beauty who in my day made a conspicuous figure both in London and on the Continent. Miss Brooke, or, as she was more generally called, Sally Brooke, was the daughter of a beneficed clergyman; she had agreeable manners, her education had been highly finished, and she always mingled in the best men's circles. For some reason which never was known, she quitted her parents' roof and came to London, where she created a considerable impression; she was most particularly noticed by the Prince of Wales, and consequently well received by those who basked in princely favour. Nor a word, however, was ever breathed against her honour; and she was always looked upon as a model of unimpeachable veracity. Her beauty was such that she became the object of general admiration, and her portrait was taken by the first painters of the day. The Hebe by Strœling, engraved by Heath, remains to enable the world to form some idea of the matchless charms of the original. Her figure was perfection, and the sculptor would have been delighted to have obtained such a model. From whence she derived her income was always a mystery: a silly story was for a moment circulated that a person of the name of Bouverie, commonly called "The Commissioner," had succeeded in captivating her; this, however, soon died away. Whatever may have been her resources, she kept up a good establishment in Green Street, and lived always like a lady, but without much show. Her house was the rendezvous of the first men in London; but to her own sex she was distant and reserved, never admitting any female to her familiarity.

On one occasion, Miss Brooke dined at the house of a noble marquis, where some of the fashionable young men of the day were invited to meet her. Mr. Christopher Nugent, a nephew of the celebrated Burke, was most assiduous in his attentions, and begged permission to pay her a visit; the request was granted, and a day and an hour named. Some of the party present incidentally mentioned this engagement in the presence of the widow of a Mr. Harrison, a lady who had access to the best circles in consequence of her remarkable beauty, and who had some right to place Mr. Nugent on the list of her admirers. Jealous of her rival, the widow dressed herself as a boy, knocked at the door in Green Street, and was admitted into the presence of Miss Brooke, who was reclining on a sofa, whilst Nugent was on his knees before her; the distinguished lady, finding her lover in such a position, rushed upon him, seized a knife, and plunged it into his breast, fortunately without inflicting a mortal wound. Whatever might have been expected when this fact was generally known, it was soon believed that love had healed the wounds which jealousy inflicted; for Nugent and the lovely widow were soon seen walking together in familiar conversation in Hyde Park.

After being the admiration of the world of fashion for several seasons, Sally Brooke, seeing wrinkles coming into her once Hebe-like face, determined to leave scenes where she no longer reigned as the queen of beauty, but found other and fresher forms admired, and went to Baden. There some scoundrels having robbed her of all she possessed, she left the place, and arrived at the Hôtel du Palais Royal at Strasburg, where she remained some years, "the world forgetting, by the world forgot." A dropsical disease ravaged her once symmetrical form, and she died in a land of strangers. Her landlord nobly defrayed the expenses of her funeral, although she was already much indebted to him. Her family, however, liquidated her debts. Her remains repose in the city of Strasburg, and her tomb is one of the memorials of human vanity.

Madame Grassini.—One of the curious types of fifty years ago was the celebrated singer, Madame Grassini. When I first met her in 1825, she still possessed some remains of the remarkable beauty which had won for her the attention and admiration of so many of the great men of the age. Napoleon and Wellington, the Marshals of France, the Generals of the allied armies, English, Russians, Prussians, Austrians, as well as the Dukes and Marquises of the Restoration, had all bowed before Grassini's shrine, and had all been received with the same Italian *bonhomie* and liberal kindness. She would often say, "Napoleon gave me this snuff-box; he placed it in my hands one morning when I had been to see him at the Tuileries, and added, '*Voilà pour toi; tu es une brave fille!*' He was indeed a great man, but he would not follow my advice. *Il aurait du s'entendre avec ce cher Vilainton.* By the bye, *c'est ce brave Duc qui m'a donné cette broche. Il me l'a apportée un matin que j'étais encore au lit. Il parlait un singulier baragouin, et je ne savais guère l'Anglais; mais nous nous entendions tout de même.*" And so she would run on, with anecdotes and remarks on a long list of admirers.

All Madame Grassini's recollections came out quite naturally, with true southern frankness, or rather cynicism; and she narrated her *liaisons* in as unconcerned a manner before every one she met, as if she were speaking of her drive in the Bois de Boulogne. Her face must have been in her youth still handsomer than that of her niece, Giulia Grisi. The eyes were larger and more expressive, and she had more regular features and finer teeth. There was a tragic dignity in the contour and lineaments of her countenance, which formed a strange contrast with her unrefined language and gipsy style of dress; every colour of the rainbow was represented in her garments, which were tied on without the smallest regard to taste, and gave her very much the appearance of a strolling actress equipped at Rag fair.

Grassini's once fine voice had, when I saw her, degenerated into a sharp, loud, unmelodious soprano, which grated harshly on the ear. She had no cleverness or wit, and the *bons mots* that are cited as hers are amusing only from the cynic *bonhomie* which inspired them, as well as the strong Italian accent with which they were spoken. One of her *mots* in the days of the Empire is often cited.

Napoleon had given the order of the Iron Crown to the famous castrato singer, Veluti, who was at that time all the fashion. This honour, at a period when decorations were given more sparingly than they are at present, created great discontent, especially amongst military men; several of whom were complaining in no measured terms that the Lombard order should have been bestowed upon a mere singer, when Grassini interposed, with great vehemence, and said, "I am surprised that you soldiers should be so ungenerous, and not take into account *sa blessure.*"

I never shall forget the astonishment of Lord L * * *, some thirty-five years ago, when Grassini laid hold of him at a party at which I was present, and began relating to him her adventures with his father, "*ce cher Charles S * * *. Il vous ressemblait, Milord. Il n'était pas beau,—bien s'en faut; mais il était plus aimable que vous—il avait plus de grâce.*"

When Pasta first made her appearance, and the whole musical world was in an ecstasy of admiration, Grassini shrugged her shoulders, and exclaimed, "*Ah bah! si vous m'aviez entendu, c'était bien autre chose.*"

Madame Grassini was the possessor of a large fortune, and died in Paris at an advanced age.

Piety of Madame Catalani.—I knew the celebrated singer, Madame Catalani, when she lived in England. Her house was the rendezvous of many of the French *émigrés;* and as she was very rich and very generous, she frequently assisted those who were in the greatest distress. At the head of her profession, with the finest voice in the world, and the admired of all admirers, no whisper had ever been heard against her fair fame, and she lived in the utmost harmony with her husband, M. de Valabrèque. She was a most admirable woman in every relation of life, and as truly pious as she was kind and charitable.

An excellent friend of mine, Mr. Fitzwilliam, so well known in Paris, informed me that as he was seated in the stage-box at the opera one night, when Madame Catalani was about to appear in one of her greatest parts, he observed her in the *coulisse*, before she had to come on, in an attitude of devotion, and evidently in earnest prayer, for the space of two or three minutes. When she had finished, she made the sign of the cross, and went on the stage, where, it is needless to say, she was received with unbounded applause. My friend, on calling upon the great singer next day, told her what he had observed; when she informed him, with a charming simplicity, that she never went upon the stage without first praying to God that He would grant her the favour to be enabled to sing well, and to meet with success ; nor did she ever fail, on retiring to rest, to return thanks to Him for that and all the other mercies vouchsafed to her.

Miss T * * *, and the Perverts.—Dean Lockyer, a great favourite of George I., after a visit which he paid to Rome, was asked by his Majesty, in a jocular manner, as they sat over their bowl of punch, whether he had succeeded in converting the Pope. "No, your Majesty," replied the Dean; "his Holiness has most excellent Church preferment, and a most desirable bishopric, and I had nothing better to offer him." The same difficulties probably prevented the success of Miss T***, an excellent young Scotch lady, who went to Rome some years ago with the express purpose of converting to Presbyterianism the great head of the Roman Catholic Church. Miss T***, instead of succeeding in her object, was herself converted, or perverted, to Catholicism, and is at this moment superior of a convent at Edinburgh.

When I was last at Rome I was much disgusted at the absurd over-zeal of the English perverts, who were first and foremost in every procession, prostrating themselves on the saliva-covered floor of the churches before the most grotesque idols or absurd relics, and kissing, with a display of the most ardent devotion, St. Peter's well-worn toe, just after the same ceremony had been performed by some filthy Trasteverine reeking of garlic and covered with vermin. It used to be said, at the time of the Restoration in 1815, that many of the followers of Louis XVIII. were more *royalistes que le roi;* and the same saying may be applied to our vulgar English perverts, who are more Popish than the Pope, and make themselves the laughing-stock of Antonelli, and the great majority of cardinals and abbés, who believe in nothing at all.

RACHEL'S DÉBUT.—When the inimitable Rachel first appeared at the Théâtre Français, M. Prévost, secretary of the theatre, and well known for his good taste and judgment in all theatrical matters, was accosted by the young *débutante,* begging him to give her a few lessons in declamation. Prévost, surprised at this request, replied, "*Ma pauvre fille, allez vendre des bouquets.*" Soon after this Rachel appeared for the first time in "Hermione." Her acting electrified the audience, and on the fall of the curtain bouquets were thrown to her from nearly every box in the theatre. She modestly courtesied, and picked them up; then, taking them to Prévost, she said, "I have followed your advice, and bring you the bouquets for sale." Upon which the secretary fell upon his knees before the great *tragédienne*, acknowledging his haste and rudeness, and expressing regret for having wounded the feelings of the *débutante*.

RACHEL AND JUDITH. — Mademoiselle Judith, the clever and accomplished actress of the Théâtre Français, was one day abusing, in no measured terms, her fellow-*tragédienne*, Mademoiselle Rachel, to a mutual friend, the celebrated Doctor D * * *. After expatiating upon her many faults, and, above all, her grasping rapacity, she wound up by saying, "*C'est une vraie juive.*" The doctor, somewhat surprised, said, "Surely, my dear Judith, that ought not to be a fault in your eyes; as you likewise belong to the same religious persuasion." "True," replied the witty actress; "but the difference is, that I am a Jewess, and she is a Jew."

This reminds me of a late saying of James Rothschild's, who, furious at the increasing prosperity of his rival, Pereire, exclaimed, with the same forgetfulness of their mutual nationality, "How can anybody transact business with such a wretched little Jew?"

ROSSINI.—Rossini has been for some time a resident in Paris; and whenever he receives, every one is anxious to be admitted to his *soirées*, where good music is sure to be heard, or to his dinner-table, where excellent macaroni is as certain to be served up. The master looks in perfect health, and has more of the Englishman than the Italian in his personal appearance. The photographs that are sold of him are perfect of their kind, and express the good-nature and sly humour for which he is remarkable. He lives a large portion of the year at Passy, where the Parisian municipality made him a present of the ground upon which he has built his villa in the Italian style.

Rossini narrates, at his dinner parties, with great glee, some of the circumstances that occurred to him in London. He was made a great deal of by the Prince Regent; and on one occasion he could not help showing how little pleasure he derived from the attempts made by his Royal Highness to execute some passages, in which he totally failed owing to his inability to keep time: for the Regent, though a great lover of music, and not a bad player on the violin, constantly put out the *maestro*, to whom he at last offered an apology. Rossini accepted it with civility, and good-naturedly said, "There are few in your Royal Highness's position who could play so well."

Rossini was not aware of a law which then existed, by which a foreigner might be imprisoned for debt without any warning, and merely upon the affidavit of a creditor affirming that the stranger was about to leave England. He was once arrested in London by a bailiff, and carried to a sponging-house, and though his incarceration was of short duration, it gave him a disgust for a city where he had otherwise been well received.

Rossini does not go as often to the opera as might be expected, preferring the agreeable society of a few friends. He has also a strong objection to go out to parties; even the Emperor's invitations have no weight with him, and he has frequently begged to be excused. Rossini is an enemy to modern innovations, and has never yet trusted himself to the railroad. No inducement could be found sufficiently strong for him to travel otherwise than in a coach drawn by horses, and that at so moderate a speed, that a week was occupied by him in his journey from Paris to Baden.

Madame Colbrand, the *prima donna* at Naples when Rossini commenced his career as a composer, exercised considerable influence on the success of his earliest operas. They were written expressly for her, at a period when the heyday of her youth was gone by, she having long been an acknowledged favourite both with the manager and King Ferdinand. "When "Elisabetta" was produced in 1815 by the young *maestro*, Madame Colbrand retained all the beauty of her voice, which, added to her physical advantages and a commanding figure, fine features, and dignified bearing, called forth a shout of applause as she appeared on the stage of San Carlo, in the character of the English queen. The duet with Leicester secured the success of this the first opera that Rossini had produced at Naples, and others which followed in quick succession were received with the enthusiastic admiration they so fully merited.

But it was reserved for that unrivalled *artiste*, Madame Pasta, to come up to the full exigencies of Rossini's musical genius. Her appearance at Her

Majesty's Theatre electrified the house; and none who are old enough to remember the great *Diva*, can forget the wonderful pathos and power of that rich-toned thrilling voice, whose somewhat husky notes seemed to deepen the effect of her singing upon the hearts of her auditors.

To descend from grave to gay, I remember hearing one of her ardent admirers at that time, when Pasta, having just come off the stage, was refreshing herself, asking her, in his most romantic tones, "*Signora, prendete limonata o sorbetto?*" "No," answered the great singer in her deep voice; "*prendo 'af-an'-'af* [half-and-half] *adesso.*"

Pio Nono's Flight to Gaeta.—All who are personally acquainted with Pope Pius IX. are aware that he is a man of extremely benevolent disposition, naturally liberal in his political views, and desirous of promoting the welfare and happiness of mankind. Political events in 1847–48 were singularly calculated to bring out the peculiar characteristics of a sovereign Pontiff who was called upon to exercise his temporal power in an exceptional period of modern Italian history. Pius IX. believed that it was not incompatible with the attributes of the Papacy, to participate in that great liberal movement which shook so many thrones in the year 1848.

The College of Cardinals, and especially the conspicuous members of the order of the Jesuits, became alarmed at the Pontiff's liberal ideas. Knowing well his character, and observing the progress of that overwhelming tide of popular opinion which was sweeping sovereigns from their thrones, and shaking the very foundations of government, they did not at first openly oppose the Pontiff's views, but gradually and insidiously set about creating alarm in his mind, and, above all, sought to awaken doubts in the conscience of "the Vicar of Christ." They calculated, and correctly, that if they could not deter him from bestowing mundane and political benefits on the Roman people, they could at least make him believe that in doing so he was betraying the interests and influences of the Catholic Church, and they succeeded in arousing a tempest of indignation and alarm in the mind of Pio Nono, until he felt it his duty to take to flight, more in the cause of the Roman Catholic Church than from fears concerning personal safety.

The golden tints of an Italian sunset had faded into that brief twilight which heralds darkness, when a female, dressed in humble attire, was admitted to the garden of the Vatican by a gentleman in the confidence of the Pope. Neither of the persons spoke as they made their way to a portion of the palace not generally inhabited. On arriving at the foot of a dark and narrow staircase, the gentleman took from his pocket one of those little knots of twisted wax-taper which the Italians carry about with them, and lighted it; then, without uttering a word, he beckoned the lady to follow him, and proceeded up the narrow stone staircase, which, after many windings, led to a door, on which three raps were given by the mysterious guide. Almost immediately the door was opened by Pio Nono himself, and the guide, making way for the lady, retired. This was Madame Dodwell, to whom

I alluded in my previous volume as one of the most beautiful women of her time; she was the widow of an Englishman, though a Roman by birth, and married *en secondes noces* to the Bavarian minister, and she had come to the Vatican in order to arrange the clandestine flight of the Pontiff from Rome.

His Holiness appeared to have lost all presence of mind, and trembled as he took the lady by the hand, and, gazing earnestly on her still beautiful face, said, "I look to you, madam, for arranging all details. I have the utmost confidence in your discretion, and I know the firmness of your character." The lady replied, "Has any plan of escape suggested itself to your Holiness?" "Yes," said the Pontiff in a low voice; "I think the best thing I can do is to put on the gown of an ordinary priest, and at daybreak to-morrow morning walk out of the gates which conduct to the Fondi road. You, madam, in your carriage, will have preceded me, and, waiting at a convenient distance, you will take me up. I have made arrangements with my good and faithful friend, Ferdinand, King of Naples, for a safe retreat at Gaeta; and I have no doubt that you, with your passport as Ambassadress of Bavaria, can pass the customs authorities with little or no difficulty." "Holy father," replied the lady, pressing the Pontiff's hand, "the scheme seems to me in every way satisfactory. I shall bring with me a confidential servant, a clever coachman, willing to brave any danger." The Pope rose, and bestowing his blessing on the lady, ushered her to the door, adding, "I retire to pass the night in prayer." "I shall be one mile from the gate on the Fondi road," said the lady in a whisper, "by four o'clock to-morrow morning."

At that hour a carriage might have been seen in a bend of the road which leads to Naples. On the box-seat beside the coachman sat a female, dressed as a domestic servant, who anxiously gazed around while waiting the arrival of the Pope. She did not wait long before she beheld approaching a thick-set and somewhat corpulent priest, who advanced towards the carriage with a rapid step, and covered with dust. In a few moments Pio Nono was seated in the carriage with the ambassadress, and the horses were whipped into a gallop, and did not halt until they reached the small custom-house of Fondi.

It was now ten o'clock, and they were immediately surrounded by the custom-house officers, who demanded their passports. The chief official, looking into the carriage, observed, "I do not find on your passport the name of the priest who accompanies your excellency." "Oh," replied the lady, "he is only my confessor." Unfortunately, the priest showed signs of uneasiness and alarm, which excited the suspicion of the officer, who said, "In these times our orders are very strict, and I cannot permit the *padre confessore* to pass. I must beg him to descend, and shall be obliged to detain him until I get permission from Rome for his release." The Pope, hearing this, was in a great state of excitement; he caught hold of the man's hand, and whispered in his ear, "*Caro amico*, you don't know who I am,—I am your sovereign and father, Pius IX." Whereupon the officer turned round to a little group of persons who had collected, and exclaimed, "Per Baccho, here is a fellow who calls himself our Pope!" The crowd peered into the carriage, and indulged in a volley of ribaldry, evidently not believing in the identity of the sovereign Pontiff. Matters were becoming serious, when the Pope placed a bag of gold coin in the hands of the officials, whilst the ambassadress threw handfuls of scudi to the mob. A loud cheer was raised by all present, and in a few minutes the carriage was going at full speed, without fear of pursuit, on the road to Gaeta.

Sudden Turns of Fortune in France.—I have seen some of those marvellous changes in France which have made all Europe wonder. Kings, statesmen, financiers, marshals, ambassadors, and ministers of state, have risen up and faded away before my eyes. An empire, an army, a city, have risen from the old foundations, through the *débris* of a revolutionary government. How long the present state of things is to last, no human foresight can tell. A *coup d'état* has once succeeded; why may not another? One army has left its much-loved sovereign; why not another? Every one believed that Charles X. was popular with the army; the Gardes du Corps and the Garde Royale seemed ready to lay down their lives in his defence; and only a few days before the revolution of July, no one had the slightest doubt that every soldier was prepared to do his duty whenever called upon. Yet how few accompanied the fallen monarch on his way to embarkation for a foreign land.

Men who are now playing an active part in life, and occupying a great position, I have known in very different circumstances, apparently not possessing the means of elevating themselves to a higher grade in society. For instance, one of the great men near the Emperor was, prior to the revolution, obliged to have recourse to the editorship of a journal, *Le Messager du Soir*, in conjunction with his friend Monsieur Brindeau, a person employed at the Bourse. A late French ambassador, whose name has so lately been before the public in connection with the march of affairs in Italy, filled a very humble position when I was first made known to him; he was then only a clerk at a small bank in the Rue Lafitte, kept by Messrs. Orr & Goldsmith, which, with many others in Paris, has vanished. My friend married a daughter of a rich London distiller.

The last revolution, no doubt, brought down some substantial houses, as it cleared away some of doubtful character. Messrs. * * * & * * * retired upon that occasion; but they have, however, again commenced separately. The railroad to Boulogne was under the auspices of that firm; but it has now become a part of the Great Northern line. The Rouen Railway also aided Messrs. * * * & * * * in regaining their lost money, though many of the original subscribers were unfortunately ruined; and the separation of the two partners of the firm appears to have been attended with good results to both, judging from the external appearance of wealth exhibited in their magnificent hotels, their splendid equipages, their powdered lackeys, and their luxurious style of living.

True, the most solid and established houses do not follow the example set by some of the moneyed gentry. Few establishments maintain such a high reputation as the old and respected firm of Mallet, whose name is associated with worth, economy, and good sense, and where everything is straightforward and honourable. They have no box at the Grand Opera, or at the Italiens, for their families, who do not seek, by gorgeous promenades in the Bois de Boulogne, to dazzle the eyes of the poor, and outvie the *demi-monde* in insolence and extravagance; creating envy and dissatisfaction in those who may have suffered from the failure of other establishments. Indeed, some of the financiers of the day have been of great public service, and their honoured names are not to be associated with those who have played a game disreputable to themselves, and injurious to their fellow-citizens.

Messrs. Rothschild and Pereire—who may not like to see their names in the same paragraph, as it is generally believed that they are by no means on good terms with each other—are amongst the leading moneyed men of the day, and both of them have been of service to the state. The Rothschilds have the credit of being very liberal to those who require their aid, although by no means allowing themselves to be imposed upon by the solicitations of the idle and dissolute. Many acts of kindness are related of them; and they are known to be generous in their hospitality, and charitable to the stranger. M. Pereire, who was once a clerk in the house of Rothschild, has made a rapid fortune, and has acquired a high reputation as a financier, by founding that successful institution, "The Crédit Mobilier;" and he has many warm friends, who speak highly of his liberality and disinterestedness. He has built a very fine hotel near the British Embassy, and fur-

ENGLISH VISITORS AT THE CAFÉ DE MILLE COLONNES.

nished it with artistic taste, and there he receives his friends with splendid hospitality.

Parisian Cockneydom.—Although I entertain a high opinion of the Parisians and Frenchmen generally, I believe that there is no human being more thoroughly ignorant and conceited than the uneducated Parisian Cockney or *badaud*. Of other countries he has scarcely any knowledge; and he is firmly convinced that the French are the masters of the world, and that no people on the face of the earth can enter into competition with them in war, literature, arts, or science: perfection is only to be found in his native land. He turns up his nose contemptuously at everything English; all his notions of England being derived from the low theatres on the Boulevards, where British, Russian, Austrian, and Prussian soldiers are invariably put *hors de combat* by the French. He is very fond of talking of an invasion of the "Little Island," and fully believes that sooner or later a Zouave will be "Duke of London," and some *employé* of the French Government, "Prefect of the Thames." He is firmly convinced that the English visitors come to Paris only to be astonished at the magnificent edifices of the city, to gaze at the Louvre and the beautiful monuments; though the great attraction to them is, in his opinion, the good dinners that are to be eaten in Paris, for he thinks that there is nothing in London to tempt the appetite but half-raw beef. As for fresh vegetables, sauce for fish, and good pastry, nothing of the sort is to be obtained there, and a French beggar would disdain to partake of the meals which the ravenous Londoner devours. But when

John Bull comes to Paris, the beautiful metropolis of France,—of Europe,—he finds apartments to lodge in superior even to those which the Queen occupies at Buckingham Palace or Windsor Castle, at a moderate price, while his table is served with a luxury nowhere else to be found.

Louis Philippe committed a great mistake, and caused much mischief, by his patronage of the *bourgeoisie*, who not only introduced vulgar manners, but conducted themselves with great insolence; aping, as far as they could, the style of persons of good blood and high rank and station. Unfortunately, the revolution of 1830 had overthrown the fortunes of one half of the aristocratic families, who were consequently compelled to shut up their hotels, discharge their servants, and retire from the world. Since that period the domestics have imitated their masters in their follies, and flaunt themselves in silk dresses and expensive bonnets, instead of the pretty muslin caps and modest dimity gowns which formerly became the *bonnes* and cook-maids. Wages necessarily became doubled; nay, even tripled; the tradesmen connived with the servants to plunder the family, and extravagance became the order of the day. Paris has rapidly increased in size, and the idle and dissolute have consequently congregated in this overgrown city. But, alas! it also became the rendezvous of all the miscreants that other great cities have expelled: here are to be found the liberated convict and the depraved harlot, rioting in luxury, and offending the eyes of modesty and rectitude. It is calculated that the population now exceeds 1,500,000 souls, and to preserve order, and give security to the honest portion of the inhabitants, it is necessary that 40,000 police should be kept in constant employment.

I cannot refrain from alluding also to the extortionate prices which, I regret to say, my fellow-countrymen are compelled to pay for every article they require. There is a league amongst the shopkeepers, the proprietors of hotels, the restaurateurs, and even the humble porter whose occupation it is to stand at the corner of the street; they have one common interest, which is to extract from the pockets of John Bull whatever money they can extort from him on any pretext.

The large and magnificent shops in the Rue de la Paix, in the Rue Castiglione, in the Faubourg St. Honoré, and the Rue de Rivoli, are sources of immense wealth; and it is a well-known fact that, in the course of six years, tradesmen who occupy them accumulate large fortunes, and are enabled to retire from business. Should a war occur between France and England, all those splendid establishments would be closed; for it is chiefly on the money spent by foreigners, and more especially by the English, that Paris tradesmen subsist. If the Duchesse d'Abrantès, whose Memoirs were so universally read during the Restoration, had been alive at the present time, she would have been horrified at the marvellous change for the worse that has taken place. The Duchess, who was evidently a person of enlarged mind, and fully alive to the iniquities of this wicked world, says in one of her volumes that there is not a more industrious class of persons than the artisans of Paris, who toil eighteen hours out of the twenty-four, and carry to the shopkeeper the produce of their labour; and, by dint of coaxing and entreaty, induce him to give enough to keep their body and soul together; immediately after, the extortionate shopkeeper obtains from some of his customers a price equal to a profit of five hundred per cent. This system prevails in every department; the industrious peasant who brings to the market the produce of his garden, is compelled by the municipal authorities to sell at the Halle (the great market), before seven in the morning, whatever he has brought. If he does not find customers, he is quickly surrounded by innumerable harpies, who induce the hard-working labourer to sell to them his vegetables and fruit at less than half their value. These harpies are themselves small vendors of these articles, and I do not hesitate to affirm that they realise a profit of four hundred per cent. on their bargains. Then the wine-merchant, who purchases his wines at Bordeaux or Macon, or the borders of the Rhone, generally receives a genuine and pure produce of the grape; but when this wine is brought to market in Paris, it has marvellously increased in bulk, for every cask of real wine is, by the aid of water and logwood, converted into three, and sold as genuine wine.

A celebrated surgeon, a resident of the Faubourg St. Germain, related to me the following fact. He accepted an invitation to dine at the house of a well-known nobleman, distinguished in the fashionable world. The dinner was all that the most delicate taste could offer; the *cuisine* was inimitable, the wines of the choicest *cru*, the dessert rich and tempting. Several of the *plats* left the table untouched; the doctor observed that pine-apples and grapes were abundant, and that so plentiful was the supply, that many plates were taken from the table exactly as they were placed upon it. The dinner being over, the gentlemen and ladies retired to the *salon*, and they had scarcely entered it, when a relation of the Amphitryon's unexpectedly arrived, after a long journey, from the provinces. He was received with the utmost cordiality by the family, and was naturally asked if he had dined; on his reply in the negative, that in fact he had tasted nothing since he left Lyons, the bell was rung, and the servant ordered to prepare something for the hungry traveller. The servant shortly returned to the *salon*, and, to the inexpressible astonishment of every one present, said that the *maître d'hôtel* had desired him to say that there was nothing left; on the *maître d'hôtel* being questioned, he confirmed the statement of the domestic, whereupon he immediately received from his indignant master orders to quit his service in twelve hours. On receiving his ill-gained wages, the man acknowledged that he had disposed of the dinner amongst his fellow-servants, as he considered that every article became his property, with the exception of the dessert, which belonged to Chevet of the Palais Royal, who farmed out the fruit and sweets that composed it at a certain sum per dinner.

The porters, or, as they now denominate themselves, the *concierges*, are perhaps the worst species of servants that ever infested a domestic establishment. They are inadequately paid by the proprietor, and consequently prey upon those who have the misfortune of living under their surveillance.

In fact, they are rogues and thieves in disguise: they compel the tradesmen who serve those who live in the house to pay five per cent. for every article that enters; wine, wood, coal, and indeed almost every article, is subject to this abominable mode of levying contributions from the residents.

Improvements in Paris.—Paris has within four or five years undergone marvellous changes, which reflect the highest honour on those who have contributed to its splendour at the present time. The melancholy, gloomy, miserable portion of the city might be very charming to the artist and archæologist, who admired mediæval pointed roofs, fantastic domes, labyrinths of galleries, and windows that seemed as if not intended to admit the air or the sunlight; whilst liquid mud and filthy streams sluggishly meandered through the dark and narrow streets and passages, from which the frightened foreigner could scarcely extricate himself. A beautiful, fairy-like city has replaced the crowded heaps of dingy, dark dwellings; the blind alleys and the fetid courts have been exchanged for lofty and elegant mansions, wide and well-paved thoroughfares, and spacious open places. A writer of antiquity denominated Paris *Leukotokia*, the white city. Well now does it merit that name. All that was may have been picturesque; but all that is must be pronounced delightful. We may have lost the identical spot where the body of Admiral Coligny fell on St. Bartholomew's day; we may inquire after the street through which passed the carriage where sat the good and glorious Henri of Navarre, when he was assassinated by Ravaillac; the narrow street has also disappeared where the assassins lurked with an infernal machine to blow up the First Consul. But upon sites once covered with cemeteries, with sewers, with pits, and with abominations indescribable, have arisen verdant lawns, squares, and gardens, where, at the vernal season, flowers charm the eye and gratify the sense, while sparkling fountains pour forth their cool streams; spaces where the sun and air give life and animation to all around; mansions where domestic or polished society can enjoy all the luxuries and comforts which art and taste have introduced.

This transformation has been effected at an enormous expense, by skilful architects and sculptors, under the control of one great sovereign; it has been the result of unremitting energy on the part of those who planned the improvements, and the indomitable toil of those who carried them out. It was indeed a sight worthy this engineering age, to see the thousand workmen congregated upon various spots, the tram-roads, and trains of horses and waggons bearing enormous weights of stone from the neighbouring quarries, the crumbling houses marked for destruction, and the deep foundations dug for new Boulevards on both banks of the Seine, the delight of Paris. Palaces have sprung up, which may give historic recollections to future generations quite as interesting as those we have received from the Tour de Nesle, where a queen carried on her licentious intrigues; or as the Hôtel de Sens, and the Hôtel des Tournelles, the residence of princes, where bravoes issued forth to murder, and in whose dungeons languished the good and the brave, as well as the criminal; or the convents of the Cordeliers, the Benedictines, and the thousand lazy monks of the olden time. One of the most glorious achievements of the present reign has been the completion of that magnificent edifice, the Louvre. Its saloons, lined with treasures of fine art, were the glory of France; but a large portion of this vast structure, only a very short time ago, wore a most ignoble aspect: columns, with rich capitals, were at their base disfigured by all that was filthy and disgusting. The square that had displayed the talents of Jean Goujon, and of Perrault,—where Catherine de Medicis and her sons, where Henry IV. and Margot, gazed from the windows,—adjoined stalls where squalid people offered for sale dogs, birds, the sweepings of *bric-à-brac* shops; spots infested by the lazzaroni of Paris, thieves, and courtesans. A more painful contrast of luxury and misery never disfigured the most attractive part of a luxurious city. Napoleon I., in the plenitude of his power, and Louis Philippe, with all the *bourgeoisie* of Paris to back him, could not drive away the human vermin that infested the place; nor did they add a single stone to improve this *chef d'œuvre* of architecture. At length, to the immortal honour of the Emperor Napoleon III., the work has been accomplished, and the Louvre is now a palace worthy of the *chefs d'œuvre* of art which enrich its interior. Indeed, the inauguration of the Louvre is an era in the annals of Paris.

The cleansing, draining, and lighting of the streets have also been admirably carried out; and the famous city of Paris now appears with renovated grace and beauty, and decorated with a thousand ornaments, which attract the eyes of the whole world.

There has been another immense improvement: the groves of the Bois de Boulogne, formerly the rendezvous of duellists, footpads, and gipsies, have been transformed as if by the hand of an enchanter, and flowers and foliage, velvet turf, cascades, and winding streams combine to delight the senses and invigorate the health of the promenaders. Here lovers, idlers, poets, the humble and the wealthy, lounge their hours away amid joyous scenes, where art and skill have successfully combined the varied charms of nature.

French Criminal Jurisprudence.—A trial for a criminal offence is one of the most remarkable scenes that France affords. In every respect it essentially differs from what occurs in England, and produces a sensation of disgust amongst those who have witnessed an offender arraigned in the British Isles. A feeling of sympathy is there entertained for the prisoner at the bar, whom the law assumes to be innocent until he is proved guilty. Seldom is any emotion exhibited, or if there be any, it is mostly in favour of the prisoner. Far different is the case in a French court of justice. An unfortunate being seems to be set up to be mentally tortured; every effort is made by the judge and by the *procureur-général* to convict him out of his own mouth; he is cross-questioned, brow-beaten, and every device is employed to entrap him into a confession. He has most probably been confined for months previously on suspicion, and during that time has been cross-examined, entreated, and persuaded by a *juge d'instruction* to acknowledge himself guilty. Enfeebled in body by long confinement, and harassed in mind, he is called upon, before an excitable auditory, to combat with highly-educated legal opponents, who watch with unwearied vigilance every change of countenance, every expression of emotion, listen with eager anxiety to any faltering of the voice or hesitation of speech, and seem to rejoice if, by accumulation of evidence, they can fix upon him the stigma of crime. He has no protection from either judge, jury, or prosecutors; he is interrogated, not with a view of ascertaining the truth, much less of proving innocence, but in order to prove him guilty. The spectators, in a state of excitement, watching with eager curiosity every phase of the scene acting before them, do not disguise their emotions; compassion, horror, disgust, vengeance, and other passions are awakened and expressed openly, often with the purpose of producing an effect upon the judge and jury.

The criminal process in France will probably be somewhat improved, and imprisonment before trial will then be no longer enforced; for the highest legal authorities are occupied with the endeavour to alleviate some of the worst features of French criminal trials; indeed, it is generally understood that the Emperor will soon sign a decree prepared by the Minister of Justice which will modify the existing practice, and that the system of finding bail, which has so long existed in England, will be substituted for preliminary imprisonment.

The banker Mires was long confined in prison before trial, and afterwards his innocence was established by a jury. In a recent notorious trial, where a rich landed proprietor at Marseilles was accused of attempting to murder his servant, the accused suffered eight months' imprisonment before he was brought to trial, and then was pronounced not guilty; but he had no redress for this long and painful incarceration. The eminent men now at the French bar are for the most part anxious for an amelioration of this and other defects in the *Code Napoléon.*

Some of the leading advocates take an active part in politics, and for the most part belong to the Liberal party. M. de Berryer, however, one of the most eloquent men of the day, and who defended Prince Louis Napoléon after the memorable affair at Boulogne, is an acknowledged and stanch Royalist; he supports the claims of the Comte de Chambord, who very wisely says, "I will come to you, if you want me, and send for me; but otherwise, I intend remaining quietly at Frohsdorff. A crown has no great charms for me; and if I put yours upon my head, Frenchmen may some time or other wish to take it off, and very possibly my head at the same time." What the politics of M. Dupin may be, now or hereafter, nobody can well guess. He was once a stanch Orleanist, then a confirmed Republican, and is now a lukewarm Napoleonist. M. Marie, an accomplished orator, remains a Republican: he became a member of the Provisional Government, but was somewhat timid; always fearing some excess upon the part of the people. M. Cremieux, one of the ugliest little men that France can boast of, seems to have retired from political life; energetic, even violent in action when speaking, he is a sound lawyer and an able advocate.

M. Jules Favre is a great favourite; an acute

and intellectual pleader, he is employed by all parties; but his ultra-liberal views are not always relished. He is a fluent speaker, and has the tact of making juries attentive to him; for he has a plain, straightforward manner of speaking, and his language is pure and correct. None of the first men at the bar at the present day have been remarkable for literary success; in fact, it would appear that literary pursuits are considered almost incompatible with legal distinction. There is an Englishman, a Mr. Jones, practising with some success at the French bar. But there is a striking difference in many points from the practice of the law of England, which renders any approximation of the courts of the two countries quite out of the question.

There is an idea in France that French literature is predominant throughout the whole of Europe; and it is the firm belief of the mass of the French people that their authors of the present day take precedence over all others. Undoubtedly French dramas and novels have lately found favour in England; Victor Hugo, Alexandre Dumas, Madame George Sand, have found translators of their more striking romances; but their historians, philosophers, and moralists are much less known and esteemed abroad than those of Germany; indeed, the German language is beginning to be studied by thinking men and women with much more assiduity than the French. French plays, adapted to the English stage, have of late years been more popular in England than the Shakspearean drama; but literary revolutions are of such frequent and rapid occurrence, that the caprice of to-day may be forgotten to-morrow. Dramas of political intrigues are now the order of the day in Paris; will they be transferred to the London boards?

Every one in France is looking to the effect that will be produced by free trade in dramatic literature; importations from England will probably be more frequent, as the censorship has generally exerted its influence to prevent the stage offering a representation of the manners and customs of the British, and has weighed heavily upon authors and managers. Freed from the tyranny that has confined the human mind to a certain class of ideas, new dramatists will arise, and we shall have fresh subjects brought on the French stage; genuine comedy may then assert her powers of depicting "the living manners as they rise."

The Paris Insurrection of 1848.—No one, who now for the first time visits Paris, can comprehend how such a magnificent city could be converted into a strong fortress, with impediments to the action of the military on every side. The magnificent, broad, and well-macadamised streets, through which successive regiments and parks of artillery can move without dread of molestation, seem little adapted for *émeutes* and barricades. But far different was the aspect a few years since. Narrow, close, confined streets, paved with huge stones, were alone to be seen; and there were quarters of the town inhabited by a desperate and poor population, in a state of squalid misery, and ever ready to fly to arms and raise barricades at the summons of a few political fanatics. When an opposition to the existing government was decided upon by a few active demagogues, there poured forth, from dens of darkness and abodes of filth, a mass of people who at other periods scarcely ever saw daylight, and who wildly expected to lessen their sufferings and improve their condition by acts of violence. No one had attempted to ameliorate their condition; it was not dreamt that, by the judicious expenditure of money, these people might be made good citizens, and enabled to throw off the yoke of crime and misery. Yet, in a few short years, a marvellous change has come over the spirit of the "dangerous classes." The spots where they congregated are covered with lofty mansions, and the former inhabitants have migrated to less densely-populated districts, and are able to obtain honest employment. The Faubourg St. Antoine, the Barrière du Trône, and the environs are no longer under the control of two or three fiery demagogues, but have become the quiet habitations of a class that has learnt to respect itself.

When, in former days, an *émeute* was decided upon, it was the result of much previous deliberation by the leading members of secret clubs, who planned a strategic movement, which they induced a number of ill-fed, ill-conditioned, discontented, and reckless men to carry out. Their object was to impede the march of troops, by the erection of barricades; to take possession of the neighbouring houses, and from the windows hurl missiles of every description upon their opponents. From the Batignolles in the north, from St. Antoine in the east, and from the Quartier Latin in the south, there simultaneously poured forth hosts of the humbler class; their great object being to meet near the Hôtel de Ville, and, gaining possession of it, to form a provisional government, and issue thence proclamations.

In 1848, Louis Philippe's government succumbed to the manœuvres of the insurgents; but when, at a later period, General Cavaignac made up his mind to support the Legislative Assembly, the tables were turned. The battle, however, was most sanguinary—the resistance desperate. In a few hours rose up, as if by the labour of Cyclopeans, masses of stone gathered from the paved streets, which seemed to defy all attempts to overthrow them; and behind these barricades stood resolute and excited men, armed with every species of offensive weapon, vociferating defiance and contempt of those who attempted to dislodge them; while every house in the neighbourhood became an arsenal of deadly missiles. The insurgents would have gained the victory had their opponents not sprung from their own ranks; for the soldiery were little inclined to act. But the National Guard, upon whom rested almost the whole of the encounter, had fortunately been recruited by many of the very men who had joined the insurrection in the previous February. Lamartine and his colleagues had, with great prudence, and more judgment than they usually exhibited, enlisted, in some regiments to which they gave the name of "La Garde Mobile," all the idle young men and *gamins* of Paris who had taken up arms on the former occasion. Animated by a love of the service they had so lately joined, and controlled by military discipline, they forgot that they were firing upon their friends and relations; and, being boldly led on, they executed their task with devotion and courage. Dreadful was the carnage and devastation: the next day the Faubourg St. Antoine and the neighbourhood of the Bastille presented the appearance of a city taken by storm.

General Cavaignac had not been sparing in his chastisement of the people, and a vivid recollection of the punishment he had inflicted was long preserved. But no beneficial results followed this terrible battle; for the Legislative Assembly were satisfied with having thus made an example of the misguided, and strengthened their own power. With the usual heedlessness of the Parisians, the whole affair was nearly forgotten in a few weeks, and the lives that had been lost were scarcely thought of. Eleven generals had been either killed or wounded, and the slaughter had been tremendous; but it produced no permanent effect: no effort was made to prevent future risings. Red Republicanism, it is true, had received a severe blow; but nothing was done to alleviate the sufferings, or enlighten the understandings of the people; nor was the good feeling of the nation appealed to. Indeed, excepting in two or three of the *soi-disant* Liberal journals, no narrative of the fatal events was published; for a great struggle for power was then going on amongst the different parties. Legitimists, Orleanists, and Liberals were only occupied in calculating their strength in the Chamber; and aspiring individuals indulged in hopes that the party to which they looked for their own advancement would triumph.

French Statesmen and Journalists in 1851.—Ever since my first visit to Paris in 1815, there has been political agitation in France; unfortunately not that of statesmen, but that of ambitious men, each one anxious to fill the highest office in the state, for which every one here thinks he has sufficient capacity. The doctrine that the humblest may rise to the highest rank is well adapted for the army, where personal courage is of the first importance; but in the state, where success depends upon intellect, such a notion is not only fallacious, but fatal. Under the reign of Louis Philippe, any one who could write a decent leading article in a newspaper immediately fancied himself versed in state policy, and felt persuaded that he had nothing to do but fly at high game in order to gratify his ambition. The success of M. Guizot and M. Thiers seemed a sufficient guarantee for the access to power of innumerable petty scribblers, who had neither the wisdom of the *doctrinaire* nor the eloquence of the historian.

M. GUIZOT.—M. Guizot, when he commenced his lectures on public history at the Sorbonne, appeared like a luminous meteor on the political horizon. The expression of his views of ancient literature, the energy and the dignity with which he explained to his admiring audience the philosophy and the religion of Rome and Greece, his ironical comparison of the present claimants to renown, were listened to with an enthusiasm which proved how thoroughly they were understood, how fully they were appreciated. It was a sight which can never be effaced from memory, when the crowded hall was filled with impatient students awaiting the presence of their much loved professor, who with difficulty threaded his way, amid immense applause, with a slow and solemn step, to the professorial chair. He poured forth, at first slowly, in a continued flow of elegant language, eulogiums upon the great writers in his own language, and then, with an impetuosity that seemed to convey an electric impetus around, his face, at first sombre and inexpressive, lighted up with supernatural animation; and as he gazed around, he inspired each of his auditors with the conviction that he was listening to a being of a superior order.

In the Assembly, M. Guizot spoke in a different style from what he did at the Sorbonne; and it was somewhat difficult to define the emotion that predominated in him: no sense either of triumph or of defeat was apparent. Cold, sombre, and meditative, he spoke with authority; and it was only at rare intervals that any great animation was visible in his countenance. It is no discredit to those statesmen that they earned their livelihood by writing for the newspapers; indeed, M. Guizot, aided by Madame Guizot, derived his subsistence for a long time from his literary labour. But they were the innocent cause of much mischief; for many a scribe who contributed a few lines to some journal anticipated the time when he might become Prime Minister of France.

M. Thiers.—It was in the Legislative Assembly that M. Thiers appeared to most advantage; but neither his matter nor his manner awoke the same feeling as those of his great competitor for power. An acute reasoner and an eloquent declaimer, though his voice is naturally harsh and shrill, his gestures are striking and animated, and he fixed the attention even of his political opponents. He marshalled his arguments with incredible skill, and brought out the caprices of his thought with energy and with decision. His countenance became animated as he spoke; and though his brilliant intelligence is tinged by a sarcastic expression not always befitting, his physiognomy is pleasing and occasionally winning. Upon the British Ambassador, Lord Normanby, he seemed to produce a great effect; for the noble Lord, who generally slumbered gently through the debate in the diplomatic *loge*, always woke up when M. Thiers commenced one of those brilliant attacks upon the administration, which at length unseated his powerful rival.

LAMARTINE.—There was a period when much was expected from Lamartine. Certainly no one did more for the safety of Paris than he did during the first days of the revolution of 1848; but there was too much poetry in his head for a statesman. He was too much absorbed in himself to think of his friends; the consequence was, that he never made up a party to support him; indeed, he always stood aloof from any associations. His *soirées* on Saturday evenings in the Rue de l'Université were most agreeable, but were only social: every one sought access to them. They were presided over by Madame Lamartine, a highly-accomplished Englishwoman, daughter of Colonel Birch of Norfolk. She was an amateur artist, and took great delight in sculpture; a bust of her husband from her chisel is one of the best likenesses we have of Lamartine. At his re-unions were to be seen the principal literary and political persons of the day, and all the distinguished artists; but amongst them were no attached friends. Many persons expected that he would be elected the first President of the Republic; and this most probably would have been the case, had not Louis Napoléon presented himself, for Lamartine was preferred to Cavaignac. The poet foresaw that the name of Bonaparte would carry everything before it, and was one of those who opposed the admission into France of all who belonged to that family.

PRINCE LOUIS NAPOLÉON.—Great was the eagerness of every one to know the opinion that had been formed in England of the Prince Louis Napoléon. It was only known that he was looked on there as a perfect gentleman; but nobody could understand why he should have had himself sworn in as a special constable on the occasion of the Chartist demonstration of the 10th of April, and various were the reasons assigned.

His first speech in the Legislative Assembly was expected to be an explanation of his policy; it was, however, brief and modest. The election of the Prince as President of the Republic may be considered as a national triumph, as it certainly proved a national benefit; for he immediately took steps to organise a competent Ministry, and commenced carrying into effect the improvements that his mind had long been engaged in studying. His speeches, his addresses, gave evidence of a vigorous intelligence, and he now and then astonished his Ministers by the boldness of his language. This was the case at the inauguration of the railroad at Dijon, on which occasion he delivered an address, which M. Leon Faucher, his then Prime Minister, took care to alter before he gave it publicity. The Prince had occasion sometimes to change his Ministry, according as circumstances permitted, but his selections uniformly gave satisfaction to the country. The station of Minister of Finance was filled for the most part by M. Achille Fould, who, amid all the varied changes in the political world, has maintained a well-deserved popularity, whilst his attachment to the Emperor has been both political and personal.

THE COUP D'ÉTAT.—The simple narrative of an unprejudiced individual who has witnessed some of the scenes of that extraordinary event, the *coup d'état* of 2d December 1851, and who has had opportunities of forming a judgment for himself of many of the circumstances attendant upon it, will, I am persuaded, be received with indulgence as a contribution of facts, for the accuracy of which I am able to vouch from my personal knowledge.

As a boy I read with infinite delight the volumes that described one of the most remarkable revolutions that history has recorded, and which was effected almost entirely by two daring women. The Empress Catherine of Russia and the Princess Dashkoff in a single night hurled from his throne the despotic autocrat of all the Russias; when his bold and ambitious wife seized his crown, and ruled the empire with uninterrupted power.

I have perused with attention most of the works that have contained a narrative of the events during the memorable days of December 1851, and I am persuaded that the public mind in England has been influenced by accounts written by persons who, not having witnessed them, or been acquainted with the state of society in Paris, have drawn inferences not justified by the actual position of affairs at that eventful period. One work, written by a man of high literary talent, appears to have been brought out for the express purpose of calumniating the Emperor and his Ministers. How fallacious are some of the contributions to the history of that time may be inferred from the fact that they affect to narrate what was passing within the walls of the palace of the Elysée whilst the conflict was going on in the streets of Paris; even so minutely, as to describe the attitude and sayings of the individual who, at the same time, is spoken of as solitary, and brooding by himself over the probable issue of the struggles.

State of Public Feeling in Paris.—Every thinking person in Paris, towards the close of the year 1851, anticipated, with considerable apprehension, that early in the ensuing spring a great change must take place in the government of the country. The constitution, which had been proclaimed with apparent enthusiasm in the year 1848, appeared likely to produce anarchy and confusion; for a new President and an Assembly had to be elected, and whatever claims the individual who had once acted as head of the state might have upon the country, he was, according to the constitution, ineligible again to fill that high position. There was every reason to fear that the Red Republicans would make a desperate effort to gain power, even should the streets of Paris again be deluged with blood; indeed, the language of some of their adherents boldly proclaimed that liberty could only be secured by means of the guillotine. In effect, a struggle for power had commenced between the Prince-President and the representatives of the people. The Assembly had refused to grant to the chief of the state the funds necessary to defray the expenses attendant upon his position; it manifested distrust of his Ministers, and jealousy of his popularity with the army, of which Changarnier had the command; and so mean were the devices resorted to to annoy Louis Napoléon, that he was compelled to wear at reviews the uniform of a general of the National Guard. A decided opposition was being organised against his re-election; and there is no doubt that his personal liberty was menaced by his opponents, and that, had not the *coup d'état* taken place, his career would have terminated in the fortress of Vincennes. The candidature of the Prince de Joinville for the Presidency of 1852, which was very popular in France, even among the Liberal party, and seemed likely to be successful, disquieted the Bonapartists; and the violent and insolent language of General Changarnier aroused Louis Napoléon to the conviction that the time for action had arrived. It was the general opinion that a crisis was rapidly approaching, and only the President had the skill and courage to place himself at the head of the movement, and act decisively.

THE PRINCE-PRESIDENT.—The Prince-President naturally looked to that great source of power in all governments, the army, as his strongest support; as military discipline secures prompt and efficient action at the bidding of one directing mind. The army, having already been disgusted by the interference of the Legislative body, felt humiliated by the Republicans, and hailed with delight the expected advent of a bold leader. At the end of November the principal military authorities met at the house of General Magnan, and unanimously resolved to co-operate in any measures necessary to secure the tranquillity of Paris, and establish a firm and resolute government. The whole army being stationed in the vicinity of the metropolis, was prepared for some decisive movement; and although its precise nature was not understood, yet there was a determination to obey any orders emanating from the military authorities, whatever might be the consequence.

Relying on the support that he was thus to receive, the Prince-President announced to some of his faithful followers that the time had at length arrived when it was necessary for the welfare of the country, as well as for his own preservation, that measures should be adopted to dismiss the Assembly, and to give into his own hands the reins of government. Upon every occasion Louis Napoléon has secured to himself many attached adherents and friends, who have devotedly followed his fortunes on desperate occasions, and have not failed him in adversity. Such fidelity and devotion, while it reflects honour on them, also indicates rare qualities in the Prince, who exercises so powerful an influence over his adherents. His winning, unaffected manners, his calm self-possession, the deliberation and coolness of his judgment, and his firm conviction of his ultimate success, which have borne Louis Napoléon through difficulties apparently insurmountable, have never failed to impress all who have been admitted to his intimacy. He has also obtained the well-merited reputation of never having alienated or forgotten a friend.

M. de Morny.—The friend who stood forward on this occasion, and in whom the President felt that he could place the utmost reliance, was M. de Morny, a man of firm determination and keen intellect, who was well acquainted with the state of political feeling in France, and was friendly with some of the most distinguished men of the day. He entered into the plan proposed with a full conviction that he was acting the part of a good citizen and an attached friend, and zealously devoted himself to the cause of the Prince; indeed, much of its success must be attributed to his admirable arrangements. Throughout he exhibited that calm but energetic and indomitable spirit essential on great occasions. He was at the Opera Comique on the very night when the storm was to burst forth; but nothing in his manner or appearance betrayed that his mind was absent from the dramatic scene.

The following anecdote is related of him, of the truth of which there can be no doubt. Being seated beside a lady of high rank, she asked him if the rumour in circulation was true, that it was intended to sweep out the Legislative Assembly; the prompt reply of the future Minister of the Interior was, "I trust that I shall be near the handle of the broom that is to produce this effect." His tact, his temper, and his moderation may be judged of by the telegraphic despatches which passed, during the tumult of the day, between himself and the Minister of Police. The celebrated Dr. Veron occupied himself for some time in copying these messages as they were transmitted ; and the experienced editor of the *Constitutionnel* has enabled the public to judge how rapidly M. de Morny entered into the ideas of the Minister of Police, and how cautiously yet vigorously he answered the somewhat hurried and imprudent communications that he received.

Major (now General) Fleury, a most gallant officer who had greatly distinguished himself in Africa, was another individual upon whose remarkable abilities the Prince had the strongest reliance ; to these personal friends were added M. de Maupas, who had, in the exercise of his high authority as Préfet at Bordeaux, shown qualifications which entitled him to be intrusted with the important office of Minister of Police. Two distinguished men of high rank in the army represented the military element ; General (afterwards Marshal) St. Arnaud accepted the onerous position of Minister of War, and General (now Marshal) Magnan was appointed to the command of the army at Paris.

THE NIGHT OF DECEMBER 1.—On the evening of the 1st of December, a gay and fashionable assembly congregated at the palace of the Elysée ; all was gaiety and animation as usual ; it was a *fête* of social life, into which care never seemed to enter : to-morrow seemed never dreamt of. The Prince joined the lively throng ; no trace of care was upon his brow : he was apparently bent only on making happy the friends by whom he was surrounded ; and, with his usual affability and kindness, he spoke to several of those who were for the first time present, giving to all a hearty welcome. At eleven o'clock the party broke up, and the visitors departed.

A BALL AT THE PALACE OF THE ELYSÉE. PRINCE NAPOLEON PRESIDENT.

Then the Prince, with his faithful friend and secretary M. Mocquard, the Comte de Morny, M. de Maupas, and General St. Arnaud, entered the private cabinet of the President, to arrange definitively the course of proceeding on the morrow. It was at this meeting that the final orders were issued to the various functionaries by whom the plan of operations was to be carried into effect. Everything had been well and maturely considered; even the minor details had been decided upon. To obtain possession of the Government press—to arrest some of those whose violent opposition was most to be dreaded—to prevent the meeting of the Legislative body—to distribute the different regiments in commanding position—to name a new ministry,—these were objects of vital importance, the failure of any one of which might endanger the success of the whole movement; and each of the members of this cabinet council had important duties to perform, which if neglected would produce irremediable confusion. Not one of these determined men failed in his purpose, and all acted in concert; each one felt that upon his own efficiency rested the lives and fortunes of his associates, and the complete success of the *coup*.

The first step taken by Louis Napoléon was to sign the dismissal of the existing ministry, the appointment of the new ministers to their respective offices, and to prepare those energetic proclamations which on the following morning were read with eager eyes by the astonished Parisians. An active and intelligent officer, Colonel Béville, had been selected to carry to the printing-office the decrees that were to be disseminated; these consisted of appeals to the people, orders to the army, and the proclamation of the Préfet of Police. He took them to the national printing-office, where he found that a hundred of the Garde Municipale had, with prudent foresight, been installed, with orders to obey his commands. The director, of course, complied with the injunctions of the Préfet of Police, and the printers were kept at work during the night under strict surveillance; and in the morning Paris was placarded with the President's decrees.

As soon as M. de Béville had left the room, M. de Morny, M. Maupas, and General St. Arnaud repaired to their several posts, prepared to act simultaneously, and with the energy and boldness essential to secure success. The account given by Mr. Kinglake of what occurred on the eve of the *coup d'état* is so far from being correct, that instead of manifesting the perturbation, nervousness, and apparent anxiety of mind so graphically described, the Prince quietly retired to rest, and simply gave orders that he should be awakened at five in the morning. He betrayed not the slightest emotion, and nothing transpired that could give the household the most remote intimation of what was about to occur: indeed, it is a well-known fact, that the domestics were as much surprised the following morning at learning that a revolution had taken place in Paris, as any other inhabitants of the city, for some of them actually sallied out to inquire of the servants of the English Embassy whether there was any truth in the reports that had reached them from without.

The Arrests.—The Minister of Police, M. de Maupas, instantly summoned all the commissioners of the different arrondissements into his cabinet, and signed orders for the arrest of the leading members of the Legislative Assembly, which were to be carried into effect before the break of day. Strange to say, there was not a word of inquiry, not a sign of hesitation. These functionaries recognised at once the authority under which they were called upon to act, and performed their duties with marvellous promptitude and with unfailing efficiency. The prisons of Paris received the men who the day before were the legislators and governors of France. Nor did the jailers hesitate (as was the case when Robespierre was overthrown) to open their gates for the reception of their late masters.

An anecdote is related, that General Changarnier was very nearly being made acquainted with the impending events. A young officer whose regiment was stationed at Courbevoie, had come up to Paris to pass the night; he was awoke by his servant, who told him that his presence was required immediately, as his regiment had been suddenly called out. The officer, surprised at this intelligence, and thinking that he ought to acquaint General Changarnier with this unusual order, went to the General's hotel; but finding that the porter was slow in opening the doors, he abandoned his intention and went to his quarters; whence he was obliged to accompany his regiment on the following day to overthrow the authority of General Changarnier and his friends. No delicacy was shown in the manner of arresting the most distinguished men of the day; and the volume of M. Granier de Cassagnac, narrating what occurred in each case, has not met with general approbation: a little more consideration for men woke up in the dead of the night to be thrown into prison, would have better become that injudicious writer.

M. de Morny, after playing at whist at the Jockey Club with Colonel Feray and Count Daru, went to the hotel of the Minister of the Interior at five in the morning, and found the actual possessor of the office enjoying a peaceful slumber, from which he was speedily awakened to find himself superseded. The Chamber of Deputies was dissolved; some of the members in vain attempted to assemble and form a house, but they were removed and imprisoned for the day in the barracks on the Quai d'Orsay, whilst others were distributed amongst the neighbouring forts. Cromwell, when he drove the members out of the House of Commons, and the first Napoléon, when he boldly turned the representatives of the people out of their chamber at St. Cloud, could not have acted with more energy and decision than was shown on this occasion; and apparently under the sanction of the law, for the ministers had their instructions direct from the President of the Republic, who, as the executive power, was invested with the authority of arrest and imprisonment. All the different *employés* of Government, therefore, whether civil or military, carried out the commands they received without a moment's hesitation, coming as they did from the quarter which they were accustomed to regard as being responsible for what they did. In short, everything worked well, and the Government was soon in the hands of those who had so adroitly planned and so boldly carried out the *coup d'état*.

It now remained to keep the people tranquil, and to preserve the public peace from those daring Republicans, who would be certain to take advantage of any movement that might afford them an opportunity of seizing power, and to whom any amount of bloodshed would be considered of little consequence, so that their ends could be obtained.

PARIS ON DECEMBER 2.—Upon the 2d of December, totally unsuspicious of what was going forward, I left my house, and was somewhat surprised to witness great agitation amongst the people in the streets, who, for the most part, seemed anxious to return to their homes. I saw various groups reading placards of a large size upon the walls of every street, that had evidently been posted up by order of Government, as they were printed on white paper; for since the revolution of 1848, all private announcements have, by order of the police, been printed upon coloured paper. Knowing that at the mayoralty of my arrondissement every authentic document would appear on the *façade*, I hastened thither; besides, I was anxious to know what was said by the street politicians, who are in the habit of daily visiting the public office, outside which the *Moniteur* is daily affixed.

I found two proclamations attracting the eager attention of the readers: one was a *plébiscite*, countersigned De Morny, decreeing that votes should be taken at the different mayoralties for or against the maintenance of the power of Louis Napoléon; the other emanated from the Préfet de Police, demanding the maintenance of order, and recommending people to remain at home. Little was said by the readers; but in the group I espied a well-known Figaro of the neighbourhood, who whilst shaving his customers usually launched out into politics. He was a stanch Bonapartist, for his father, a soldier, had been raised to the rank of sergeant in consequence of a brave but ineffectual attempt to rescue Prince Poniatowski from a watery grave at the battle of Leipsic. I determined to submit my chin to the operation of this worthy during the afternoon, feeling sure that I should hear information from him as to what was the general opinion of his customers. In the meantime I strolled into the Faubourg St. Honoré, where a squadron of the 12th Regiment of Dragoons was stationed before the British Embassy, another being drawn up in front of the palace of the Elysée, whilst there was a third doing duty at the garden gate. A few individuals stood gazing on the unusual military display; but not a word was uttered, and they soon passed on. Now and then a carriage drove up to the gate, and after a scrutiny from the porter, was admitted or rolled away. So far as I could learn, no demonstration of any kind was made that day at the fashionable end of the town; but it was said that the Republicans were to have, at ten o'clock at night, meetings to take into consideration the incidents of the day; and that in the Faubourg St. Antoine, the Barrière du Trône, and the Faubourg du Temple, cries had been heard of "*Vive la République sociale!*" and "*À bas le Prétendant!*"

After reconnoitring the principal streets, and seeing nothing remarkable, beyond the anxiety and curiosity written upon the faces of most persons, and witnessing, what is not unusual in the streets of Paris, the marching by of several regiments evidently in high glee, I adjourned to the barber's, and seated myself in his chair. He was in a state of great excitement, and expatiating on the many virtues of Prince Louis Napoléon, with which he had become acquainted from having on two occasions dressed the hair of the chambermaid whose duty it was to lay the fire over-night in the cabinet of the President, which he himself generally lighted at an early hour in the morning. The excellent *soubrette* could never speak in sufficiently high terms of the gentleness and amiable temper of her master, and the worthy barber had caught the infection. Deriving his information from her as to the Prince's domestic virtues, and inheriting his father's admiration of the great Napoléon, he launched out in no measured terms against all those who opposed the re-election of the President, though his animosity to the Republicans was somewhat restrained by the presence of two doubtful-looking statesmen in blouses, who now and then interrupted him, by expressing their faith in General Changarnier. My eloquent friend, however, soon resumed his discourse, anathematising M. Thiers as having obliged King Louis Philippe to resign, that he himself might become Prime Minister to the Duchess of Orleans, and hurling strong language against M. Emile de Girardin, for abetting Prince Napoléon, the cousin of Prince Louis, in his views of succeeding to the Presidentship: he had heard some cries in the street of "*Vive l'Empereur!*" from the military, and they had delighted him. Some of the surrounding persons, waiting to have their beards trimmed, differed from the knight of the brush ; doubts were expressed of the talent of the Prince-President, and there was evidently a Republican tendency springing up ; but the announcement that the Prince, attended by a numerous staff, was passing by, put a stop to the conversation ; away every one rushed out to see the passing show, and upon their return there was a universal opinion expressed, that the Prince-President looked like a noble soldier, and "every inch a king :" his gallant bearing had evidently produced a strong impression upon the spectators, the majority of whom from that moment were evidently in favour of the changes that had taken place.

Louis Napoléon at the Elysée.—It has been asserted that the Prince-President remained in his cabinet, during these eventful days, solitary and gloomy, and, like the Roman emperor at Capreæ, solely occupied in issuing his edicts for the destruction of his opponents. This story originally emanated from an author more distinguished for the brilliancy of his imagination than for the soberness of his judgment, or the accuracy of his knowledge ; and who was conspicuous for his political malevolence, and the virulence of his speeches in the Legislative Assembly. He has been followed by some who, whilst they claim to write history, have no hesitation in copying the errors and exaggerations of others ; but it can safely be asserted that, so far from Prince Louis Napoléon being left to himself, the Princesse Mathilde remained with him the greater part of the day ; King Jérôme and most of the new ministers were admitted, and the Elysée was not closed to any visitors who had a right to present themselves to the President. Those who were received, found him calm, collected, and urbane as usual; and as notes and messages were placed in his hands, he received them with coolness, and quietly read their contents; but never, by his countenance, his gestures, or his words, could the effect or import of these communications be inferred. He addressed all with his customary affability and kindness, and conversed freely upon various topics. The Emperor, it is true, does not possess that volubility for which Frenchmen are remarkable; he thinks and weighs his words before he speaks, and what he says is concise and to the point: his manner is quiet and reticent, like that of a grave and thoughtful man; but this quietude is amply made up for by the flattering attention which he gives to the words of all with whom he speaks: nothing escapes him; he listens intelligently to all that is said, and his replies and observations evince a wish not to express his own opinion, but to learn that of others; and he never fails to appreciate at their due the value of the views and opinions brought before him. Upon these eventful days the Prince maintained his usual equanimity, and was not more grave and silent than usual; he never for an instant flinched from possible danger; he was always prepared to meet it; indeed, the man who had so boldly advanced into his enemy's country at Strasbourg and at Boulogne, was not likely to be daunted or quailed when so much was already accomplished; and his followers had seen enough of his conduct in such emergencies, to be satisfied of his presence of mind and personal courage.

M. de Persigny, whose attachment to the Emperor is such that he would at any moment lay down his life for him and for his dynasty, was constantly at the Elysée; for to him had been intrusted the task of effecting an honourable retreat, in case of an adverse turn of circumstances. His duty it would have been, had the day gone against the President, to have collected the household, and to have conducted the Prince, with all the troops that were faithful, to the palace of the Tuileries, where the active leaders were determined to make a last stand, and succeed, or perish with arms in their hands. This was the only alternative proposed; no preparations had been made for flight; no horses and carriages kept ready, no money had been sent to foreign countries, and nothing had been packed up to be carried off at a moment's notice. There was a firm resolve that death or victory was to be the result of this great enterprise.

In the course of the first day, I paid a visit to an old comrade, that distinguished officer Sir de Lacy Evans, who had just come to Paris, and was residing in the Place de la Madeleine; the conversation naturally turned on the events passing before our eyes, and the General expressed much satisfaction at the apparent promptitude with which the affair had been carried out; for we believed that public tranquillity had not been disturbed. He observed that the enemies of the Prince-President had brought the whole thing upon themselves, by their shameful treatment of the chief of the state; adding, that he felt persuaded that if Louis Napoléon would give the people a liberal constitution, which should include the freedom of the press, he would prove himself a greater man than his uncle.

I had been told that a column of the National Guard had marched with the infantry, but I found that this was not the case; in fact the utmost care had been taken not to call out the National Guard, for it was well known that in some of the regiments there were Republicans, who might be induced to leave their brethren and join the insurgents, if they were disposed to raise barricades. The consequence was that everything depended upon the regular troops.

Reception of the Prince-President.—When the Prince, attended by a numerous staff, accompanied by the ex-King Jérôme and by Count Flahault, rode through the streets, he exhibited that bravery which has never deserted him in the hour of danger; notwithstanding the calumnies of his traducers, who choose to assert that he is deficient in personal courage and nerve. He was remarkably well received by the army, and shouts of "*Vive le Prince!*" were heard from every regiment, as he cantered along the Champs Elysées. The people of Paris are never demonstrative in their reception of their monarchs; even the ordinary token of respect to royalty, the lifting of the hat, is rare, and on this occasion there was no observable departure from the usual habit. The Prince-President returned at an early hour to the Elysée, where M. de Persigny received him with the intelligence that all the steps hitherto taken were successful, and that the military were fully prepared to fulfil the orders of their superiors; indeed, so obedient were the sentries to the commands which had been given, that when the President, preparing to leave the garden of the palace, presented himself at the gate, the advanced guard of the 12th Regiment, then on duty, would not allow him to pass without giving the countersign. The orderly officers and the aides-de-camp gave proofs of their courage, zeal, and devotion. At one moment false reports were rife, that some of the regiments exhibited an unwillingness to act; General Rollin was summoned to express his opinion, and explain the state of affairs; he found the Prince firm and resolved, and prepared to take upon himself any personal responsibility for any steps that might be necessary. In short, every one who approached the Prince—and these were many—were struck with admiration at his dignified equanimity and self-possession.

Alarm of the Parisians.—The news of the imprisonment of so many persons of great political importance spread like wildfire throughout the whole of Paris, whilst the suddenness and the boldness of their arrest astonished and struck terror into the minds of many. Much sympathy was felt for them individually; and the horrors of the great French Revolution, the massacres in the prisons, the slaughter of priests, the banishment to Cayenne, rose up before the affrighted imaginations of the friends and relations of those who had been imprisoned. In the *cafés* a profound silence was observed; all communication from man to man seemed suddenly to have ceased; and anxiety was depicted on every countenance. The *salons* of the gay world were necessarily closed, as few dared to venture forth in the evening, no one knowing the extent of the danger that might be incurred. Were there to be Roman proscriptions? Was the guillotine to be erected once again on the Place de la Concorde? Lists of the prisoners (which of course abounded with errors) were eagerly circulated, and surmises were made as to their probable fate. It must be acknowledged that these alarms were natural, for the real disposition of the Prince was not known, otherwise there would have been less uneasiness, as was evinced by the fact that the gentlest treatment had been recommended, and that not a single individual arrested received the slightest insult or injury. Indeed, as soon as quietness was re-established, and the influence of the members of the Assembly could no longer be of consequence, every one was liberated; and not a person was in any way interfered with who was willing to submit to the new state of things. Some who menaced the newly-established government, were necessarily exiled for a short period, to prevent their entering upon schemes which could be only injurious to society and themselves. But as soon as possible a complete amnesty was offered; and those who announced their intention to remain quiet were at once allowed to return to their homes. Those who were taken with arms in their hands, and had proclaimed the Republic, were handed over for trial to the established tribunals, and only those were removed from the country whose character as disturbers of society had been previously acknowledged. In the conduct of the new government throughout, there was nothing that could justify the attacks that had been made, and the assertion that cruelties were inflicted upon innocent and harmless persons. In all great emergencies there are circumstances which, in the more peaceful states of society, would be highly reprehensible; the moment called for the establishment of a Dictator: *Nequid respublica detrimenti caperet.* Democracy, Socialism, Red Republicanism were to be combated, and success attended the grand attempt. Property and intelligence have been rendered secure; the boldness and energy of one man have crushed dangers to society which were seen to be fast approaching, and which, if not arrested, would have produced anarchy and confusion, and destroyed the peace and prosperity of the nation. The measures that the Prince-President was compelled to take, naturally excited the wrath of the very men who would have overthrown him; and every means were resorted to, by a small knot of aggrieved persons, to excite the indignation of the people at the recital of the misfortunes that fell upon those who exposed themselves to peril on an eventful day. Much was necessarily done in the defence of order which those who live where tranquillity has been for centuries established cannot fully comprehend; and the sympathy that is felt for the weak and suffering, has been called into activity by some who are incapable of judging fairly of the circumstances.

THE LEGISLATIVE ASSEMBLY.—But whatever sympathy may have been felt for individuals, none whatever was expressed or shown for the body to which they belonged. The abrupt dismissal of the Legislative Assembly was not regretted by any one; on the contrary, it was considered as a benefit to the country. The Assembly had never gained or deserved the confidence of the people, and not one of its acts could be cited that was worthy of a great nation. Even the Provisional Government, during its short and feverish existence, had shown some proofs of its desire to benefit society; it had abrogated the laws that punished political offences with death; it had ameliorated the hardships of the debtor; carried out some excellent improvements in the direction of railways, and had boldly met the financial exigencies by additional taxation, whilst it had removed the vexatious *octroi*. But the Legislative Assembly seemed to take a delight in repealing every statute that had given satisfaction to the nation; its aim appeared to be to return to the legislation of MM. Molé, Guizot, and Thiers; and it was remarkable for its ingratitude to any man who had done the state service. M. Lamartine, to whom Paris was so much indebted, whose eloquence had controlled the fierce democracy when the mob would have supplanted the tricolor by the red flag at the Hôtel de Ville, could scarcely command attention; nothing that he said was listened to. Cabals against General Cavaignac, the man to whom they were indebted for their existence, prevented his influence having due weight, and he was forsaken as soon as he ceased to be useful. Their presidents were utterly disregarded; the high-minded and finished gentleman, Armand Marrast, could not control the debates; M. Dupin was only regarded by them as a clever jester, whose caustic wit and epigrammatic reproofs served to amuse; his judicious admonitions and calls to order were unheeded, and the Assembly was too often the scene of virulent dispute and indecent violence. The tumult and clamour attending the appearance of any unpopular member in the tribune were disgraceful. When Victor Hugo attempted to speak, bursts of laughter followed some striking remarks which were not in accordance with the sentiments of the Assembly; the taunts and marks of ridicule lashed the speaker into a fury, and the more vehement his speech and gestures, the more his auditors derided him. There were many men of great ability in the Assembly who were esteemed by the country at large, but general opinion was not in favour of the body, and its disorganisation was regarded with much the same indifference as was the breaking up of the Rump Parliament by Oliver Cromwell; the announcement of its dissolution, therefore, was favourably received. There had been so many changes in the ministry, that people hardly knew who filled the respective offices; Leon Faucher was almost the only one who enjoyed public confidence, and even he was regarded by a large party with suspicion, for they beheld in him only a warming-pan for the advent to office of M. Thiers, who was supposed to be ready to take advantage of any change, and offer himself as candidate for the Presidency of the Republic. Rumours widely circulated that a *coup d'état* was preparing on the part of the Assembly, and many of its acts seemed to support this idea: such as the attempt to place under the authority of the Assembly a large military guard, and the defiant and menacing language of General Changarnier, then in command of the army. The apprehensions of the people were constantly aroused, and conflicts were daily expected; foreign statesmen looked with anxiety at what was passing, and the alarm upon the Continent was increased by the expedition to Rome; for, however much such a check upon the policy of Austria might be necessary, French interference with the Republican party in Italy was looked upon with suspicion. In fact, the National Assembly had lost the respect and confidence of the nation, and no one was anxious to see it reassemble. The protests and appeals to the people, made by some few members on the morning of the 2d of December, were received with apathy, and elicited no exhibition of feeling in their behalf; for, when at the Mairie arrests took place, no rescue was dreamt of; the spectators gazed on quietly, and were perfectly indifferent to the consequences.

THE 3D AND 4TH OF DECEMBER.—Slight barricades were formed in some of the streets, but the people took little interest in these manifestations on the first day; on the 3d of December, however, greater resistance was offered. But evidently M. de Maupas received exaggerated reports from his *employés*, which he somewhat hastily communicated to the Minister of the Interior; and these, unfortunately, led to the decisive and energetic course taken on the melancholy 4th of December. M. de Maupas, unaccustomed to the amplifications of police agents, was alarmed by false reports; he actually communicated a telegram announcing that the Prince de Joinville had disembarked at Cherbourg, and that other Princes of the house of Orleans had arrived at different parts of France. He also believed that the same opponents were in the field as those who had fought against Cavaignac, and that they were fighting at the barricades with determination; that Ledru Rollin, and a whole army of Red Republicans, had reached Paris from Rouen; in short, upon reading carefully the telegraphic despatches, the only conclusion that can be arrived at is, that the fears of M. de Maupas, and not the orders issued from the Elysée, were the principal cause of the fatal 4th of December.

On Thursday, at a quarter past one, M. de Maupas, as Préfet of Police, transmitted a telegram to the Minister of the Interior, in which appears these words:—"*Voilà le moment de frapper un coup décisif. Il faut le bruit et l'effet du canon, et il les faut tout de suite.*" The Minister of the Interior at this very time, when it has been asserted that the most sanguinary orders were issued, was exerting himself to see that the execution of all commands should be performed as inoffensively as possible:—"*N'arrêtons pas légèrement.*" "*Cet ordre sera exécuté avec beaucoup de politesse.*" "*Faites fermer avec douceur la réunion.*" "*Je ne veux pas que vos agents arrêtent légèrement.*" Such words, combined with other proofs, show that there was no intention on the part of the adherents of the Prince to act with brutal force. The poor Préfet of Police seems, indeed, to have lost his head. Among other of his despatches I find the following:—"It is said that the 2d Dragoons (the very regiment that was guarding the Elysée) has arrived from St. Germain, and that the Comte de Chambord is in its ranks as a private. I scarcely believe it." The only answer by M. de Morny was, "And I do not believe it." Even at the end of the fatal day, when everybody was regretting what had occurred, the frightened Minister of Police begs that the troops should guard him, that they should not be allowed to enter their barracks; and at half-past five on that 4th of

December he announces new barricades, and states that fresh insurgents are coming up by the railroad. It is impossible to read the bulletins which passed on this occasion without arriving at the conclusion that M. de Morny, in obedience to the wishes of the Prince-President, acted with forbearance and lenity; that, had he listened to the fears of the Minister of Police, the occurrences would have been of a much more fearful character. Even when this zealous chief of an active department pointed out to M. de Morny where Victor Hugo was concealed, and wished to make an examination of the house, the answer was, "*Ne faites rien.*"

That the 4th of December was a melancholy day for France, and will long remain remembered by Europe, is not to be denied; but it is neither just nor honest to attribute the lamentable events which then occurred to cold-heartedness on the part of Louis Napoléon. No man ever more deeply deplored them; and where the opportunity offered, he gave what indemnity he could to the families of those who had suffered. There are young persons who lost their parents on that day who have been educated at his expense, the cost being defrayed out of his private purse; and I know myself one instance in which the children have had a regular quarterly stipend paid to them, from their infancy, and which is continued, without interruption or diminution, to this day.

The first impression made upon the minds of people in England as to what occurred on the 4th of December, was the result of a letter which appeared in the *Times*, from an officer of the British army, who, from a window on the Boulevard Montmartre, was a personal witness of the scene that took place in the street beneath him, where many persons fell victims to the fire of the soldiery. The infantry, quartered in sub-divisions, suddenly fired, not only upon the men, women, and children in the footpath, but at the windows above them, and with sad results: volley succeeded to volley, and it was evident that a panic had taken possession of the soldiery. Their officers had given no commands; for, as Captain Jesse observes, they were quietly smoking their cigars when the firing began.

From the reports of the agents of the Minister of Police in the quarter of St. Denis, firing from the windows took place at the commencement of the military impulse. "*Des maisons sont déjà occupées par l'émeute; on a tiré des fenêtres,*" were the words transmitted from the office of the Minister of Police. It was this alarm that produced the fatal consequences. The windows of the houses had on former occasions been filled by insurgents who fired upon the troops, when the soldiers suffered so severely as to be under the necessity of watching for concealed foes, and had been obliged to rush into a house with the hope of dragging forth their enemies. In 1848, in the Rue Castiglione, two soldiers were killed by shots from the third storey of a house, whilst a lady was quietly standing on the balcony above. The soldiery, too, remember that, in the days of Louis Philippe, from a window of a house upon one of the Boulevards, not very far from the spot where Captain Jesse was standing, a deadly volley was discharged, by which many military were killed; amongst them Marshal Mortier, as brave a soldier as ever drew a sword for his country. It is not to be denied that considerable irritation existed amongst the military, from the recollection of what had occurred during the Revolution in 1848, when they were most shamefully treated;—they recollected the carnage and the burning alive of the brave men in the guard-house before the Palais-Royal; they bore in mind the treachery which some of their comrades experienced in the Champs Elysées; and there existed amongst them a strong feeling against the Parisians generally. The firing of the soldiers at the house of M. Sallandrouze, near which was Captain Jesse's apartment, was occasioned by some persons standing on the steps cheering at what they supposed was the employment of blank cartridge by the troops.

What the Author Saw.—I happened on that day to pay a visit, in company with my friend Mr. Paget of the British Embassy, to my banker in the Rue Basse du Rempart: M. Charles Lafitte then gave us to understand that orders had been given to the military to act with great moderation; but if there existed the slightest disposition to riot, they were to "take the bull by the horns," and to destroy all barricades with cannon. During our short interview the bugles were heard close at hand, the windows were opened, and we took up a position on the balcony, whence we saw marching, in good military order and at double-quick time, the Chasseurs of Vincennes. M. Lafitte, without anticipating what was about to occur, good-naturedly said, "If you wish to see the fun, you had better follow the troops; for I am confident, from the information I have this moment received, that they are bent on mischief."

Mr. Paget and I then bent our steps towards the Rue Richelieu, where the rattling of musketry was distinctly heard. My friend left for the British Embassy, saying that, as a diplomatist, his place was in the Faubourg St. Honoré and not upon the Boulevards. Immediately afterwards a brigade of Lancers, commanded by Colonels Feray and Rochefort, arrived opposite the spot where I had placed myself, at the angle of the Rue Grange Batelière and the Boulevards. A considerable crowd had there collected; and such was their hostile attitude, and so loud their vociferations, that I was convinced the Lancers would not long remain inactive, especially if the slightest insult was offered them. From amongst these persons thus collected came a pistol ball with a loud detonation, and a soldier was wounded. Col. Rochefort immediately charged at the head of his regiment; the consequence was that several of the crowd were severely wounded, and a bad feeling sprang up amongst the soldiery. I thought it prudent to quit this scene and return to my home, which I reached with considerable difficulty.

Certainly, all that occurred was of a nature to excite uneasiness and alarm; but "that it was seen with frenzied horror by thousands of French men and women" is an absurd exaggeration. The upper classes of Paris were no doubt exceedingly angry and irritated, because during every *émeute* in the metropolis, the Boulevards on the Madeleine side of the Rue Richelieu always continued to be the resort of the *flâneur*, and had escaped the slaughter consequent on the erection of barricades; and they went there attracted by "the pomp and circumstance of war," and thought themselves safe; for they looked upon the soldiers as their national defenders against insurgents, and they were maddened at the idea of the slaughter of unarmed saunterers, who had gone out as it were under the shield of the military, to see what was going forward.

Groundless Fabrications.—The occurrences of that day undoubtedly struck terror into the hearts of the people of Paris which will never be obliterated, and they certainly have tended to affect the popularity of the Emperor Napoléon in the capital; more especially as his political adversaries have never failed to throw upon him the responsibility of events over which he had no control. So dishonest have been some of the writers who have furnished the public with their tales, that it has been stated that in the gardens of the Tuileries, and the Luxembourg, military executions of prisoners took place in the dead of night! The overthrow of a pile of the chairs, which in winter are generally to be seen in the garden of the Tuileries, and the consequent alarm given by the sentry, was even magnified into an attack upon the palace and the consequent carnage of the assailants. As for the statement that platoons of soldiers performed the office of executioners in the night, it is a pure invention; and the rumour alleged to have been credited in Paris, that during the night of the 4th and 5th of December prisoners were shot in batches and thrown into pits, is an equally groundless fabrication. I never heard that such a falsehood was propagated, until I read this shameful insinuation in a volume which claims to be a contribution to history. As for the "nine kinds of slaughter" which the eccentric writer discovers that military men may unhesitatingly indulge in, I do not think that any of these have relation to the melancholy events of the 4th of December.

Those events are deeply to be deplored; but they arose out of accidental circumstances. No one has ever attempted to defend them; and they ought not to be exaggerated, either for the purpose of exciting the sympathy of nations, or for the sake of blackening political enemies. There was no wanton massacre of the people, as has been asserted; there were sad mistakes, and people ran into danger notwithstanding the warnings that were distributed everywhere—for placards were upon the walls in every direction, entreating every one to stay at home. There were insurgents, there were barricades, there was firing upon the soldiers; there was therefore a necessity for martial law to be enforced; but the Emperor is not chargeable either with the wild excesses of the soldiery, or the credulity of the Minister of Police.

The Parisians, even at the height of their excitement, did not hold the Prince-President responsible for these deplorable consequences; neither had he the least apprehension of being the object of vindictive feelings. So far from entertaining any personal fear, his calm self-possession was never more conspicuous than during these eventful days. I will only mention one corroborative circumstance in proof of this.

On the fourth night after the *coup d'état*, my daughter and myself were present at a ball, given by the Duchess of Hamilton in honour of the Prince-

President, at the Hôtel Bristol, Place Vendôme. At ten o'clock precisely, the President entered the ball-room, accompanied only by Count Bacciochi, when a quadrille was formed; the Prince dancing with the Duchess of Hamilton, Lady Poltimore and the Duke of Hamilton being the *vis-à-vis*. The second quadrille soon followed; when the Prince chose the Princess Mathilde as his partner, Lord Poltimore and Lady Cowley making the *vis-à-vis.*

The Prince appeared perfectly cool and collected; he conversed with a great many persons, but more particularly with Lord Cowley, who had only arrived in Paris that morning, to fill his post of British Ambassador. Lords Francis Gordon, Strangford, Halliburton, Ernest Bruce, with their wives, were present; together with many foreigners of distinction. The instant the clock struck twelve, Count Bacciochi, in a low whisper, said that the Prince's carriage was ready; whereupon the Duke of Hamilton, taking two wax-candles, conducted his imperial guest down-stairs, and handed him into his plain brougham. On the return of the Duke to the ball-room, he observed to several friends who had collected round him, "How extraordinary! There were neither military nor police in the court-yard of the hotel, to protect the President in case of danger." In fact, the Prince returned at midnight, without an escort, to the Elysée, in a one-horse brougham.

And this is the man whom Mr. Kinglake, in his account of the *coup d'état*, has insinuated to be constantly occupied in guarding himself against attacks from assassination, and living in fear and trembling.

Let those who have been influenced by these calumnies, consider what have been the results of the *coup d'état* upon the position and prospects of France. The nation enjoys greater prosperity and happiness, and its power and influence are stronger and more undisputed than ever in Europe; while the Emperor of the French holds a firm and lofty place amongst the monarchs of the world, in right of the wisdom with which he governs the people and develops the resources of the country.

Camp Life during the Peninsular War.—There was a wide difference in the camp life of the English and French armies.

An English soldier in camp appeared to be the most uncomfortable of mortals; there was no plan laid down for his recreation, or the employment of his leisure hours, and you might see him either brushing his clothes or cleaning his accoutrements, or else sitting on his knapsack, smoking his pipe to pass the time. We had no large tent wherein the men could congregate to converse, read, or otherwise amuse themselves, and when the weather was wet, they huddled together in small tents, where the atmosphere was worse than that of the Black Hole of Calcutta. The pipeclay system of tormenting our men, by requiring them to keep their kits clean, and punishing them by extra drills if the firelock or belts were not as spotless as on parade at the Horse Guards, was (to say the least of it) extremely injudicious.

The French soldiers, on the other hand, had small tents, amply large enough for five or six men, or, in default of these, they constructed tents with earth, trees, and rushes. Streets were formed, with squares; places of amusement were planned, and large trenches were dug in every direction, to drain the ground thoroughly. The officers, if near a town, took possession of the best lodgings, for the convenience of coffee-houses and kitchens; but, although they had every luxury they could afford or procure, their motto was, "*À la guerre comme à la guerre.*" On entering a French camp you saw as much order as in the best regulated towns. Gendarmes kept strict watch over the soldiers, a fire-brigade was always in readiness, and everything was arranged methodically. The dress of the French soldier was not only loose and comfortable, but easily cleaned, and his knapsack was remarkable for its convenience. A *cantinière* was attached to the camp, and supplied the officers and men with wine and spirits according to regulations.

The French soldier marched quicker than the English, both in advance and retreat; and after a victory by our troops few prisoners were taken. The Duke of Wellington, with all his wonderful foresight and genius, could never get at the secret why so few stragglers were met with in following the enemy; whereas at Burgos, after our raising the siege of that town, indescribable confusion arose, and nearly half the English army were either left behind or taken prisoners by Soult and Clauzel.

The system of outposts in the French army was on a different footing from ours. Before the enemy, the French sentinel was relieved every hour; whereas our soldiers remained on duty two hours!—the extra hour caused great fatigue, and in cold weather induced sleep. A troop of the 11th Light

Dragoons on duty in front—that is, at the extreme vedette, in the immediate presence of the enemy—was once caught napping. The French officer in command, observing the bad guard kept, ordered forward a sergeant and five men, who entered our lines and found Captain Wood and his men fast asleep; when the dragoons awoke, they were compelled to surrender themselves prisoners of war. Now, if the vedette had been changed every hour, this disgraceful catastrophe would not have occurred. Doubtless all these matters are better arranged now: the Crimean war ought to have taught us many valuable lessons, and our experience, so dearly bought, should be made profitable for the future. Were we to take a leaf out of the French book of tactics, instead of following the German school in all its pedantries, our armies would be better prepared for active service than they now are.

I may here mention an incident which befell Captain George Mansel, R.N., who related it to me. He was deputed by the Duke of Wellington to accompany the French army, under Marshal Clauzel, to the siege of Constantine. The expedition proved a failure, owing to causes which it is superfluous to mention; the French army raised the siege, and commenced a most disastrous retreat. It happened that Mansel on one occasion slept in the tent occupied by the commanding-officer of the Engineers, who showed our countryman every possible attention. This French officer was rather loquacious, and among other things he said that the defence of Burgos had been intrusted to him by General Clauzel when it was attacked by the army of Wellington, and that the British army had been foiled on that occasion. Mansel, like a brave and gallant Englishman, defended the honour of the British arms, and at the same time begged to know the causes that led to the disaster. The French officer replied, "I have seen a great deal of English soldiers, and better and finer troops do not exist; with the exception of your Engineers, whom I consider the worst of any troops I have ever met with. It was to them your defeat before Burgos was owing."

When Captain Mansel returned home, he was invited by Lord Bute to pass some days with him, and to meet the Duke of Wellington. The Duke naturally asked the gallant Captain several questions respecting the retreat, and said, "Clauzel is the best general, perhaps, that the French have; I never, during the period he commanded the French army, caught him napping." Captain Mansel then requested permission to relate what had occurred in the tent of the commanding-officer of Engineers. "By all means let us hear it," replied the Duke. Captain M. then stated what the French officer had said; when his Grace observed, "There is some truth in what the Frenchman asserted; but it was not entirely the fault of our Engineers. We were almost destitute of siege-cannon at Burgos; we had few tools, and many things requisite for a siege were wanting. It is true that the officer who commanded the artillery in the rear was removed from his post, but Captain Dixon, who succeeded him, proved a good officer: a stoppage of communications necessitated our retreat."

The great Duke was in this, as in most cases, correct. Had he acted on his own responsibility, the siege of Burgos would never have been attempted; or would have been attempted with proper tools, at a later period, and under more favourable circumstances.

A Foraging Party on the Adour.—Early in the spring of 1814 I was ordered to proceed with Lord James Hay on a foraging expedition. Our party consisted of fifty men, armed with firelocks, and mounted upon mules. It would be impossible to give any adequate idea of our zigzag march and our wanderings in the dark; at last, after proceeding in tolerably good order for about nine hours, we came in sight of a village called Dax, consisting of a few pretty houses, about a mile distant. At break of day, wanting our accustomed breakfast, we determined to seek quarters there; but gave directions to the non-commissioned officers to prevent the slightest disorder or pillage. My batman, Proyd, who spoke nearly every European language, advanced into the market-place with a saucepan, which he had brought with him from camp, and began striking it with a thick stick with all his might. The noise awoke the inhabitants, some of whom approached our party, and, after much persuasion, one of them was prevailed upon by Lord James to show us the Mayor's house; and presently this personage, "dressed in a little brief authority," made his appearance. We told him that one object of our coming was to procure provisions for ourselves, and forage for our horses and mules, but that everything supplied should be paid for. The Mayor regarded us with suspicion, until Proyd entered with our teacups and boiling water, and asked in good French for some plates for "my lord." The title of "my lord" electrified the Mayor, and in less than a quarter of an hour the whole of his family appeared, and offered us and our men everything that we required.

With a heart full of thankfulness I sat down to an excellent breakfast of cold meat, eggs, coffee, and bread and butter; and, to crown all, one of the daughters of the Mayor, an extremely elegant young lady, entered the room with some delicious comfitures, of which she said her mother begged our acceptance. The wife of the Mayor soon after joined us, and, to our astonishment and delight, began conversing with us in English. She said that she had been brought up in England, and that her mother was English, but had left her native land for France when she was about sixteen.

Having refreshed ourselves, and seen that the horses and mules had been properly groomed and baited, we gave orders to return, and our troop put itself again in motion; the animals being laden with straw, Indian corn, and forage of every description, for which we paid the Mayor in Spanish dollars. After we had marched some hours, finding that, hampered as we were, we could not march well in the dark, we determined to halt at the first village we fell in with, and continue our march the next morning to Bayonne; whence we were then about eight leagues distant. We soon struck a little bourg about two leagues from Dax, but could see no one stirring in the place: in fact, it seemed deserted. However, Proyd, ever alert, heard a dog bark in one of the houses, a sign that the inhabitants were hiding. We knocked first at one house and then at another, until our patience began to be exhausted; when a sleepy-looking fellow popped his head out of a window and asked us in a most insolent manner what we wanted. While we were parleying with him, one of the sergeants, an active young fellow, scrambled up to the window from whence this Caliban was jeering at us, bolted down the stairs, opened the front door, and admitted us into the house. It turned out to be the cabaret of the village, and it was the landlord who had just greeted us in this abusive manner. He was evidently an inveterate enemy of the British, for he would neither give us any information as to how our men were to be billeted, nor show us even common civility. However, finding our host so contumacious, we ordered him to be placed in durance vile, determining to carry him off to headquarters as a prisoner.

The next morning a council of war was held to devise a plan for transporting our prisoner. Proyd, the Figaro of the party, suggested placing him upon a mule; but the question was, how to get him mounted on the back of one at so early an hour in the morning, without creating a disturbance in the village. Hay, however, had no scruples on that score, and gave instructions to have the prisoner tied upon one of the animals. Proyd, approaching the fellow from behind, threw one of the regimental bags over his head, and with the aid of his comrades fastened him securely on a mule. When all was arranged to our satisfaction, the man began to bellow, and his neighbour, finding we were in earnest, came out and begged for mercy; but to no purpose, for we were determined to make an example of the disobliging brute: so off we started with our prisoner.

We arrived in camp just in time to report the result of our expedition to the commanding-officer,

ENGLISH MILITARY UNIFORMS (CAVALRY) 1821 & 1822.

who was much amused at our bringing, in addition to an ample supply of forage, &c., an impertinent fellow, with his head tied up in a bag. The next morning, after a severe lecture, our prisoner received his *congé*, and was desired to return home and tell his friends that we differed entirely from other soldiers who had occupied the country, for we paid ready money for everything we required, and expected to be treated with civility by the inhabitants.

A few days afterwards, another foraging party was organised, and on their arrival at the same village every door was opened and provisions, corn, hay, &c., offered in abundance, while the greatest civility was paid to our men. The proprietor of the inn was foremost in proffering his services, and expressed his regret for what had occurred before, stating that the cause of it was that, in the dark, the inhabitants mistaking us for a body of men belonging to the Spanish army, had fled; as a party of soldiers belonging to that nation had a short time before robbed them of their pigs, poultry, and linen, and ill-treated their wives and daughters. After this, our soldiers, when on foraging expeditions, were ordered to dress in uniform, to show the country people that they belonged to the British army.

General Sir Warren Peacocke, Governor of Lisbon.—During the British occupation, the Governor of Lisbon was Sir Warren Peacocke, a soldier who enjoyed the utmost confidence of the Duke of Wellington. This officer was born in 1776, and when at school was given a company in a regiment his uncle had raised. He subsequently entered the Coldstream Guards, and was at the time of his death one of the oldest general officers in the British army. While at Lisbon, his duties were arduous in the extreme. He had to reconcile the Portuguese Government and authorities to a military occupation, which they always looked upon with suspicion; and he had to control and direct all the transport service of the navy: but his most onerous labours were in connection with the many questions arising with regard to the army. Lisbon, at the period to which I refer, was a sort of hospital for the army of the Peninsula, whilst it was at the same time the basis of those glorious operations the effect of which was to drive the French out of Spain, and General Peacocke was referred to on all occasions by the Portuguese and English.

No small part of his duties consisted in dealing with the friends and relations of officers in our army, a crowd of whom came over from England, each with a special object in view. Some wanted a prolongation of leave for a son or brother; others that their friends or relations might be permitted to return to England on account of urgent domestic affairs; while with the rest the excuse was, that ill health, owing to change of climate, ought to influence the Governor to permit some stalwart soldier to visit his native land. To all these importunities Sir Warren was wont to reply, that "he could not, on any account, permit domestic affairs to interfere with the duties of the service." Whilst tormented with these petty annoyances, he was constantly engaged in the most important correspondence with the British Government, the Duke of Wellington, and the Portuguese officials. Many of the services he rendered his country at that time were such as cannot be transferred to the pages of history, being of the most delicate and confidential character. Throughout all, Sir Warren was remarkable for his urbanity of manner, his untiring business habits, and a keen judgment, which made him alike an accomplished statesman and an intelligent soldier.

Some of the complaints made to the gallant officer were frivolous in the extreme. On one occasion an assistant-surgeon complained, in no measured terms, of the quarters allotted to him, stating that he was obliged to sleep in a pigsty; upon which Sir Warren inquired of one of his subalterns if he knew anything of the said pigsty. The answer was, that the quarters which the surgeon complained of were very good, in fact, better than the majority of the officers occupied. "Oh, then, sir," said Peacocke, turning to the injured medico, "if you are a prince in disguise, declare yourself; but if you are only what your diploma states you to be, I consider the quarters you have quite good enough."

Lisbon, owing to the Continental war then raging, was the only port open to the English, and thither our countrymen and women flocked; in fact, Lisbon was then what Paris and Rome are now, and some of our most celebrated men show there to advantage. It was there that the immortal poet Byron first touched foreign soil, and where some of his daring, powerful poetry was written; he became the idol of the women, and the lionising he underwent there might have made him exceedingly vain, for he was admired wherever he went. His favourite resort was the opera, where most of the young men of fashion in Lisbon congregated in the evening. He was generally accompanied by his friends, Dan Mackinnon, Hervey Aston, Colin Campbell, and William Burrell. The opera at Lisbon was its chief attraction, and it was there that the celebrated singers, Catalani, Collini, Naldi, and Ambrogetti, with Presle, Angiolini, Deshayes, and the rest of the *corps de ballet* riveted the attention of hearers and beholders; and thence those artistes were engaged for the London Opera-house. Byron well describes these "amusing vagabonds," as he calls them, and their English admirers :—

> "Well may the nobles of our present race
> Watch each distortion of a Naldi's face!
> Well may they smile on Italy's buffoons,
> And worship Catalini's pantaloons.
> . . . .
> While Gayton bounds before the enraptured looks
> Of hoary marquises and stripling dukes,
> Let high-born ladies eye the lively Presle
> Twirl her light limbs and spurn the heedless veil;
> Let Angiolini bare her breast of snow,
> Wave the white arm, and point the pliant toe;
> Collini trill her love-inspiring song,
> Strain her fair neck, and charm the listening throng."

During the war, Colonel Gould, the factotum of the English lady patronesses, and manager of Her Majesty's Theatre in London, went once a year to Lisbon to hire his *troupe;* as Waters, Ebers, Laporte, and others, subsequently went to Paris and engaged singers and dancers.

I have been informed that the Duke of Wellington, during the Peninsular War, visited Lisbon only once, remaining three days at that town, at the Palace of Necessidades; and on this occasion he was received in the most enthusiastic manner by the Portuguese and English. Unfortunately, Marshal

Beresford and our Minister, Sir Charles Stuart, afterwards Lord Stuart de Rothsay, were at this time at variance, and hated each other most cordially. The Marshal wanted to lodge our great commander at his own house, and thereby monopolise his society; but to no purpose, as the Duke went to the palace. The Duke did not disguise his displeasure at the inefficiency exhibited by many of the superior officers in the British army then at Lisbon, and sent several of them back to England, saying, "It is not my fault that they are sent home, but the fault of those who sent them out."

Whilst the Duke was insisting on Sir Warren Peacocke's acting with severity against the skulkers from the army, these gentlemen were complaining bitterly of the Governor for not allowing them to shirk their duties, alleging that, on account of "ill health" (unfortunately a common excuse in the service), they ought to be allowed to remain at Lisbon to recruit it: this "recruiting of health," be it understood, generally consisting of a minimum of work, combined with a maximum of dissipation. Sir Warren was so disgusted with the amount of extra work and anxiety entailed upon him by these useless officers, that he several times requested the Duke to find some one to supply his place as Governor; but the answer he generally received was, "You are too valuable here to be replaced by any one. I cannot possibly spare you."

FRANK RUSSELL AT THE BATTLE OF THE PYRENEES.—After the battle of Vittoria our army marched to the Pyrenees, where took place those operations in the passes, and that brilliant succession of victories, which have given historical character to the names of Picton, Lowry Cole, Adam, Colville, and a hundred others. At that time nothing was thought impossible for British soldiers; after those victories the French soldiers were not to be compared with the English, although our adversaries were commanded by Soult. From Torres Vedras to the Bidassoa we carried everything before us, and we were only momentarily checked at the battle of the Pyrenees, where Lord Wellington found that the French were not disposed to allow us to invade their country without a severe struggle. At that memorable battle, Soult made a desperate effort to drive us back again into Spain; but he found to his cost that the fiercer he fought the more desperate was the resistance he had to encounter, till at length he saw it was impossible to withstand our invincible phalanx.

One of the heroes of that bloody day was Frank Russell, "the Pride of Woburn Abbey," whose character it would be as difficult to over-estimate as it would be to give an idea of his chivalrous bearing in presence of the enemy. He possessed all the requisites for a good soldier. Of noble birth, good-looking, and with a splendid figure, he was valiant in the extreme. He was gazetted in the 7th Fusiliers at the age of sixteen, and forthwith sent with them to Spain, where he followed the fortunes of his corps up to the time of the battle of the Pyrenees. One of the most furious attacks made by Soult on our position at this celebrated conflict was directed on the left wing of the British army. The Fusiliers were posted on the right, and ordered to maintain themselves against all odds, and not to budge a foot. The French General being determined to turn our right, sent an overwhelming force against Frank's regiment, which was posted against a mountain wall. The Fusiliers defended themselves with obstinate courage, but their Colonel, for some reason which was never explained, declared it prudent to order a retreat, though his line was unbroken. Frank Russell, however, shouted out, "Not yet, Colonel," and with the colours of his regiment mounted the wall and cheered our men on; the French meanwhile renewing their attack with redoubled vigour. During this fierce struggle, however, our hero kept his position, till the fierce energy with which the French had been fighting began to cool: for Wellington had meanwhile broken Soult's centre, and the retreat of the French forces was ordered. Before Russell quitted his post of honour, Lord Wellington with his staff happened to pass by the wall, and saw Russell standing on the wall, holding the colours of his regiment, which were riddled with bullet holes. On the following day, when the gallant young officer's conduct was reported to our great commander, he exclaimed, "Ah! there's nothing like blood."

The chivalrous bearing of Frank Russell affords a memorable example of the feeling which actuated young officers at the time of which I am now speaking. As a man of the world, Frank was a great favourite with the fair sex, and enjoyed in a remarkable degree the confidence of his friends; for his temper and disposition were eminently sociable, and he was noted for his kindness of heart. He died at an early age, holding a company of the Guards, and was universally regretted. A pretty compliment was paid to him by the Duchess of York, who presented him with a ring, made by Lawrier, the jeweller in St. James's Street, having for a motto, "None but the brave deserve the fair."

HUNTING IN THE PYRENEES, 1813, 1814.—The Commissary-General, Marsden, who belonged to headquarters, succeeded in collecting from England a kennel of splendid hounds. On the Marquis of Worcester's (the late Duke of Beaufort) leaving the army, he promised to send some of his father's dogs to Marsden; other gentlemen followed this nobleman's example, and before we crossed the Bidassoa the pack was complete, and in fine condition. The hunting in the Pyrenees reminded me of my native Wales; it was all up hill and down dale, and for that reason, when a fox was found he was seldom if ever killed. The best riders belonging to the hunt were the officers of the 14th and 16th Dragoons, who were, as a rule, well mounted. I have seen at a meet in the Pyrenees about two hundred officers assembled, some (as I have said) well mounted, but the majority on "screws," ponies, or even mules—a strange contrast to the Quorn and Pytchley gatherings. The greatest character of all was Lascelles, on his immense horse, on which he used to delight to race up hill for a lark; and many were the scrapes he got into with the whipper-in for riding over the hounds.

One fine morning in October 1813, Reynard took it into his head to cross the Bidassoa, and the dogs and huntsman, heedless of danger, followed. The notes of the hounds and the cheering of the huntsman alarmed a French drum-major and some twenty boys whom he was instructing in a secluded spot on the banks of the river. Instead of showing fight, the drum-major with his young pupils scampered off; the dogs meanwhile, accompanied by the huntsman, were in full cry, and shortly afterwards killed a fine dog fox. The field had remained on our side of the river, enjoying the sport without incurring any danger; when all of a sudden the enemy, wondering what the deuce we were about, came down in force, with a battery of field-pieces, and opened fire, which made us all scamper off as if old Nick had been at our heels. Marsden, however, advanced to the water's edge, and with his white pocket-handkerchief as a flag of truce, asked permission of the French officer in command to cross and explain what we were doing. This request was acceded to, and when our gallant foe had heard the reasons why we had advanced out of bounds, he very graciously permitted the huntsman and dogs to recross the river and join us.

Dysentery in the Peninsula.—Early in the year 1812 the Duke of York despatched to the seat of war the 3d Battalion of my old regiment. It was considered by military men to have been the finest in his Majesty's service. All the men, with the exception of the grenadier company, were strong, active young fellows, but had not seen active service. They were conveyed to Cadiz in men-of-war, and arrived there without any accident; but owing to change of diet, and the substituting the horrid wine of the country for the porter they had been accustomed to at home, before the expiration of a few weeks, five hundred of these fine fellows died in the hospital at Vizu, and were buried in the churchyard there. I mention this to show how careful commanding-officers ought to be to prevent similar consequences from decimating bodies of fresh troops: although warnings of this sort have occurred all over the globe.

On joining my regiment in the Peninsula, one of the grenadiers, a tall and well-built man, was recommended to me as the best person to employ for pitching my tent. This man had been brought up as a carpenter, but through some misunderstanding with his relations had enlisted. While cutting the trench he entered into conversation with me, and said he hoped, as I appeared very young and unaccustomed to bivouacking, that I would forgive him for being so bold as to offer a little salutary advice: which was to drink every morning on rising a small glass of brandy or rum, as by so doing rheumatism, dysentery, and many other camp disorders, would be prevented. He added, with tears in his eyes, that he had lost his brother at Vizu, owing to his not following the advice he was now giving me. I was so struck with the earnest manner of the man that I adopted his panacea, and during the whole time that I was in camp I never had a day's illness.

A Daring Exploit.—Among the incidents that occurred in the war in Spain, the following will no doubt surprise the reader:—In Picton's division in the Pyrenees, there was an Irishman of extraordinary courage, by name O'Keefe, who was addicted to all sorts of irregularities, which brought him more than once to the halberds, but who performed a feat worthy of the heroes of antiquity. Near the pass of Roncesvalles the French occupied a peak or impregnable mountain called the Boar's Head, at the top of which a company of the enemy was posted. To drive them away appeared impossible; Picton thought so, and determined to invest this natural fort, to prevent useless bloodshed. During a reconnaissance, the General said, in a loud voice, which was overheard by the men below, that the French could, if they pleased, pelt us away with stones from the top of the mountain. O'Keefe stepped up, touched his cap, and addressed Sir T. Picton thus: "If your honour chooses, I will take the hill alone." This speech astonished all who heard it; but not the General, who had frequently witnessed the daring and intrepidity of O'Keefe. "If you do so," replied Sir Thomas, "I will report it to Lord Wellington, and I promise you your discharge, with a shilling a day for life." O'Keefe stole away, having whispered to the commanding-officer of his company to follow him, and climbed up the goat-path, the English sentinels firing at him, thinking he was deserting to the enemy. O'Keefe having entered the stronghold of the French, was received with open arms, as a deserter. He then began to play his part, by showing signs of imbecility, laughing, dancing, singing, &c.; so that the enemy thought that they had actually received a madman instead of a deserter, and told him to decamp, as there was not food enough there to feed him. During this farce, our men quickly got up to the summit, where they found O'Keefe occupying the attention of the enemy. They rushed in and took possession of this stronghold without losing a man. O'Keefe (I believe that was his name) received for this act of daring the nomination of one of the warders of the Tower from the Duke of Wellington.

My Soldier-Servant.—When in Spain with my regiment, it fell to my lot to receive from the ranks a soldier born in Sicily, of Sicilian parentage, by name Proyd. When the Guards occupied Catania, this individual, having lost his father and mother, was adopted by the regiment, and through the instrumentality of Lord Proby, became a soldier, and was inscribed on the muster-roll of the 1st Foot Guards. He was an excellent servant, and perhaps the best caterer in the army; for when we were invading the Pyrenees, he supplied me with every delicacy, while the army generally was living on salt beef and biscuits: in fact, poultry, mutton, and fresh bread at my table were the rule, rather than the exception. With all these accomplishments, he possessed one fault—a too great admiration, unqualified with respect, for the charms of the fair sex, and he seldom lost an opportunity of stealing a kiss from any pretty girl that came in his way.

On our return from the Peninsula, I took this Figaro with me to White Knights, the seat of the Duke of Marlborough, where I was invited to spend some days. At this charming house I found a great number of visitors, among whom were Lord and Lady Grenville, Lord and Lady Macclesfield, Mr. Mathias, the author of the *Pursuits of Literature*, Lord William Fitzroy, Mr. Garlick, and others. It happened on the day of my arrival that my servant met the maid of Lady Macclesfield on the staircase, and without the slightest ceremony he attempted to kiss her. The maid, unaccustomed to such behaviour, screamed, ran downstairs, and then up again, with Proyd close at her heels; he even followed her into her lady's room, where she flew to take refuge. Her ladyship, alarmed at seeing a strange man in her room, shrieked loudly; many persons ran to her assistance; and her noble husband, more dead than alive, thinking some sad disaster had befallen the Countess, inquired with caution, "What is the matter?" Her ladyship replied in a faint voice, "The man is under the bed." Pokers and tongs were seized, and the noble Lord made use of his weapons to such purpose that the delinquent quietly surrendered. This incident, which created great confusion, rendered it necessary that the Sicilian should be sent to rejoin his regiment. Poor Proyd soon after applied for his discharge, and returned to his native land to make love to his own countrywomen.

Sir Thomas Styles.—Poor Sir Thomas Styles, who fought with the poet Shelley at Eton, received a commission in the 1st Foot Guards. Had it been in the time of peace, poor Styles would have shone to advantage on parade and at the mess-table; but the active life of a soldier proved too fatiguing for him, as will be seen by the following anecdote. In course of time he was sent with a detachment of his regiment to Portugal; but on his arrival at Lisbon, the Guards had left to join the army in the neighbourhood of the Pyrenees; accordingly, our young Guardsman received orders to march through Portugal and Spain until he came up with his regiment. The heat was excessive; and on his falling in with the brigade, poor Styles was more dead than alive. All his brother officers hastened to congratulate him on his safe arrival after so long a march; but he spoke little, saying, that, ever since he had left Lisbon, he had not closed his eyes for half-an-hour, and that his health was in such a state that he feared he could not long survive. Observing that something extraordinary had happened, he was pressed to be more explicit, and to tell what had occurred to make him so miserable. He replied, with a very grave countenance, that the fleas and vermin on the march had nearly driven him mad; and that when the peasant girls observed him scratching himself, they would laugh, and shaking their petticoats over pails full of water, tell him how much more they were to be pitied than he. Our doctor, Mr. Bacot, a very kind fellow, anticipating brain fever, placed Styles in his camp bed, covered his head with wet towels, and desired his batman to watch over his master, and not to leave him for an instant. However, the servant fell asleep, and during the night poor Styles got out of bed, unlocked his trunk where his razors were kept, and with one of them deliberately cut his throat from ear to ear.

Sir John Elley of the "Blues."—In previous pages I have had the pleasure of relating several anecdotes of this gallant officer; and I also mentioned his having commenced his military career as a private in the Blues. I have received a letter from a gentleman who knew him personally, giving me the following information respecting this dashing hero:—"I spent some time at Harrogate with this gallant soldier, whom I admired not only for his bravery, but for his talents; he was replete with wit and fun, and full of the most interesting anecdotes. On my leaving him, he said that he had an old acquaintance residing not far from my father's place, whither I was going, and he would feel obliged if I would ride over some day to a certain toll-bar in the west of Cumberland, and deliver a message to his old friend, the sergeant who had enlisted him in the Blues. I did not forget a promise which might lead to some anecdotes respecting Sir John's early life; and shortly after arriving at home, I mounted my nag, rode to the toll-bar, and saw the old sergeant, who kept the turnpike and appeared to be seventy-five years of age. When he came to take the toll he appeared much astonished at receiving the message from Sir John, and asking after his health, said that it was true that he had enlisted him into the Blues, and he related the circumstance :—'The sergeant, having charge of a recruiting party at Barnet, one fine day a tall and respectable-looking young fellow addressed him, stating he wanted to enlist; the shilling was therefore given, and on the following day the recruit was sent to headquarters, where he was passed and duly enlisted in the Royal Guards.'"

The old man being asked what he knew of Sir John's antecedents said, that the appearance and manner of the recruit proved him to have been a gentleman. He declined affirming as to the truth of what he had heard; but added that the report current in the regiment after his entering it, was that the new recruit had held a cornet's commission in the Scots Greys, then quartered at Doncaster; but owing to a misunderstanding with an officer about a lady, he had thrown up his commission in disgust, and having spent all his money, enlisted as a private in the manner described. In the barrack-room he was "hail fellow well met" with all his comrades, who nevertheless treated him as their superior. As a swordsman and rider, he was considered the best in the regiment; and in consequence of his gentlemanly deportment, and being a good penman, he was taken into the adjutant's office, whence he was promoted to a commission in the regiment.

Perhaps the most distinguished service ever performed by Sir John Elley was in the cavalry engagement at the battle of Vittoria, when he was assistant adjutant-general to the cavalry under the immediate command of Sir W. Cotton. Sir William had given directions to the 3rd Light Dragoons to charge a superior force of the enemy, which proved disastrous; for the regiment was almost entirely cut to pieces. Sir John Elley, observing this disaster, got together as many of the 14th and 16th Dragoons as he could, and charged at the head of them through the enemy; thereby saving many of the fine fellows, who were dispersed and unable to act. In the charge he was knocked down, together with his horse, the fall breaking his leg; and although continually ridden over by friend and foe in the *mêlée*, Elley, nothing daunted, cheered on his men to fight for the honour of old England, and at last, catching hold of Sergeant Cooper's stirrup, was dragged to the rear.

Jack Talbot of the Guards.—Poor Jack Talbot, after leaving Eton, entered the Coldstream Guards, and accompanied his regiment to Spain, where he evinced great courage, and was foremost in every fight. Though he possessed many imperfections, he was the manliest and kindest of human beings, and was the idol of the women; and their champion, also, for he was one of the few men who would never hear improper epithets applied to them under any circumstances, or allow their failings to be criticised by those who were in all probability the cause of them. There was a charm in Talbot's conversation that I never found in that of any other man; his brave good heart, and love of punch, made him an agreeable companion, and many friends. When in his cups, or rather bowls, he would talk facetiously about his rich father in Ireland, Lord Malahide, spending that nobleman's money all the time. He was foolishly generous. I have often seen him, at a club or in a coffee-house, pay for the whole of his friends present; and his liberality to women of all classes was profuse. He used to say, "I would rather disoblige my father or my best friend than a pretty woman."

Whether in the Guards' Club or at private assemblies, you were always sure to find Jack surrounded by a circle of friends, amused with his witty conversation and charmed with his good-humour. He had always a smile on his face; in fact, everybody acknowledged him as their friend, from Beau Brummell to Theodore Hook.

During his last illness, Alvanley asked the doctor of the regiment what he thought of it. The doctor replied, "My Lord, he is in a bad way, for I was obliged to make use of the lancet this morning." "You should have tapped him, doctor," said Lord Alvanley; "for I am sure he has more claret than blood in his veins." The late Duke of Beaufort one day called upon him at his lodgings in Mount Street, and found him drinking sherry at breakfast: the Duke remonstrated with him, saying, "It will be the death of you." Talbot replied, "I get drunk every night, and find myself the better for it next morning." Talbot was a great favourite of the late Duke of Cambridge, who frequently called to inquire after his health. Upon one occasion, the Captain's servant, in answer to the Duke's interrogations, told his Royal Highness that his master did not want to see either doctor or parson, but only wished to be left to die in peace. The Duke, with sad forebodings, sent Dr. Keate to see him; the doctor, on his arrival, found Talbot seated in his arm-chair dead, with a bottle of sherry half-empty on the table beside him. He was only twenty-seven.

"Teapot" Crawfurd.—Crawfurd was brought up at Eton, and subsequently entered the 10th Hussars. He possessed immense strength, was a handsome fellow, and his bravery was proverbial. His riding to hounds particularly, when a boy at Melton Mowbray and Belvoir Castle, was plucky in the extreme. He was called "Teapot," because of his predilection when at Eton for brewing tea in a black pot, which he kept and cherished when a soldier; though some would have it that his handsome head looked like those on old-fashioned teapots. He was noble-looking to the last day of his life, though worn down by disease. As a companion, he was charming; his bewitching manner found him friends everywhere, and he was courted by the dandies and men of fashion. He married Lady Barbara Coventry, a very beautiful woman, with whom he lived happily many years. The Prince Regent was very partial to him; and on the occasion of the 10th Hussars being paraded before their departure for Spain, the Prince said to him, "Go, my boy, show the world what stuff you are made of. You possess strength, youth, and courage; go, and conquer." Crawfurd arrived in Spain, and his first rencontre with the enemy was at Orthes, where he was foremost in the charge, and behaved splendidly. A brother of his, equally brave, was killed at Waterloo, whilst defending the château of Huguemont.

THE GUARDS' CLUB.—In order that my readers may understand what I am about to relate, it is desirable for me to advert to the causes which induced the officers of the Foot Guards to form their Club. Circumstances which it is unnecessary to enter into had for a long time prevented those gallant sons of Mars from carrying out the object they had in view. Unseemly broils and quarrels often took place in the room at the St. James's Coffee-house, at the bottom of St. James's Street, where the officers of the Guards used to congregate, and these were caused mainly by the admission of (or rather the impossibility of excluding) Irish bullies and persons of fashionable exterior but not of good birth or breeding. Consequently the officers were obliged, on the return of their regiments from the Peninsula, after the disaster at Corunna, to establish a club of their own. Arrangements were made, and the Guards' Club was formed, the subscription to which was at first only £5 per annum for each member.

Among those who first patronised this new institution were the Dukes of York, Cambridge, and Gloucester, and nearly all the general and field officers then in London. The room where the meetings of the officers of the Guards used to be held at St. James's Coffee-house was a miserable little den, the floor sanded over like a tap-room now-a-days: a strange contrast to the luxurious apartments now occupied by the officers in Pall Mall; but notwithstanding this, among the people who used to assemble might be found all the wits of the day—Brinsley Sheridan, Jekyll, Wyndham, and others, whose choice sayings over their punch and pipes would fill a volume. The rules of the new Club excluded gambling; and from 1812 till 1821, when I left it, I cannot recollect any serious quarrel occurring among the members, who were composed of the best men England could boast of. So great was the loyalty that pervaded them, that when the trial of Queen Caroline took place, and the *Times* made use of disrespectful language towards her, that paper was, at a meeting of the Club convened by Sir Henry Hardinge, late Lord Hardinge, expelled. *Tempora mutantur et nos mutamur in illis.*

GENERAL THORNTON AND THEODORE HOOK.—On the return of the British army from Spain in 1814, the Prince Regent, desirous of rewarding the personal associates of the Duke of Wellington, decided on removing the Generals of the Guards, and giving their places to officers of the Duke's staff who ranked as Colonels. The Generals were mostly either useless and decrepit veterans, or officers whose ideas of service consisted in attending as little as possible to their regiments, and giving the balance of their time to pleasure. One of them, General Thornton, was afflicted with the idea that of all persons in the world he was the only one who understood the art of waltzing. In fact, it was quite a mania with him, and he might be seen at nearly every party of note, making himself exceedingly ridiculous by teaching young ladies to waltz: this dance having only shortly before come into fashion. Theodore Hook gave him the *sobriquet* of the "waltzing General;" this occasioned a violent altercation between them at a ball in Portman Square, where, it is said, the General received a more personal affront from Hook: which, however, the soldier did not resent according to the then received notions of honour, by calling him out. The inquiry into this affair by a committee of the other officers of the Guards, no doubt caused the sweeping change proposed by the Prince Regent; it was found that General Thornton had been guilty of cowardice in not demanding immediate satisfaction of Hook, and he was therefore desired to quit the regiment forthwith. His resignation, and the comments on it at the time, paved the way to the proposed changes in command; and when Hook heard that the companies had been given to the Duke's Colonels, he said, "I rejoice to hear that they have adopted the Wellington over-alls, and discarded their inexpressibles." These Colonels were ever after called the "Wellington over-alls."

THE HEROIC LADY WALDEGRAVE.—When the British army was about to enter France, I was struck with the beauty and attainments of the chivalrous Lady Waldegrave, who accompanied her lord throughout the war. Her conduct was the theme of the army, and she won universal praise and admiration. She was a perfect heroine.

Since the peace, I have had the honour to receive invitations to her house in the Champs-Elysées. She used to speak of her campaigns with the same energy that an old soldier would talk of battles wherein he had distinguished himself, and would tell you of the innumerable risks she had been exposed to in the several charges of cavalry which her husband had led. She felt much, she used to say, for those poor fellows who were left wounded on the ground, and her description of their sufferings was so natural and touching that it frequently brought tears into the eyes of those who heard her. The heroine was nearly taken prisoner upon one occasion; but, upon presenting her pocket-pistol at the breast of the French cavalry soldier who menaced her, he dropped his sword, and suffered her to escape.

The Countess of Waldegrave was not only young but beautiful; she had a splendid figure, and was one of the best riders I ever saw. She was not at all masculine in her style; her voice and manner of speaking were remarkable for sweetness and grace. I cannot hope to see her like again.

COLONEL, *alias* "JEMMY," COCHRANE OF THE GUARDS.—This gentleman was, in the fullest sense of the word, fearless—in fact, he dared danger; yet, although so brave, he was an amiable and quiet man, and an enemy to every species of disorder. Looking at him, one would have thought that he was fit only for a drawing-room, as he had most delicate hands and feet; but his figure was perfect symmetry, and his strength was prodigious. He had neither vanity nor ambition, and was a firm friend to all his comrades.

Fifty years since, my lamented friend was sent to Bristol with a recruiting party of the 3d Guards. Frequent quarrels arose between the soldiers and sailors at that place; and upon one occasion he observed a mob of brutal fellows ill-treating his recruiting-sergeant. Regardless of the immense odds against him, he ran to the rescue of the sergeant, who lay bleeding on the ground, and, alone, attacked the furious mob that surrounded them. Every blow he dealt brought one of his adversaries to the ground, till at length they ran away right and left, leaving him master of the field. I was told by a gentleman who arrived on the ground a few minutes after this unequal fight, that he saw three men unable to move, owing to the punishment they had received:—one had his jaw broken, another his shoulder dislocated, and the third was so frightfully disfigured that his own mother would not have known him.

"Jemmy" Cochrane married a lady near Bath, where he resided many years, and died a lieutenant-general.

Mr. Cornewall and the Provost-Sergeant.—A large army is accompanied, not only by the sutlers and others who make their living by so doing, but by curious or scientific men, who seek to acquire either materials for small talk or solid information useful to the world at large. Our army in the Peninsula was not an exception to the practice, and many wealthy and educated men set out from England to follow its fortunes; but Lord Wellington set his face against all these intruders, with the exception of Mr. Cornewall, who was favoured with his especial patronage.

This gentleman, the eldest son of the Bishop of Hereford, having letters of introduction to his Lordship, on arriving at Lisbon, provided himself with horses, &c., and, thus equipped, reached the headquarters of the army in the Pyrenees. He was present at all the battles, down to that of Toulouse, and upon all occasions he exhibited before the enemy the greatest *sangfroid*. At Toulouse Lord Wellington requested Cornewall to be more careful of his person, saying, "If you are killed or wounded, the army will not pity you; for you are unnecessarily courting danger." "Well, my Lord," replied Cornewall, "I think the odds are in my favour now; having up to this moment escaped being hit, I care not for what may happen."

Cornewall happened to dine at headquarters that day, and when returning home at a late hour, he saw a soldier suspended by the neck from a pair of halberds. He naturally hastened to the spot, where he found the provost-sergeant and a few soldiers and peasants; and, on inquiring what it all meant, the sergeant replied, "Sir, the man you see hanging there has been found guilty of robbing and ill-treating some of these poor peasants, and was sentenced to be hanged by a drum-head court-martial, and there he is expiating his crime." Cornewall went the next morning to headquarters, and related to Lord Wellington what he had seen; upon which our illustrious hero said, "Discipline must be maintained at any cost, or my soldiers may become a rabble of thieves." "True, my Lord," replied Cornewall, "but the provost-marshal's power appears to me to be too great; for he acts as judge and executioner, without the culprit having time to appeal for mercy." Lord Wellington replied, "My orders are peremptory on that score; and I would recommend you to be careful not to get into the provost-sergeant's clutches, or you will inevitably be strung up." "Thank you, my Lord, for the hint. I will never more trust myself within a hundred miles of such danger; for I would rather be riddled with the enemy's bullets than be placed between a pair of halberds."

ARMA VIRUMQUE CANO.—Towards the close of the Continental war, viz., in 1814, the militia of that epoch were full of military ardour. The Marquis of Buckingham, who was enormously fat, and not unlike the pictures which are represented of Falstaff, volunteered, in conjunction with his friend Sir Watkin Williams Wynne, to take their regiments, the Buckinghamshire and Flintshire Militia, to the seat of war. Permission was granted them to join the Duke of Wellington's army, and off they started for Bordeaux. But they arrived "a day after the fair," for the treaty of peace had been signed by the allied sovereigns; so, as the King of France with forty thousand men

> "Marched up a hill, and then marched down again,"

our patriotic warriors were obliged to retrace their steps without having fired a shot at the enemy.

Before they re-embarked for their native land,

however, they took good care to impress upon the inhabitants of Bordeaux their value as soldiers, by parading their battalions with all the pomp and circumstance of war, both in the morning and at noon. Those for whose benefit this spectacle was intended never failed attending these military parades; not with the idea of gaining any hints as to evolutions, &c., but to gaze on the commanding officers, whom they denominated, "*Les bœufs-gras anglais.*" The militia regiments appeared but a sorry sight in comparison with British veterans who had marched through Portugal and Spain, fighting a hundred battles, and afterwards remained some time at Bordeaux, where they gained the respect of the inhabitants by their orderly conduct and manly bearing. Unfortunately, too, our militiamen did not conduct themselves in a becoming manner; for, delighted at the cheapness of the wine and brandy, and happening to be officered by men incapable of looking after them properly, when off duty they were constantly tipsy, and getting into all sorts of scrapes and broils with the inhabitants; so much so, that their conduct was reported to the Commander-in-Chief, who ordered them home without delay.

The wine-merchants, who had not done badly during the stay of our warlike friends in Bordeaux, persuaded the Marquis and the Welsh baronet, on the eve of their departure, into buying a quantity of stuff they designated claret. Proud of their purchase, they had it carefully shipped; and when it arrived in due course at London, it was stowed away in the cellars of Stowe and Wynstay. Orders were eventually given to have the precious liquid bottled; but when the casks were tapped it was found that an acetous fermentation had taken place, converting the "delicate Bordeaux wine" into very bad vinegar. The two heroes, doubly disappointed of the wine they had bought and the honours they hoped to win, commenced legal proceedings against the vendors of the liquor; but they were non-suited, and had to pay costs, amounting to a considerable sum.

Sir Jerry Coghlan.—Sir Jeremiah Coghlan's name, and the daring acts performed by him, are familiar to every naval man. Beginning life as a cabin-boy on board a trading sloop, running between Cork and Neath, Coghlan was treated by the captain in a most inhuman manner. The brutality of this man becoming unbearable, Jerry determined on quitting the vessel at Neath, but was caught by the police, and brought before one of the magistrates of the county, a relation of the author. The boy said that, owing to the cruel conduct of his mother, he had been obliged to leave home, and went to Cork, where he was bound as cabin-boy to the master who had treated him so ill. Under these circumstances, he was allowed to leave the sloop, and obtained employment in Neath as a bricklayer's lad in the building of a few houses which were in course of erection on the Parade. Not contented with this mode of gaining a living, he offered his services as ordinary seaman to a captain about to sail for Plymouth; he was engaged, and arrived at that port, where a terrible storm was raging. Coghlan went on shore, and found his way to the beach, where a number of persons were assembled to look at a large East Indiaman, which was in danger of being wrecked. Among the crowd was Sir Edward Pellew, afterwards Lord Exmouth, who, perceiving that the vessel was already aground, offered a prize to any one who should carry a rope through the breakers to those on board. No one venturing, Jerry thrust himself forward, stripped, tied the rope round his waist, dashed through the waves, and succeeded in establishing a communication between the shore and the ship. This heroic deed won the admiration of all who witnessed it, and among them that of Sir Edward Pellew, who took Coghlan on board the man-of-war that he commanded, and made him one of his midshipmen.

In a few years Jerry was sent into the Mediterranean, where he displayed such coolness and daring in cutting out prizes from the enemy's ports, engaging with success French vessels larger than his own, and running into the best guarded harbours, that the Admiralty were induced to give him his lieutenancy, and the command of a sloop of war. The exploits Coghlan performed with this small vessel are matters of history; and his achievements furnish instances of the wonders that can be wrought by the union of skill, presence of mind, and energetic daring: qualities which have distinguished the British navy for the last century. Coghlan's bravery elicited many commendations in the despatches of Lord St. Vincent, the Admiral of the Fleet. In one place the noble Lord says:—"I did not think the gallantry of Sir Edward Hamilton and Captain Patrick Campbell could have been rivalled, until I read the enclosed letter from Sir Edward Pellew, relating the great services performed by Lieutenant

Coghlan of the *Viper* cutter, which has filled me with pride and admiration." Lord St. Vincent also addressed the following letter to Lord Spencer, the First Lord of the Admiralty :—

"My dear Lord,—I shall not trouble your Lordships with a word more than is contained in the enclosed private letter from Sir Edward Pellew, on the subject of the intrepid Coghlan, except to say (not out of ostentation, but to prevent the city or any body of merchants making him a present of the same sort) that I gave him a sword of one hundred guineas' value,—Yours faithfully, St. Vincent."

Poor Coghlan died young, owing to the wounds he had received in the service; but some years previous to his death the quondam cabin-boy became a Knight of the Bath. I had the honour of being well acquainted with him, and can speak with pleasure of his varied attainments, extraordinary in a self-educated man, and the manly bearing he always exhibited.

Lord Jersey and an Officer of the Guards.—When duelling was at its height in England, the most absurd pretexts were made for calling a man out. I recollect that at one of the dinners at the Thatched House in St. James's Street, Mr. Willis, the proprietor, in passing behind the chairs occupied by the company, was accosted by a Captain in the 3d Guards in a rather satirical manner. Mr. Willis, smarting under the caustic remarks of the gallant Captain, said aloud,—"Sir, I wrote to you at the request of Lady Jersey, saying that as her Ladyship was unacquainted with you, I had been instructed to reply to your letter by stating that the Lady Patronesses declined sending you a ticket for the ball." This statement, made in a public room, greatly irritated the Captain; his friends in vain endeavoured to calm his wrath, and he sent a cartel the following day to Lord Jersey, requesting he would name his second, &c. Lord Jersey replied in a very dignified manner, saying that if all persons who did not receive tickets from his wife were to call him to account for want of courtesy on her part, he should have to make up his mind to become a target for young officers, and he therefore declined the honour of the proposed meeting.

LORD CASTLEREAGH AND SIR E. PAKENHAM.—The following incident occurred in London in 1814. When the war had terminated in the Peninsula, Sir Edward Pakenham, with his physician, Dr. John Howell, arrived in England, *en route* to North America, where Sir Edward had been named by the Duke of York Commander-in-Chief of the British forces. Before the departure of the gallant General, he had promised Lord Castlereagh to breakfast with him, and at the same time to introduce his physician to the minister. After breakfast, Lord C. inquired of the Doctor the precise place where the jugular vein was situated. Dr. Howell explained it to the satisfaction of his Lordship, stating that it would be a dangerous experiment for any man to take the slightest liberty with that artery, for death would inevitably follow if it were pierced. When the General and his friend were returning to their hotel, the former said, "I am afraid, Doctor, you were too explicit about the jugular artery, for I observed Castlereagh to be in a strange mood when you finished your anatomical lecture." It is needless to state that many years did not elapse before Lord C. committed suicide by cutting his throat with a penknife.

Dr. Howell related this incident to me at Brighton in 1849.

Louis Philippe at Twickenham.—Early in this century Louis Philippe lived with his brothers in a small cottage at Twickenham, where, though fond of conviviality, he practised the most rigid economy. They had only one man-servant and a maid-of-all-work. Towards the end of his chequered life he was heard to say in passing the cottage, "There I passed some of the happiest days of my life; but during that period I had to struggle against poverty, without receiving aid from any one." The three royal brothers had a tilbury, which they drove by turns; but they gave both man and horse a holiday on Sundays.

I received this little anecdote from a friend who when young resided at Richmond and was intimately acquainted with the fallen monarch. Louis Philippe resided in England till 1808, when he embarked for Malta, carrying thither, for change of climate, his surviving brother, the Count Beaujolais, then in a rapid consumption. The Count's health was such that it was found necessary to stop at Gibraltar, where H.R.H. died. Louis Philippe afterwards proceeded to Sicily to return thanks for various favours he had received from the King of Naples, and there he met his future wife in the king's second daughter, the Princess Amélie. There can be little question but that it was a love match, as at that period there did not appear to be the remotest chance of Louis Philippe succeeding to his patrimonial estates, much less to the crown of France; and it was by many considered a foolish marriage. There were many difficulties in the way of their being married; but these were, however, surmounted, and the royal pair were united on the 25th November 1809, at Naples.

After the downfall of Napoleon the First, Louis Philippe returned to Paris, contrary to the wishes of Louis XVIII., whose jealousy was sharpened by the wily Talleyrand. There he occupied himself with the culture of his vast estates, the education of his children, and the formation of a political party, which a few years later placed him on the throne of France.

Eton College in 1810.—When Dr. Keate, the head master of the Lower School, was elevated to the Upper, he did not bring with him a popular name; his abrupt, blunt, and somewhat rude manner, which contrasted strongly with the mild and polished bearing of his predecessor, Dr. Goodall, did not tend to remove the unfavourable impression his antecedents had produced. The consequence was a good deal of disaffection, which showed itself in various ways. The most remarkable and successful trick which was played off on him, by some bold and skilful boy whose name to this day remains undisclosed, I will endeavour to describe. The head master, when he came from his private chambers to the upper schoolroom, had to pass through the old library by a private door, the key of which Keate always carried in his pocket. One morning coming to his accustomed duties, on reaching the door he tried in vain to insert the key into the lock; the key could not be forced into it: and no wonder, for it was afterwards discovered that a small bullet had been dexterously inserted into the wards of the lock. The little autocrat (for Keate was diminutive in stature), thus compelled to sound a retreat, descended the private stairs, and after making a long detour under the colonnade, entered the upper schoolroom: he strode along full of ire and breathing vengeance; which, however, was never gratified. But the game was not yet played out; for when the Doctor got to the upper end of the school, and ascended the steps which led to the pulpit, he found the door which led into it was screwed up. Keate was considered to be a sort of pocket Hercules, but nevertheless all his efforts to force open the door proved ineffectual. Foiled here, he rushed to the other side; but the same result awaited him. The well-known Eton cry, "Boo, boo," was now reiterated from one end of the schoolroom to the other, which naturally added fuel to the flame of the Doctor's wrath. Plucky to the last, with one bound he vaulted over the doorway into his sanctum, his face glowing with rage like a fiery meteor. Off flew his three-corner cocked-hat, and down he sat; but his seat being smeared all over with cobbler's wax, the little man found that he could not rise without an awkward rent in his silk breeches. I leave it to the reader's imagination to picture the result of this species of practical joking: it certainly did not improve the Doctor's temper, for he grew more unpopular with the school, and he avenged himself upon the persons of delinquent boys.

Flogging at Eton, under Dr. Keate.—Eton under Dr. Keate was conducted on a system of brutal severity, which never ought to have been permitted. I recollect that a row—or, as it was foolishly denominated, a rebellion—took place there in 1809, owing to the vexatious and tyrannical conduct of the head master, who had ordered an extra muster roll during the summer months, by which the boys were precluded from amusing themselves as before at cricket, boating, &c. On this occasion, no fewer than ninety grown-up boys were flogged for the crime of declining to comply with the irksome regulation. Though this affair occurred nearly sixty years ago, I really cannot think of it without indignation; for I remember that the fear of the birch was so strong at the time that no boy went up with his lesson without trembling with apprehension of being put in the bill for a flogging.

Keate, however, paid the penalty for his excessive severity, for he never got on in the Church; while the late excellent Archbishop Sumner, who was a tutor under Keate, and never got a boy flogged, owed his position to his kindness towards those who afterwards became public men.

George IV. when Prince of Wales.—When everybody took snuff, the Prince of Wales followed the fashion; or rather led it, for he was known to possess the finest collection of snuff-boxes that were to be had for love or money. His Royal Highness never permitted his friends or acquaintances the liberty to take a pinch out of his box, so that every one had his own particular *tabatière*. How different this was to times gone by, when a great man delighted in nothing so much as to offer any one he was acquainted with a pinch of snuff: for instance, the greatest dandy of the time to which I am referring, thought it an honour to take a *prise* from the poet Dryden's box; but there was unfortunately a wide difference between the Prince and the poet.

Mrs. Fitzherbert, who was considered by many to be the wife of the Prince Regent, lived in a magnificent house in Tilney Street, Hyde Park, in great state, her carriages and servants being the same as those H.R.H. made use of. Brummell, who was then on good terms with the Prince, called on this lady one day accompanied by his friend Pierrepoint, and found the Prince seated on a sofa. The Prince, according to the Beau's statement, appeared sullen and evidently annoyed at the visit of the two gentlemen, and on Brummell's taking a pinch of snuff and carelessly placing his box on a small table nearly opposite H.R.H., the Prince observed, "Mr. Brummell, the place for your box is in your pocket, and not on the table." Another specimen of H.R.H.'s rudeness may be cited. Lord Barrymore called at Carlton House one day, and was ushered into the Prince's private room; on entering he placed his hat on a chair, when H.R.H. observed, in a sarcastic manner, "My Lord, a well-bred man places his hat under his arm on entering a room, and on his head when out of doors."

BEAU BRUMMELL'S AUNT, MRS. SEARLE.—At the small entrance of the Green Park, opposite Clarges Street, and close to the reservoir, there stood some years back a neat cottage, surrounded by a court-yard, with stables for cows. The exterior of the cottage betokened no small degree of comfort and modest affluence; nor did the interior disappoint those who formed that opinion. Its inmates were two old ladies, dressed in the style of Louis XV., with high lace caps and dresses of brocaded silk.

In the autumn of 1814 I happened to stroll into the Park to see these cows, which were famed for their colour and symmetry. It was the hour for milking them, and one of the old ladies, observing my curiosity to see that operation performed, came up to the palings and begged me to walk in. I readily complied, and remained some time, then, thanking her for the honour she had done me, I took my leave, having accepted her invitation to pay her a visit the next evening; which I did. After saluting Mrs. Searle and inquiring after her health, I led her on to talk on divers matters. She had an excellent memory, was replete with *esprit*, and appeared to possess a knowledge of everything and everybody. I soon discovered that the old lady was proud of her blood, and she told me that she was aunt to George Brummell, the Beau; that George III. had placed her as gate-keeper of the Green Park, and that the Princess Mary had kindly furnished her little cottage. Her description of the royal family was somewhat interesting. She said, that one day the Prince of Wales, accompanied by the beautiful Marchioness of Salisbury, called upon her, and as it was a beautiful summer's evening, stopped to see her cows milked. Her nephew George Brummell, who had only a day or two before left Eton, happened to be present.

The Prince, attracted by his nice manners, entered into conversation with him, and before he left said, "As I find you intend to be a soldier, I will give you a commission in my own regiment." Tears of gratitude filled the youth's eyes, and he fell on his knees and kissed the royal hand. Shortly after, George Brummell's commission in the 10th Hussars was made out, and he was soon quartered with his regiment at Brighton. Mrs. Searle added, "But what is most singular, a striking change took place in my nephew's behaviour; for so soon as he began to mix in society with the Prince, his visits to me became less and less frequent, and now he hardly ever calls to see his old aunt."

One Way Out of a Dilemma.—I recollect when a boy seeing a strange couple, a Mr. and Mrs. Turbeville, who were famed for their eccentricities. Mr. Turbeville was related to Sir Thomas Picton, but did not possess the talent or discretion of the gallant General. Upon one occasion, at a dinner at Dunraven Castle, after the ladies had retired, Mr. Turbeville observed to a gentleman present, that the woman who had sat at his right was the ugliest he had ever seen; upon which the gentleman said, "I am sorry to hear that you think my wife so ill-looking." "Oh, no, sir, I have made a mistake; I meant the lady who sat on my left." "Well, sir, she is my sister." "It can't be helped, sir, then; for if what you have said is true, I must confess I never saw such an ugly family during the course of my life."

Anecdote of a Lord-Lieutenant of Ireland.—In times gone by, when Lords-Lieutenants thought more of love and beauty than the land they were sent to govern, and considered they had a right to monopolise every pretty girl who appeared at the Castle balls, two sisters, the beautiful Misses Gunn, were the objects of the Viceroy's assiduous attention. Of course, they were much envied both by mothers and daughters for the attention shown them by the Viceroy and his family. All went on swimmingly until one day a young lady, only about sixteen years of age, and of surpassing beauty, a Miss Woodcock, made her appearance at one of the drawing-rooms. She came as if from the waves of the Channel, for nobody knew her name or family, and she was known by the cognomen of the beautiful Venus. The Lord-Lieutenant at once discarded the Misses Gunn, and lavished jewellery and presents upon the youthful Venus in so barefaced a manner, that society began to be alarmed, and gave the new beauty the cold shoulder. Bunbury, the celebrated caricaturist, happening to be at Dublin, turned the scandal to good account, by drawing a capital likeness of the Viceroy, dressed as Robinson Crusoe, carrying a *Gun* upon each shoulder, and a *Woodcock* at his left side; denoting that his affections lay in that quarter.

Mr. Lawrence, the Celebrated Surgeon.—It was my good fortune to have known Mr. Lawrence, who was allowed to have been the most scientific, as well as one of the most skilful surgeons England or Europe could boast of at that time. The opinion entertained of him by the faculty was evinced by the many high encomiums passed upon his talents by his contemporaries. He was the most accomplished and gentlest of mankind, and ever ready to render the slightest service to a friend in distress. Upon one occasion I called upon him at his house in Whitehall, opposite the Admiralty, and told him that half-an-hour before I had seen a pretty girl, an opera-dancer, unable to move from her sofa owing to "soft corns," which precluded her from appearing on the stage. "Bring her here, my friend Gronow, and I will endeavour to cure her; but do not mention to any one that I have turned chiropodist." I lost no time in calling upon the *danseuse*, and prevailed upon her to place herself under the care of my skilful friend. Some few days elapsed, when I met Lawrence in his carriage and was invited by him to take a drive, during which he asked me if I had seen the young lady, whom he had operated upon and completely cured. Upon my replying in the negative, he said, "It is always so when you render a service to persons possessing neither principle nor feeling; you are sure to be treated with ingratitude." This lady became immensely rich, and I regret to add that the surgeon's fee was never paid, which I had good reason to know amounted to twenty guineas.

ESCAPADE OF AN OFFICER OF THE 3D FOOT GUARDS.—It is nearly fifty years since a young officer in the 3d Guards, smitten with the charms of Lady Betty Charteris, who was remarkable for her beauty and attainments, determined at all hazards to carry her off and marry her. Her father put a stop to any legitimate, straightforward wooing, by forbidding her to encourage the attentions of the young officer, who was too poor to maintain her in the position in which she had been brought up. When the London season was over, the family left for Scotland, and my friend, Andrew C * * *, decided on following his lady-love. Andrew was young, handsome, romantic, and sentimental; but a brave fellow, and had fought gallantly at Waterloo. After consulting several of his intimate friends, who recommended perseverance, he determined to further his scheme by disguising himself. So, with the aid of a black wig and a suit of seedy clothes, he engaged the services of an Italian organ-grinder, and took his place beside him on one of the Edinburgh coaches.

In the course of a few days the pair arrived at a village close to the mansion of the lady's father, and a correspondence was carried on between the lovers. They met, and after a great many urgent entreaties on the part of the enamoured swain, a day was arranged for the elopement. Andrew next gained over the head gardener, by stating that he had just arrived from Holland, and was up to the latest dodges in tulip-growing; then a mania in England. By this means he contrived to be constantly on the premises, and to obtain frequent interviews with the charming Lady Betty. The day fixed at length arrived, and the organ-grinder (then a rarity in Scotland) was introduced on the scene; his sprightly airs fascinated the servants, who thronged to listen to him, and meanwhile a post-chaise and four was driven up, out of sight of the house, according to a previous understanding between the lovers, who were ready for instant flight. Unluckily, there was an excessively vigilant governess in attendance on Lady Betty, and at the moment when affairs seemed most prosperous, this duenna was at her post at the young lady's side in the garden. Andrew, feeling that everything depended on some decisive action, suddenly appeared, and ejaculating, "Now or never!" caught hold of his dulcinea's arm, and attempted to hurry in the direction of the chaise. The dragon interposed, and clung to the young lady, screaming for assistance; her cries brought out the servants, the enraged father, and the inmates of the house to her assistance, and poor Andrew and the organ-man with his monkey were ejected from the premises. The young Guardsman, however, soon got over the sorrow caused by the failure of his scheme; but the nickname of "Merry Andrew," bestowed on him by his brother officers, stuck to him afterwards.

THE GOOD FORTUNE OF A PRETTY WOMAN.—More than half a century ago a lady, conspicuous in the aristocratic world, on returning from a courtly *fête* and arriving at her mansion about four o'clock in the morning, was informed by her servants that a female child had been left at the door, wrapped up in a blanket. She desired that the infant might be taken care of; and, in the course of time, the child became a servant in the establishment. The girl grew to be a remarkable specimen of female beauty; her form was exquisitely modelled; her complexion was delicate and blooming; her features were regular, and she was remarkable, for her large, blue, thoughtful eyes. But her greatest charm consisted in a most engaging and lovable smile. It was difficult to gaze upon that face without feeling an interest in Clotilde far beyond that which generally accompanies the contemplation of ordinary beauty. Although educated in the servants' hall, yet, by that singular instinct which some women possess, she had learned to make her conversation and manner acceptable and engaging to educated persons, whether male or female. The titled lady whom she knew as her protector made her her confidential maid, and Clotilde soon became the companion of her mistress.

She was not more than eighteen years of age when an Admiral of the British navy, who visited the house, fell desperately in love with her. It was during the period of the great wars of Napoleon the First, and the Admiral, being employed in cruising about the Mediterranean, was absent from London for long periods; but he never failed to correspond with Clotilde, and his letters were regularly placed before her mistress. The girl used to turn into ridicule the passionate language of the old sailor; but time passed on, and the Admiral returned, having distinguished himself, and become known as the intimate friend of the immortal Nelson; and, within six months afterwards, Clotilde became the wife of one of the most distinguished officers of the British navy.

As frequently occurs when a young and beautiful woman of humble extraction is allied to a man in advanced years, and finds herself surrounded by men occupying the highest position in society, Clotilde became susceptible to attentions which were paid with a view to undermine her virtue. Amongst her admirers was a royal Duke, who afterwards ascended the throne of Great Britain; and there is every reason to believe that many public acts of the navy and army originated in her influence. In short, the marriage was anything but a happy one, although the lady had daughters who were married to rich and noble foreigners. In the course of time the Admiral ignored her amours; and it was well known in London society that my lady had her friends, and the Admiral his.

As Clotilde advanced in life, she fascinated and formed an intimacy with one of the most wealthy of British peers. By pandering to the eccentricities of the noble Lord, her authority over him became absolute. It was through this nobleman that she bestowed magnificent dowries on her daughters, and became possessed of a colossal fortune. Although her conduct was notoriously immoral, she was countenanced and visited by persons who, as is too frequently the case, permit their morality to become exceedingly elastic in the presence of wealth. Later in life, she thought it advisable to remove to Naples, where accident threw her in the way of a French lady's-maid, who in course of time obtained an alarming influence over his Lordship. Ever adroit, and possessing intuitive perception and forethought, the lady made friends with the Frenchwoman; and when his Lordship's will was opened, it revealed an engagement which the rival ladies had previously concocted: Lady S * * * became the legatee to an immense fortune, whilst her maid was moderately provided for.

Her great aim, after the death of the nobleman in question, was to become a respectable member of society. She invited people to magnificent dinners, became very devout, gave away a great deal of money in charity, and indeed did everything that such women do under similar circumstances. Her career is another illustration of what a pretty and clever woman, without heart or conscience, can accomplish, if smiled upon by fortune.

COLONEL, OR "BULL," TOWNSHEND.—When the Grenadier Guards returned to London from Cambrai, where they had been quartered some considerable time, the first thing that was proposed by the officers, was to invite their colonel, the Duke of York, to a banquet at the Thatched House, St. James's Street. His Royal Highness, in a letter full of feeling and good taste, in which he alluded to the gallantry of the regiment he commanded, accepted the invitation, and, as was the custom upon such occasions, the army agents of the regiment were also invited. After dinner, Colonel Townshend, commonly called the Bull, addressed the Duke, stating that, as he was then in command of the old battalion, he hoped H.R.H. would permit him to propose a toast. The Duke bowed assent, when the Bull bellowed out, "I propose the health of Mr. Greenwood, to whom we are all of us so much indebted." This toast was ill chosen, for the Duke of York owed his army agents at that moment nearly fifty thousand pounds; but Townshend considered it a good joke, for he used frequently to boast of having astonished the Duke with his witty toast. Townshend was the brother of Lord Sidney. He was considered by the officers and men of the regiment to be intrepid and brave. He was unfortunately a slave to good cookery, which was the principal cause of his death. Townshend, despite his imperfections, was generous and full of compassion to the soldiers he commanded; he stooped to no flattery, disdained all disloyal arts, and, in a word, was replete with sterling and splendid qualities.

Many of my old comrades can remember the excellent dinners Townshend used to give his friends at Cambrai. I can call to mind that at one of those banquets, a young officer wilfully placed some ipecacuanha in one of Townshend's favourite *entrées*, of which he ate rather voraciously. The consequence was, the Colonel was obliged to quit the dinner-table sooner than the rest of the *convives*. In the hurry of the moment he sat down upon a brittle vase, which broke, and caused a wound so severe that he was confined to his room for many weeks, and the doctor of the regiment was apprehensive of mortification, for it baffled for a considerable time his skill in effecting a cure; but, fortunately, the gallant colonel recovered.

This unlucky accident became the subject of general conversation all over London, and the Duke of York happened at one of his dinners to allude to the awkward wound inflicted upon "the Bull," when Alvanley, who was dining at the royal table, observed in his off-hand manner, it was a "*filet de bœuf sauté.*"

THE MARQUIS D'ALIGRE AND THE DENTIST.—In a previous page I alluded to the Marquis d Aligre, who, though enormously rich, was known as the miser. When in England, during the war with France, he lived in great penury; and his costume and appearance, half military and half Moravian, aided his assumption of the character of an impoverished *émigré*. Having lost nearly all his teeth, he determined to have a set of false ones, and accordingly called on Mr. Spence, a celebrated dentist, who lived in Arlington Street, Piccadilly, to whom he represented himself as an *émigré* in urgent need of a set of teeth, but without means to pay for them. Mr. Spence, commiserating the poor Frenchman, said he would make him a present of them: a day was fixed for their completion, and d'Aligre joyfully promised to keep the appointment.

It happened that a countryman of d'Aligre's overheard the interview, and seeing Mr. Spence in a thinking attitude, after the cunning old miser had left, said, "I suppose you are wondering why that old gentleman should be so ill-dressed, instead of being clothed like the generality of his countrymen." Mr. Spence, not understanding the drift of the remark, begged he would be more explicit; upon which the gentleman repeated his remark, adding, "His penurious habits make us blush for our country." "What do you mean, sir?" reiterated the dentist. "I have promised to supply him with a new set of teeth *gratis*, for he represents himself as a poor nobleman without means; and unless you can prove that all he has said is false, I shall keep my word; on the other hand, if I find that I have been imposed upon, I will make him repent it." The Frenchman said no more, but bowed and left. It happened, however, that among the many foreigners who participated in Mr. Spence's hospitality, was the Duc de Bourbon, who, although very proud, was glad enough to dine with the dentist when invited; and at table one day, about this time, d'Aligre's name was mentioned. Mr. Spence, anxious to learn more about the man, asked his Royal Highness if he could enlighten him on that point. The Duke said, "d'Aligre's wealth is unbounded; he possesses more than all the *émigrés* from France."

Mr. Spence's wrath and indignation on discovering the imposition were great; and he determined to revenge himself. On the day appointed for the teeth to be ready, the Marquis made his appearance, and wished the dentist good morning in a most obsequious manner. Mr. Spence took out of his pocket a piece of paper upon which was written, "The Marquis d'Aligre to Mr. Spence for a set of false teeth, £200," at the same time holding in his other hand the coveted articles. D'Aligre again attempted to enact the "poor man;" but the dentist gave him till the following day to pay for them. The money not being forthcoming, Mr. Spence, in the presence of several persons, broke in pieces the false teeth he had made, saying, "Rather than be cheated and robbed in such a manner, I would discontinue my profession. But this affair will only hurt the Marquis; for he will have to live upon slops until he finds some dentist whom he can defraud."

The French Émigrés.—We must all acknowledge that the self-denial and patience exhibited by the refugees from France at the time of the Revolution was worthy of the highest praise; nearly all the nobles and proprietors of that country quitted it during that fatal period, and the greater part came to England. Among them I recollect the Counts Forbin d'Offède, Choiseul, la Rochejacquelin, de Marin, and d'Aubenton, who gave lessons in

French or music; while the nobles De la Rochefoucauld, De Sainte-Aldégonde, and others, became linen merchants; others, with equally great names, kept furnished lodgings, or *cafés*; while youths extremely well born and educated were obliged to seek situations as clerks in mercantile houses. One of the most remarkable men alive was obliged to emigrate to London—I mean Auber, the great composer. He became clerk in a bank, where he remained some years: it was the same establishment where the rich Greffulhe laid the foundation of a fortune which, it is said, exceeds at the present moment six millions sterling.

I have already mentioned the Marquis d'Aligre's conduct with regard to tradespeople; and towards his own countrymen he was equally mean in refusing them any assistance, although then in the enjoyment of a princely income. After the affair with the dentist, London becoming too warm for him, he took his departure for Germany with his wife, whose death occurred there. It is the custom in that country, on such occasions, for an official to call at every house proclaiming in a loud voice the age and titles of the deceased, and the day fixed for the funeral; the Marquis, desirous of avoiding expense, and being in a measure compelled to respect the rule, employed his servant to announce these particulars. Accordingly, the flunkey, dressed in a sorry threadbare suit of black, carried out his master's orders by knocking at every door, and exclaiming in a loud voice, "*Hier à six heures du soir, Madame la Marquise d'Aligre caput.*" As "caput" in the German language means destroyed and broken to pieces, this announcement rather astonished the natives.

LORD WESTMORELAND. COLONEL ARTHUR UPTON. TOWNSHEND. (THE BOW STREET RUNNER) TOM RAIKES.

PUBLIC CHARACTERS.

The avarice of the Marquis so disgusted the inhabitants of Carlsbad that they determined by hook or by crook to get rid of him. Every sort of practical joke was played on him, and he at last quitted the town just as a concert of rough music, or, in other words, a *charivari*, which had been preparing for some time, was about to be given in his *honour*.

THE EMPEROR ALEXANDER.—The Emperor Alexander was considered one of the politest men of his age. When attending the Congress at Aix la Chapelle, he would, out of compliment, put on the Prussian uniform when he visited the King of Prussia, the Austrian when he visited the Emperor of Austria, and the English uniform, in honour of our country, which was represented by the Duke of Wellington.

It is known that, prior to the disastrous Russian campaign, his Majesty was an enthusiastic admirer of Napoleon, and it is said that when, according to custom, orders were exchanged between the sovereigns of Russia and France, the Emperor Alexander was so proud of the grand cross of the Legion of Honour, that, not content with wearing it in his button-hole, he had another cross made which, on grand occasions, was hung round the neck of his favourite horse. When Napoleon heard of this eccentricity he said, "My brother the Emperor can do what he likes at St. Petersburg; but if he adopted that plan in Paris, my Minister of Police would feel it his duty to consign him to Bicêtre (the madhouse), to prevent his being mobbed and laughed at by the public."

AN INCIDENT AT THE BATTLE OF BORODINO.—At the bloody battle of Borodino, the news of the great redoubt having been taken was carried to the Emperor Napoleon by a staff officer. The Emperor inquired whether the bearer of the message had been sent by General Caulaincourt, and the officer had begun his reply thus, "No, your Majesty; I saw the General receive his death-wound on entering the battery"—when he himself received a terrible wound, and fell from his horse insensible through loss of blood. The Emperor took off the cross of honour which he wore, and directed his aide-de-camp to place it on the poor fellow's breast. The wound was so severe that all the surgeons could do to resuscitate him proved for some time of no avail; but happily, on one of the grenadiers slapping his hands, he opened his eyes and beheld the cross of the Legion of Honour with which he had been decorated by order of his sovereign, and was told that if he survived he would be promoted. Fortunately, youth and health carried him through, and the promise made to him was kept.

Colonel Jacqueminot.—In 1814, soon after the return of the Bourbons, Colonel Jacqueminot and three other officers of the Bonaparte school dressed themselves like *émigrés,* went to the Café Hardy, asked for the carte, and looking it over observed an *entrée* called "*Poulet à la Marengo,*" upon which Jacqueminot observed, "No, that won't do; it smells too much of the Revolution." A gentleman, sitting at the next table, who had served under the Emperor at the battle of Marengo, jumped up and exclaimed, "What the devil do those *émigrés* know of our battles? They ran away from France when there was danger, but come back when it is over." Jacqueminot pretended to be very irate; but going up to the gentleman in question said, in a low voice, "You are one of the right sort. I admire both your courage and frankness; and if all men of our party would follow your example, there would not be a Bourbon left in Paris twenty-four hours longer."

Unfortunately for the young men who had acted the part of *émigrés*, it happened that one of the waiters was a policeman in disguise. He denounced them to the Government, who ordered the whole of them to appear before a court-martial; they were tried, and condemned to lose their rank and pay in the army. Jacqueminot was so enraged with the police spy, that he caught hold of the man in the presence of the court, and would have murdered him, had not the President, who had formerly known Jacqueminot in Russia, cried aloud, "You are too brave to hurt that villain. All hail, Jacqueminot, as a hero!" Suddenly Jacqueminot recollected that the President had been saved by him at the battle of Borodino.

THE EMPEROR'S FUR CLOAK.—When Napoleon I. assumed the title of Emperor, he received from the Emperor of Russia a magnificent fur cloak, which, it was reported, cost a fabulous sum. The Princess Pauline, being desirous of possessing this costly mantle, by exercising her bewitching fascinations, prevailed upon her imperial brother to give it her. It was generally believed that she had given her affections to a young officer, who was considered very handsome; but he, not content with being thus favoured, was very jealous of her, and objected to her wearing the mantle, as she thereby attracted great attention: the Princess, therefore, made him a present of it.

This gentleman, a M. de Canouville, vain of his good looks, which the superb cloak set off to advantage, determined on wearing it at a grand review of the Guards, prior to their departure for Russia. He was riding a very young horse, which had not been sufficiently broken, and when the Emperor arrived on the ground with his escort, the sudden burst of music and the firing of cannon so frightened the animal that he bolted at railroad speed across the review ground. Unluckily for the coxcomb, this *contretemps* did not escape the keen eye of the Emperor, who recognised the imperial gift; and, on his return to the Tuileries, he gave orders to send the culprit to join the army, saying that the fur cloak would keep him warm amid the snows and ice of Russia, from whence it came.

A Marriage Quickly Arranged. — When the expedition was about to sail from France for St. Domingo, the First Consul named his brother-in-law, General Leclerc, commander-in-chief of the invading army. The General went, as is usual in such cases, to make his bow to his superior, prior to his departure. Bonaparte addressed him in rather a laconic tone, saying, "You must quit Paris to-morrow evening." "But, sire, it is impossible," replied General Leclerc. "Nothing is impossible: my orders must be obeyed. I have no objection to your taking my sister Pauline, your wife, with you; but go you must." "But, sire, *my* sister will be left behind in France, without money or friends." "Oh! is that all?" replied the First Consul. "I will send her a husband to-morrow, with rank and money. Begone, sir, and come back in the course of to-morrow, and all will be arranged to your satisfaction." General Leclerc left, muttering, "*Nous ne devons plus qu'obéir. Nous avons trouvé un maître là où nous ne voulions qu'un protecteur.*"

Meanwhile General Davoust entered the First Consul's cabinet, when Bonaparte said to him, "I am glad you are come, for I have found you a wife, young and accomplished." "But, sire, I am engaged to a young lady, and have promised to marry her as soon as I have procured your consent." "Not a word more, Davoust, about your promise; but come here to-morrow morning, and you shall know more about your future wife." It was no use to kick against the pricks, so Davoust arrived at the palace the next morning, where he met Leclerc; neither being aware of the relation in which they were about to stand to each other. They sent in their names; and Bonaparte calling them in, told Leclerc to accompany Davoust to St. Germain, where he was to introduce the latter to his sister. Madame de Campan, in her position of directress of the convent, was to accompany them back to Paris with the young lady in question, and all were to present themselves at the Tuileries at a given hour. There the marriage-contract was signed. Napoleon settled a large dowry on the bride, and agreed to provide her with everything necessary for her *corbeille de mariage*. Thus, in twenty-four hours, one General found a brother-in-law in a rival, the other a brother-in-law in an engaged lover, and the young lady a husband in the man who was justly called "the bloody Davoust."

NAPOLEON THE FIRST'S LOVE OF MUSIC.—The Emperor Napoleon I. was passionately fond of Italian music, and wherever the court stayed, several of the best *artistes* of the day might be found, who were treated with the greatest consideration. Paesiello was the Emperor's favourite amongst them; indeed, he took an unbounded interest in his success, and was so enchanted one day by a song Paesiello had just written, that he caught him by the hand, saying, "Without doubt you are the greatest composer that ever lived." "No, sire, I am not," replied he; "while Cimarosa lives, to him must be given the palm."

Paesiello wrote the opera of *Proserpine*, which was brought out at Paris under the auspices of the Emperor; but somehow or other it did not suit the French taste, and proved a failure. Napoleon was furious at the non-success of his *protégé's* opera, and observed, "It is not to be wondered at, for the French understand nothing of music." Paesiello thought so too; for though so highly patronised by the Emperor and court, he quitted France in disgust. It was with difficulty that a man of musical genius could be found to replace the Italian as the Emperor's *maître de chapelle*; Méhul was at last thought of, and summoned to the Tuileries. When he was informed of Napoleon's wishes, the composer solicited an interview with the great man, and after the usual salutation, informed the Emperor that he could not accept the proffered honour unless allowed to divide the perquisites with his friend Cherubini. This was refused; Napoleon saying, "I can never permit that, for I hate the man." "It is a pity, sire, that you do not like him, for he is my superior in every way." "I care not for that. I still persist in refusing to have that man near me, and nothing can change my determination." "Then," replied Méhul, "I am compelled to decline the flattering offer your Majesty has made me."

The reason why the Emperor was so inimical to Cherubini was that, when Napoleon returned from the Italian campaign with only the rank of General, he on one occasion offered a remark not very flattering to the composer; and Cherubini retorted, "*Mêlez vous, Général, de gagner des batailles; c'est votre métier. Laissez-moi faire le mien, auquel vous n'entendez rien.*" For this Cherubini was never pardoned. Méhul, though he had refused the Emperor's offer, still remained in favour at Court, and his pieces were criticised by the Emperor; who often told Méhul that his compositions were too German, and not to be compared with those of the Italian school. "The Germans, in composing, think too much of science, but are unmindful of that which touches the heart. This fault is also shared by the French composers: all their operas want grace and gaiety." On the appearance of the opera *L'Irato*, which is written in the Italian style, Napoleon, ignorant as to who the composer was, begged Méhul to be present. After some demur he consented. The overture was much applauded, and the Emperor observed to Méhul, "Now, you see, there is nothing like Italian music." The opera then proceeded, and was throughout much admired by the audience; and when at the end the authors of the piece were called before the curtain, Méhul, the composer, and Marsollier, the writer of the piece, appeared, and were received with boisterous applause. The Emperor, delighted, sent for Méhul, and cried out, in a tone loud enough to be heard by many present, "*Attrapez-moi toujours de même, mon cher Méhul, et je m'en rejouirai pour votre gloire et mes plaisirs.*"

PARTING OF NAPOLEON AND MADAME MÈRE.—Talma was present at the last parting at the Malmaison between the Emperor and his mother, and he said that it was one of the most tragic scenes he had ever witnessed. When the last moment arrived, the Empress-mother, prostrated with grief, and with tears streaming from her eyes, could only utter, in a tremulous voice, "*Adieu, mon fils! adieu!*" And Napoleon was so affected, that he caught hold of both her hands, cried, "*Adieu, ma mère!*" and burst into tears as he left her. The mother was destined never again to meet the son—

"Whose filial piety excels
Whatever Grecian story tells."

PRINCE EUGÈNE BEAUHARNAIS.—Soon after the fall of Napoleon, the Emperor of Russia, together with the other allied sovereigns, desirous of showing their respect and admiration for the conduct of Prince Eugène, offered him the Duchy of Genoa. The following was the reply sent by the Viceroy to the letter he had received making the offer:—

"SIRE,—I have received your Majesty's propositions. They certainly are very flattering, but they will in no way change my determination. Neither the duchy nor the kingdom of Italy will induce me to become a traitor; and rather than follow the example of Murat, I would prefer entering the ranks again as a private soldier.

"You state that the Emperor Napoleon was not kind to me. I have forgotten all this. I know, however, that I owe everything to him—my fortune, my rank and titles. If he should require my services again, I would serve him with all my ability; for my body belongs to him, as does my heart.

"I flatter myself that in refusing to agree to the offer you have done me the honour to make, your Majesty will appreciate my conduct, and assure me the continuance of your esteem.

"EUGÈNE BEAUHARNAIS."

THE PRESENT EMPEROR OF THE FRENCH WHEN A BOY.—Prince Louis Napoléon, when at the age of six, lived with his mother, Queen Hortense, at the Malmaison, with whom resided the Empress Joséphine; who, it will be remembered, received the allied sovereigns there in 1814, after Napoleon I. was exiled to Elba. The Emperor of Russia when in Paris scarcely passed a day without visiting those exalted ladies, and on each occasion he breakfasted or dined with them. The Queen told her children, that when the Emperor Alexander called, every mark of attention and respect was to be paid to his Imperial Majesty; for to him, and him alone, they owed everything they possessed in the world. Prince Louis listened to his mother's precepts with great attention, but said nothing. The next time the Czar came, however, the little fellow sidled up to him and quietly placed on one of the Czar's fingers a ring, which his uncle Prince Eugène, the Viceroy of Italy, had given him. The boy, on being asked by his mother what he meant, said, "I have only this ring, which my uncle gave me; but I have given it to the Emperor Alexander, because he has been so kind to you, dear mamma." The autocrat smiled, and placing the gift on his watch-chain, said he would never part with it, but would keep it in remembrance of the noble trait of generosity shown by one so young. The Queen replied, "Sire, my son Louis keeps nothing for himself: the other day I gave him some pretty buttons, but he gave them away to some of his playmates; and when I reproached him for so doing, his answer was, "*Vous voulez, maman, me procurer un plaisir en me les offrant, et vous m'en procurez deux; celui de recevoir de vous, maman, une jolie chose, et ensuite le plaisir de la donner à un autre.*"

Another anecdote, showing the good nature of Louis Napoléon, was related to me by the late M. Mocquard, with whom I was well acquainted. After leaving the Malmaison, Queen Hortense settled by the Lake of Constance, where the young Prince was constantly in the habit of relieving poor people by giving away his pocket-money. One day he observed a family in the greatest distress, but having no money to give them, he took off his coat and boots and gave them to these poor people, saying that he was sorry that he had not any money for them, as he had given away the allowance his mother made him to some other poor persons who had just passed by the house; but he hoped they would dispose of his clothes to relieve their wants. The weather at this time was very cold, and the ground covered with snow; the Prince, nevertheless, trudged through it towards home, and when near the house was met by Mocquard, who expressed his surprise at seeing him in that state. The little fellow, then ten years old, replied, "I have given away my clothes to some poor people to prevent them from starving." Mocquard added, that "the Emperor is never so happy as when he can relieve the distressed."

JÉRÔME BONAPARTE AND CARDINAL FESCH.—Jérôme, the youngest brother of the great Emperor, was when young extremely wild and extravagant. He was always in debt, and would borrow money of any one who would trust him. Upon one occasion he called upon his uncle, the Cardinal Fesch, who invited him to dinner. The Cardinal was a great amateur of paintings, and his gallery contained some of the finest specimens of the old masters. After dinner, the Cardinal was on the point of quitting the dining-room, when Jérôme followed him, and asked for the loan of 500 francs. The old Cardinal refused to lend him the money, whereupon Jérôme became furious, drew his sword, swore vengeance against his uncle, and began cutting at everything about him. Unfortunately his sword fell upon a *chef-d'œuvre* by Vandyke, which the Cardinal, upon his return to the dining-room, observing, called out in a loud voice, "Stop, young man! sheathe your sword, and here are your 500 francs!"

THE CZAR AND THE APPLE GIRL.—In the neighbourhood of the Tuileries there used to be a small fair, where apples, toys, cakes, &c., were sold. When the Emperor Alexander was in Paris, he one day strolled through it, and remarking a very pretty fascinating girl staring intently at him from one of the stalls, he asked her the reason. "I am looking at you, sir," she replied, "because you are the very counterpart of the Emperor of Russia; but you cannot be that great personage, or you would not lower yourself by talking to a poor apple girl." The autocrat replied, "Whether I am the Emperor or not, rest assured, my dear, that were I to stay much longer in your company I should lose my heart; but, however," continued he, presenting her with a louis d'or, "can you tell me the address of the Emperor of Russia, for I am anxious to find it out?" She gave up her stall to one of her friends, and volunteered to accompany the great man to find himself. On their arrival at the hotel, he begged she would walk in. "No, sir: I have shown you where the Emperor lives, which I think is all that you require; so good morning, sir." "No, no, that is not all, my little angel; you must now tell me where you live." "Well, sir, I am to be found at my stall." The result of this was, that the girl found her way to St. Petersburg, where she lived for some time under the Emperor's protection: she afterwards married a great nobleman, and became the mother of the man who played the most prominent part in the Crimean war.

De Souza, the Portuguese Ambassador.—The fame of De Souza for the piquancy of his wit and his readiness in retort was general at every court in Europe. When in England, he had the *entrée* of Carlton House, and was on terms of intimacy with the Prince Regent. At that time his Royal Highness's life was spent in great dissipation, and those at court followed his example. A hundredth part of what actually occurred at Carlton House would afford rare materials for anecdote; though it is only right to add that much of the scandal propagated respecting this period was pure invention.

De Souza, though perhaps the ugliest little man I ever saw, was nevertheless remarkable for the charm and grace of his conversation; and there was no one then in the diplomatic world, Talleyrand excepted, who attained greater perfection in what is called the *art de vivre* than the Portuguese ambassador. Our hero revelled in the gossip and scandal of society, and he used to amuse the Prince Regent with frequent anecdotes and witty sayings from both Lisbon and the Brazils. His sayings made everybody laugh, and his droll manner was inimitable. He had a mania for relating stories about women, which sometimes made even the Regent blush. At dinner at Carlton House one day he observed that some men were addicted to extraordinary tastes, and commenced a story in illustration, when the Prince exclaimed, "Halt! no more at present, De Souza. You shall tell us the rest when the cloth is removed." After the servants had retired, the Prince said, "Now, De Souza, continue the story which you began during dinner." "Well, your Royal Highness, my story will not occupy much time; it is merely that a friend of mine in Lisbon was exceedingly fond of peacock's tails." "Well, what then?" "Ah! your Royal Highness, he preferred those ornaments to the most beautiful women: indeed, he was so infatuated with them, that he sometimes fancied himself a peacock." "Come, come, De Souza, this is too much:

we cannot swallow such nonsense." "Well, sire, I can only vouch for what I saw, and that was, a nun rubbing down the tails upon my friend's back, and saying, What a beautiful bird you are!"

Lord Hay and the Prince Regent.—At the Prince Regent's first levee, in 1815, Lord Hay, eldest son of the Earl of Errol, was presented with other officers of the Guards to have the honour of kissing hands. When the Prince gave his hand to be kissed, the young nobleman, unversed in court etiquette, caught hold of it and shook it with all his might. The Prince, though a very proud and formal personage, seeing the youth of the young soldier, took the salute in good part, and inquired how the Earl of Errol was. Lord James Murray, observing that something had occurred which was creating a laugh at the expense of his young countryman, good-naturedly took him by the arm and removed him from the royal presence. "What have you been doing, Lord Hay," inquired Lord James Murray, "to be the cause of so much mirth?" "I don't know, unless it was that I shook the Prince's hand with all my might." "Only that, my Lord!" replied Lord James; "why, you have committed a flagrant breach of etiquette." "How so?" inquired Lord Hay. "Why, you ought only to have placed the royal hand to your mouth, instead of shaking it." "Oh, my Lord, I will make amends. I will return and apologise to his Royal Highness." "No, no, Lord Hay; that will make matters worse." The same evening Lord James Murray dined with the Prince, and mentioned to his Royal Highness what Lord Hay proposed doing, by way of making amends for his *gaucherie*. The Prince was extremely amused, and observed, he never had seen so handsome a young soldier in the uniform of the Guards.

Lord Hay, a few days subsequently, left England for Brussels, to join his regiment, the 1st Foot Guards; and at the battle of Quatre Bras, whilst gallantly leading his company in a charge against the French sharpshooters, this young nobleman received a musket ball in the heart, which, of course, caused instant death.

In those days the 1st Foot Guards were officered by some of the handsomest young men that England could boast of. I recollect with pride the names of several of them, viz.:—The two Foxes, William and Sackville; the two Bridgemans; Johnny Lyster, Augustus Dashwood, Cradock, Daniel Tighe, Douglas, Erskine of Mar, Alix, Thoroton, Lord Hay, Barrington, Langrishe, and many others whose names, alas! I now forget. But as nothing is perfect in this world, I must in justice state, that notwithstanding the noble list I have particularised, there were in the regiment one or two of the ugliest men, perhaps, that the world ever beheld.

THE PRINCE REGENT AND CARLTON HOUSE.—One of the meanest and most ugly edifices that ever disfigured London, notwithstanding it was screened by a row of columns, was Carlton House, the residence of the Prince Regent. It was condemned by everybody who possessed taste; and Canova the sculptor, on being asked his opinion of it, said, "There are at Rome a thousand buildings more beautiful, and whose architecture is in comparison faultless, any one of which would be more suitable for a princely residence than that ugly barn." This building was constantly under repair, but never improved, for no material alterations were made in its appearance. The first step towards improvement should have been to give it a coat of "lime-wash," for it was blackened with dust and soot. *A propos* of the alterations: the workmen engaged therein were a great source of annoyance to the Prince, who, pretending that he did not like to be stared at, objected to their entering by the gateway. It is certain that the Prince Regent kept himself as much aloof as possible from the lower class of his subjects, and was annoyed by the natural curiosity of those who hold that as "a cat may look at a king," permission for that luxury should not be denied to bipeds.

I recollect that, having called, when on guard, upon Sir Benjamin Bloomfield about the sale of a cob, which he gave me to understand he wanted for the Prince Regent, while conversing we were interrupted by the entrance of the Prince, attended by M'Mahon and the eccentric "Tommy Tit." His Royal Highness was in an angry humour, and blurted out in his rage, "I will not allow those maid-servants to look at me when I go in and out; and if I find they do so again, I will have them discharged." I could hardly believe my ears, that a man born to the highest rank could take umbrage at such pardonable curiosity. But while riding in Hyde Park the next day, I was joined by General Baylie, who it seemed had been a spectator of this outburst of wrath: he told me that the Prince constantly complained of the servants staring at him, and that strict orders had been given to discharge any one caught repeating the offence.

Lord Barrymore.—This nobleman came of a very old family, and when of age succeeded to a fine estate. He acquired no small degree of notoriety from his love of pugilism and cock-fighting; but his *forte* lay in driving, and few coachmen on the northern road could "tool" a four-in-hand like him. His Lordship was one of the founders of the "Whip Club." The first time I ever saw Lord Barrymore was one fine evening while taking a stroll in Hyde Park. The weather was charming, and a great number of the *bon ton* had assembled to witness the departure of the "Four-in-hand Club." Conspicuous among all the "turns-out" was that of his Lordship, who drove four splendid greys, unmatched in symmetry, action, and power. Lord Barrymore was, like Byron and Sir Walter Scott, club-footed. I discovered this defect the moment he got off his box to arrange something wrong in the harness. If there had been a competitive examination, the prize of which would be given to the most proficient in slang and vulgar phraseology, it would have been safe to back his Lordship as the winner against the most foul-mouthed of costermongers; for the way he blackguarded his servants for the misadjustment of a strap was horrifying. On returning home, I dressed and went to the Club to dine, where I alluded to the choice morsels of English vernacular that had fallen from the noble whip's mouth in addressing his servants, and was assured that such was his usual language when out of temper.

In addition to his "drag" in the "Four-in-hand Club," Lord Barrymore sported a very pretty "Stanhope," in which he used to drive about town, accompanied by a little boy, whom the world denominated his tiger. It was reported that Lord Barrymore had, in his younger days, been taken much notice of by the Prince Regent; in fact, he had been the boon companion of his Royal Highness, and had assisted at the orgies that used to take place at Carlton House, where he was a constant visitor. Notwithstanding this, Lord Barrymore was considered by those intimately acquainted with him to be a man of literary talents. He certainly was an accomplished musician, a patron of the drama, and a great friend of Cooke, Kean, and the two Kembles; yet I have heard a host of crimes attributed to his Lordship. This, if not a libel, showed that the connection existing between the Prince Regent and this nobleman could not have been productive of good results, and tends to confirm the impression that the profligate life led by his Royal Highness and those admitted to his intimacy was such, as to make it a matter of wonder that such scandalous scenes of debauchery could be permitted in a country like ours. Indeed, his acquaintance with the Prince ruined Lord Barrymore both in mind, body, and estate. While participating in the Regent's excesses, he had bound himself to do his bidding, however palpably iniquitous it might be; and when he was discarded, in accordance with that Prince's habit of treating his favourites, he left Carlton House ruined in health and reputation.

Lord Barrymore during his last years was a martyr to the gout and other diseases; and on his deathbed he was haunted by the recollection of what he had been, and the thought of what he might have become: indeed, the last scene of his profligate life, when tortured by the inward reproaches of his accusing conscience, was harrowing in the extreme.

LORD BYRON AND DAN MACKINNON.—During Lord Byron's sojourn at Lisbon, he was much amused with Dan Mackinnon's various funny stories. Upon one occasion Dan's time was entirely taken up by presenting women with tooth-brushes, a supply of which he had received by the packet from London. Opposite his quarters there lived two very pretty Portuguese ladies, who, unmindful of Dan's proximity, and of the fact that his windows commanded a view of their chamber, dressed, undressed, and went through their morning ablutions and toilet. Dan's astonishment was great when he perceived that the fair ones never brushed their teeth; and he lost no time in sending his servant with two tooth-brushes in paper, well perfumed and sealed up. The ladies opened the packet, and appeared delighted with the present; but judge of Mackinnon's horror in beholding those dainty creatures perseveringly brushing their raven locks with the tiny brushes!

Lord Byron was a great admirer of well-formed hands: he preferred a pretty hand to a pretty face. He was asked whether he admired pretty feet: his answer was, "that he never went so low;" "and as for teeth," said he, "a blackamoor has as white a set of teeth as the fairest lady in the land." His Lordship added, "A Frenchman thinks very little of the teeth, face, or colour of the hair; provided a woman put on her cashmere veil in a graceful manner and is well shod, then he is in raptures with her."

Dan Mackinnon was ever in good spirits and good humour, and he was a great swell both in Lisbon and London. His calm smile, black eyes, and splendid figure, when he strutted in uniform down St. James's Street, struck every one with admiration. He was the most active man I ever saw: he would run, jump, and climb against the most expert professional gymnasts.

An Englishman's Visit to St Petersburg in 1815.—Now-a-days, everybody who has the means can start from London and travel all over the Continent, without being more of a linguist than to be conversant with such phrases as can be culled from the vocabularies for travellers. In fact, the facility with which the Continent may now be traversed affords a satisfactory proof of the advancement of civilisation in Europe during the nineteenth century. In 1815, when harebrained youths took it into their heads to travel, their relations bade them farewell on their departure, as if they were starting for the antipodes; and many and amusing were the scrapes which these inexperienced young gentlemen got into.

I recollect among others, an adventure of which a friend of mine, a Mr. Kington, the son of a rich Bristol merchant, was the hero. My old school-fellow took it into his head to visit the Continent, but being above following in the tracks of other tourists, who did the grand tour in a mechanical way that was perfectly ludicrous, he determined on visiting St. Petersburg, then a *terra incognita* to the ordinary run of British travellers. Fully equipped with purse, portmanteaus, and the usual supply of stiffly-starched neckcloths, he left his friends at Bristol, after receiving the usual cautions respecting damp sheets, wet feet, and the neglect of flannel, and in due course of time arrived at St. Petersburg. There he had some difficulty in making himself understood as to the hotel he wished to put up at, for he could not speak a single word of any Continental language; he was on the point of being consigned to the care of the police as a madman, when one of the officials, who could speak English, came to the rescue and conducted him to one of the best hotels, where, according to the notice appended to its cards, English was spoken. After recovering from the fatigues of his journey, my friend hired a guide and proceeded to view the lions of the Russian metropolis, and also to visit our vice-consul (the only diplomatic agent England could boast of at that time), for the purpose of having the necessary forms gone through with regard to his passport.

In the course of conversation, Mr. Kington inquired whether he could see the Emperor, and was told in reply that possibly an interview might be obtained, if he called at the palace and left his name. Off started our ambitious tourist, and on arriving at the porter's lodge, instead of writing his name down, he gave in his card, on which was inscribed in large characters, "MR. KINGTON, *Carlton House.*" The following day, one of the equerries of the Emperor dashed up to the hotel where my friend was staying, bearing an invitation for him to dine with the Emperor that evening. Kington, although surprised at the deference with which he was treated by the officer, and the honour conferred upon him, bade one of the servants at the hotel to interpret his thanks to the bearer of the invitation, and his grateful acceptance of it. At the appointed hour, Kington, rigged out in best suit, presented himself at the palace, and was ushered into the Imperial presence. The Emperor received him very graciously; and speaking English perfectly, asked him a thousand questions about London, which city he had visited the year before: in short, he appeared to treat him as an equal.

At dinner, there were many ladies, personages of the highest rank, and officers in uniform, and the conversation became general. But what puzzled Kington was the constant allusions made to "Carlton House" and the Prince of Wales; and his answers to the questions put to him on these subjects were naturally vague and unsatisfactory. To crown all, the Emperor observed to one of the ladies, in French, "He is evidently a natural son of the Prince of Wales, or he would not be so shy." On retiring from the dining-table, Kington was called aside by the lady, who spoke English, and asked what mystery it was that surrounded him and made him so diffident. He replied that he himself did not know why the allusions to Carlton House and the Prince Regent were made, but that they were no doubt intended as compliments to his country. "No doubt you wish to preserve your incognito," observed the lady; "but I must tell you frankly the opinion of the Emperor, in which I fully coincide—viz., that you are a natural son of the Prince of Wales: is it not so?"

The truth instantly flashed across Kington's mind

that he had come to the palace under false colours; a discovery which was succeeded by a terrific vision of what was usually the fate of impostors: he rushed from the palace, haunted by the idea that he was pursued by Cossacks, lance in hand, for the purpose of being consigned, first to the knout, and then to Siberia.

The card given by Kington to the porter had been handed to an equerry, and by him laid before the Emperor; who, seeing "Carlton House" on it (which was the name of the country residence of the father of our hero), fell into the mistake of supposing that Kington was in some way or other connected with the Prince Regent; and hence the invitation.

Fearing to be arrested by the police, Kington bribed the landlord of the hotel to hide him in a garret while the necessary forms were being gone through to facilitate his departure; and after passing two days without sleep, he succeeded in providing himself with a berth in a vessel bound for England. When on board he exclaimed, "Thank God, I am saved! Never, never will I trust myself in a foreign country again." Poor Kington was so overcome with anxiety and fright that he arrived in London more dead than alive; for I was among the first persons who saw him on his arrival, when he recounted his adventures in such a doleful manner, that for the life of me I could not contain my laughter. But the climax was reached when he said, "It is all very well for you to quiz me, but how would you have acted, sir, if you were in a strange country, among a horde of barbarians, and were called virtually a bastard, without being able to revenge yourself? Confound it! my father and mother were honest people, and this insult affects me more than all." Poor Kington found his way back to his anxious family; but, either from "funk," or some disease contracted on his voyage, he died a very short time after his return. He was considered, when at Eton, to be an extremely well-built and powerful boy; he was a famous cricketer, and one of the "cocks of the school."

CARICATURE ON THE ALLIED SOVEREIGNS.—I recollect a droll caricature in Paris, which created much amusement among the crowds that thronged the Boulevards. It represented the Emperor of Austria seated in a magnificent carriage, with the Emperor of Russia on the box as coachman, the Prince Regent of England as postillion, and the King of Prussia as footman. The Emperor Napoleon was portrayed as a running footman, holding the handle of the carriage door, and saying to the Emperor of Austria, then his father-in-law, "*Beau père, ils m'ont mis dehors—et toi ils t'ont mis dedans.*"

It was stated in well-informed circles, that, up to the very moment the Bourbons entered Paris, the Emperor of Austria had not the slightest idea that the dethronement of the King of Rome, and the banishment of his father, were contemplated by the allied Sovereigns. But the English declared that the Bourbons were the legitimate royal family of France; and by the aid of a bribe to Metternich, and the exercise of their Continental influence, which was then unlimited, the claim of the son of the Emperor Napoleon was set aside.

Breguet, the French Watchmaker.—This celebrated man was greatly encouraged by the Allies in 1815. The Emperor Alexander purchased several of his unequalled watches, and the Duke of Wellington also had one which, on touching a spring at any time, struck the hour and minute. The Duke carried it for many years, and it proved of great service to him on many occasions: it cost, I was told, three hundred guineas. The Duke and Duchess of Berri, the Marquis of Londonderry, Lords Beauchamp, Chesterfield, Bruce, and many others, were also customers of Breguet; who was, without doubt, the best and most scientific watchmaker known. I frequently visited his shop, and had many conversations with him; and, although at that time getting old, he was full of energy and vivacity. He was not an advocate for flat watches, as he said they impeded the proper action of the wheels and could not be depended upon as time-keepers: he defied any one to make a watch so good as those made on his own principle. The prices he paid to his best workmen were enormous; there being few to whom he could confide his watches, as so many were drunkards, and could only work a day or two in the week. He told me that he paid some of them thirty francs a day, and none less than a napoleon; and that throughout Paris there were only fifteen or twenty able to execute the delicate work necessary for such watches as he made.

Breguet was a great encourager of merit: he used to say to his young workmen, "Don't be discouraged, or allow a failure to dishearten you; accidents will happen, miscalculations cannot altogether be avoided: be persevering, industrious, sober, and honest." Such was the advice he gave, and he frequently enabled those in his employ who were skilful, steady, and industrious, to arrive at opulence. Breguet, besides his scientific knowledge and mechanical skill, possessed great general information. Napoleon himself, knowing his abilities, frequently went incognito to the workshop and conversed upon the improvements which he was anxious to effect in cannons and fire-arms. The Russian campaign and its disasters put an end to all projects on that score.

Labédoyère and the Number Thirteen.—In 1815 Labédoyère, one of Napoleon's aides-de-camp, paid a visit to the Malmaison prior to the fallen monarch's departure for Cherbourg. The dinner hour arrived, and when the company were seated, Queen Hortense observed that the ominous number of thirteen had assembled, and that, according to the prevalent superstition, one of them would inevitably die before the expiration of a year. Labédoyère remarked, "In all probability your Majesty's prediction will be verified in me; for the Bourbons will never forgive the part I played in joining the Emperor on his return from Elba." The dinner proceeded, and nothing more was thought of the speech; but before a year was over, poor Labédoyère's anticipations were realised: he was seized by the police, brought before a court-martial composed of Legitimists, and condemned to die, for having all his life espoused one cause, and fought for it bravely.

Fouché and Carnot.—During the latter part of the reign of Louis XVIII. his Majesty nominated

Fouché as his Minister of Police. To propitiate the Bourbonists, this man desired many of his former friends and associates to quit France, without assigning a cause. Among those who received this unexpected *congé* was the celebrated General Carnot, who wrote the following laconic epistle to Fouché: "*Où veux tu que j'aille, traitre?*" to which the following answer was given: "*Où tu voudras, imbecile.*" Both Fouché and Carnot had voted for the death of the unpopular Louis XVI., but had subsequently served as ministers to the Emperor.

L'ENFANT DE TROUPE.—A sergeant in the 16th Dragoons, dying suddenly, and leaving his child, a fine boy, entirely unprovided for, without any one to take care of him, the officers of the regiment interested themselves in the little fellow's welfare, and adopted him. He was brought up with great care, and received a very good education; and as he was a remarkably clever youth, and his conduct was unimpeachable, he made great progress in his studies. He became a thorough musician, and could play upon several instruments, and his aptitude for learning languages was astonishing: he could speak fluently Spanish, Portuguese, French, and German, and had a fair knowledge of almost every Continental language. Having attained to the rank of sergeant in the Peninsula, on the return of the regiment to England he was sent, under the charge of an officer, to continue his military studies at Clifton House; and he afterwards attended Colonel Peter's drill in Pimlico to learn the German method of riding (thanks to the Prince Regent's love of change in every department of the army).

Having obtained an *entrée* into the houses of several city families, and being a remarkably clever horseman, and possessing a fine figure and good looks, he became somewhat neglectful of his military duties, passing most of his time among the citizens' wives and daughters. A young lady, the daughter of a rich merchant, fell desperately in love with him, and the end of it was that our dashing young sergeant married her privately; absenting himself for the purpose several days from Colonel Peter's drill without leave, and when he returned it was to give himself up as a deserter. His wife, who was very beautiful, and who had returned with him, flung herself on her knees before the commanding-officer to implore pardon for her husband, who was, notwithstanding, placed under arrest; but at the court-martial held on the matter he was, on the certificates of the officers of his regiment, acquitted. His discharge was obtained with his wife's money, and he was afterwards appointed second in command of one of our Indian Irregular corps; in which country he ended his somewhat eventful life.

Incident at a Ball at the British Embassy in Paris, 1816.—During the reign of the Bourbons, society was, as now, divided into two or more classes; the nobility on the one hand, and the rich mercantile men on the other. The latter studiously copied their betters in dress, manner, and style of living; but as a system of exclusiveness was observed, which militated against their being admitted into the best *salons*, great interest was necessary to overcome the obstacle to their admission. A beautiful woman, the wife of a rich banker, being desirous of getting an invitation to a *bal costumé* given at the British Embassy in Paris, induced Mr. James Rothschild, the great financier, to ask Lady Elizabeth Stuart, the Ambassadress, for an invitation. The *entrée* being obtained by means of a ticket obtained by stealth from Sir Charles Stuart, the lady set about choosing a costume, and decided on appearing as Diana; but, not having been classically educated, she did not bear in mind that chastity was a distinguishing characteristic of the goddess she intended to represent. The consequence was, that her appearance was such as to lead any one, not versed in Greek mythology, to suppose that the country in which Diana hunted must have lain in some happy region near the equator, where the scantiest drapery was the most agreeable costume. The lady, with a triumphant air, that was regarded as effrontery, entered the ballroom dressed, or rather undressed, as described, and approached the British Ambassadress, who, astonished at the exhibition, turned her back, and studiously avoided compromising herself by even looking at the lady during the rest of the evening; informing the visitors present, her friends, that the "Jew" was alone responsible for the immodest appearance of this representative of the chaste goddess.

UNKNOWN PERSONS AT A BALL AT THE BRITISH EMBASSY, PARIS.—When the late Lord Cowley was Ambassador in Paris, Lady Cowley, during a ball that was being given at the Embassy, observed a face in the crowd of visitors that she was unacquainted with; she accordingly interrogated his

Lordship's private secretary and the master of the ceremonies, but neither could find the slightest clue as to who the gentleman was. Mr. Bulwer, perceiving her Ladyship in trouble, offered his services to find out the name of the unknown guest, and boldly advancing towards him, accosted him in French, saying, "I am sent by Lady Cowley to know your name." Whereupon the stranger replied, "Before I gratify you with mine, perhaps you will let me know yours; for your manner is excessively impertinent, and you require to be made an example of." Bulwer replied, that his rank as Secretary of the Embassy authorised him to make the inquiry, as the Ambassadress did not know him. This elicited the stranger's name and address: he was the Marquis D * * *.

The following morning this nobleman called upon me, and mentioned what had occurred the previous evening; he swore that he would run Bulwer through the body for the insult offered him, and requested me to be the bearer of a challenge to the offender. I, however, took upon myself the responsibility of arranging the matter without consulting any one, and succeeded in calming the fury of the irate Marquis; I assured him that Bulwer was the last man in the world intentionally to insult any one, especially a French nobleman with whom he was totally unacquainted, and used other arguments to convince him that no affront was intended; thus preventing a meeting.

During the same evening, Lady Cowley discovered another stranger, and applied to Windsor Heneage to enlighten her respecting him. Heneage replied, "I know but one thing of him; that he lives in the Rue Basse du Rempart, and sold me a silver teapot not later than yesterday." The master of the ceremonies was sent for, and desired to request the silversmith to inform him how he dared appear at the ball without an invitation. The man replied, "But I had one: I received a ticket." "Then be pleased to produce it," was the request of the master of the ceremonies. "I left it on my mantelpiece," said the intruder. "Then go and fetch it." The intruder departed on the errand; and it is hardly necessary to say that he did not return.

A Musician's Reproof.—Among those of the fashionable world in London who patronised music, early after the peace, no one was more conspicuous than Lady Flint; whose charming concerts, given generally on Sunday at her house in Birdcage Walk, delighted all who had musical tastes and enjoyed the honour of an invitation. Among the musicians present there were Dusseck and Cramer, who played on the piano, and were accompanied by Viotti and Jarnowickz, the celebrated violin players. Lady Flint's desire to gratify her friends, however, was often frustrated by the annoying conduct of those who had no taste for music, who disturbed the enjoyment of some of the most beautiful pieces by the rattling of their cups and saucers, and the tone in which their conversation was carried on. Jarnowickz, the violin player, having upon one occasion commenced a concerto by Beethoven, accompanied by his little orchestra, consisting of Cramer, Spagnoletti, Lindley, and Dragonetti, suddenly ceased playing, and apologised for so doing by stating, that the discord caused by the tea-drinkers was such as to mar the effect of the immortal composer's music.

He added, that those who thus showed that they did not understand music, would perhaps appreciate better the piece which he was about to play,—viz., "God save the King," to which they would listen at least with respect. The reproof had a good effect, for always afterwards a complete silence reigned during the performance.

Lord Alvanley.—When Alvanley was at college, he was smitten with a sudden thirst for military glory, and a pair of colours in the Coldstream Guards, then commanded by the late Duke of York, was given him. He became the Duke of York's bosom friend, and this unfortunately led him to become reckless in money matters. Upon one occasion George Anson, afterwards General Anson, asked Alvanley at White's if he felt disposed to join a water party on the Thames, at which his cousin, Lord Ellenborough, and several pretty women of fashion, would assemble. He assented, inquiring where they were to dine. Anson replied, he never thought of dining. "Well, never mind, Anson; I will give instructions on that head." Accordingly, he told Gunter to supply the party with a good dinner, to hire the largest boat on the Thames, to have it carpeted and covered with an awning, and make it as comfortable as possible, and to hire twelve boatmen: in short, nothing was to be wanting. The *fête* succeeded to the satisfaction of all parties; but Alvanley paid Gunter two hundred guineas for his folly.

Apart from his extravagance, Alvanley, the magnificent, the witty, the famous, and chivalrous, was the idol of the clubs, and of society, from the King to the ensign of the Guards. All sorts of stories used to be told of his recklessness about money. When Lord Alvanley succeeded to his father's fortune, he inherited an income of eight thousand pounds a year; when he died, he did not leave to his brother, who succeeded to the title, above two thousand. Armstrong, full of biting sarcasm, well knowing that the noble Lord never paid ready money for anything, asked him the price of a splendid hunter he had just purchased. "I owe Mathe Milton three hundred guineas for it," was the characteristic reply.

There is another amusing story of Alvanley's extravagance. His dinners were considered perfect, and the best in London. He had given directions to have a cold apricot tart every day throughout the year, and his *maître d'hôtel* remonstrating with him upon the expense, Alvanley replied, "Go to Gunter's, the confectioner, and purchase all the preserved apricots, and don't plague me any more about the expense."

The great charm of Alvanley's manner was its naturalness, or *naïveté*. He was an excellent classical scholar, a good speaker, and whatever he undertook he succeeded in. He had lived in nearly every court of Europe, had a vast acquaintance with the world, and his knowledge of languages was great. When he was recommended to pay his debts, he gave a list of them to his friend "Punch" Greville, but forgot to insert one of fifty thousand pounds which he owed.

Sir Astley Cooper and the Troop Horses.—Sir Astley Cooper, independently of his great skill in surgery, was a very clever and humane man. He was exceedingly fond of horses, and whenever an opportunity occurred, would operate on these animals with the same judgment and skill that he bestowed on his human patients. After the battle of Waterloo, all the wounded horses of the Household Brigade of cavalry were sold by auction. Sir Astley attended the sale, and bought twelve which he considered so severely hurt as to require the greatest care and attention in order to effect a cure. Having had them conveyed, under the care of six grooms, to his park in the country, the great surgeon followed, and with the assistance of his servants, commenced extracting bullets and grape-shot from the bodies and limbs of the suffering animals. In a very short time after the operations had been performed, Sir Astley let them loose in the park; and one morning, to his great delight, he saw the noble animals form in line, charge, and then retreat, and afterwards gallop about, appearing greatly contented with the lot that had befallen them. These manœuvres were repeated generally every morning, to his great satisfaction and amusement.

Italian Brigandage in 1815.—In the sober age we now live in, when Englishmen can travel from Dan to Beersheba almost without molestation, John Bull hears with surprise that his friends on an excursion in Italy, not half a mile from a populous town, were seized by a party of brigands, and only liberated on paying a ransom of some thousands of pounds. In 1815, however, these occurrences were very common. In fact, at that time both Italy and Spain swarmed with banditti, and travellers in those countries were generally accompanied by an escort of cavalry when in dangerous districts.

Two English gentlemen—Lord Valletort, son of Lord Mount-Edgecumbe, and the Hon. Mr. Collyer, only son of Lord Milsington, and heir to an immense fortune—decided on visiting Italy. In those days Englishmen exhibited more ostentation when travelling than they do now; and these two young scions of nobility proved no exception to the rule, for they started from London carrying baggage enough to stock a clothes-shop, and money in their pockets sufficient to form the capital of a provincial bank: nothing was forgotten, in short, that might mitigate the hardships of travel. They carried all the luxuries of Pall Mall and St. James's Street with them. Of course, they had engaged a courier; and as character was not so much an object as cleverness and insolence, some of the greatest blackguards and thieves in the world were often candidates for such a situation; although, from the accounts of Italian brigandage appearing daily in the papers, the cause of the misadventures that befell travellers was invariably traced to the couriers who accompanied them, and who gave notice to the bandits if they were worth robbing. Our young friends had picked up from the purlieus of Leicester Square one of these fellows, to accompany them on their travels, —an Italian, without a character as usual, but of engaging manners. But how men could be so deluded as to walk into a trap in the manner these two tourists did is incomprehensible. However, they embarked for the Continent provided with baggage and money enough to tempt the brigands, even without a courier to victimise them, and after visiting several continental cities *en route*, at length found themselves at Rome, where they engaged an old palace and lived in splendour for some time, spending their money like princes, and making themselves the talk of the city.

At length they determined on making an excursion to the south of Italy, and ordering their baggage to be packed up, they started on their journey, accompanied by their courier. Immediately before reaching Fondi, the carriage was stopped, a party of brigands made their appearance, and our travellers, with pistols held at their heads, were commanded to give up all that they had. Lord Valletort, who was very hot-headed, made some show of resistance, and had his brains blown out instantly; while poor Collyer, exasperated at the foul deed, snatched a pistol from the hands of one of the gang and shot him dead; he was then dragged out of the carriage and brutally murdered on the way-side. It is hardly necessary to state that every article of value was taken from the persons and baggage of our murdered countrymen, and that the courier disappeared with the assassins, and was never more heard of.

This foul deed, among hosts of others, was never avenged; for we could not then, any more than now, afford to quarrel with a nation like Italy on a personal matter. Very different would have been the conduct of France in such an emergency. A frigate would have been despatched to the scene of the outrage, and a dozen of the peasantry (who are generally either brigands or in league with banditti) would have been hanged or shot in reprisal. When

Napoleon I. was in Italy, he issued orders that for every Frenchman or French soldier ill-treated or killed by brigands, a dozen villagers should be shot; and after finishing off about 700 of those pests in Italy, he established a respect for French lynch law that lasted the whole time of his occupation of that peninsula. As soon, however, as the French left Italy, this state of things was instantly changed, and brigandage has existed from that time up to the present: for England is held, as a power by itself, in sovereign contempt by the whole of the hordes that infest Terracina and the spots so graphically described by Washington Irving.

Madame de Staël and Mr. Canning. — Madame de Staël, with all her talents and attractions, was somewhat of a toady. At one of the Duchesse de Castries' *soirées* I witnessed a quarrel between her and Mr. Canning. Madame de Staël thought that by abusing Lord Castlereagh she would obtain favour from our great statesman; he, however, coolly informed her that the manner in which she had spoken of his political adversary prevented him from continuing to converse with her, and then made his bow, to the surprise of those present. Madame de Staël was so angry that she actually foamed at the mouth.

The Duchess of Duras.—The Duchess of Duras was considered a clever and witty woman. She disliked Wellington very much, for having allowed the pictures and the statues in the Louvre to be removed and sent as presents to the sovereigns among the allies. The Apollo Belvidere, which had been given to the Duke by the Pope, was once the cause of a dispute between Wellington and this high-spirited lady. On meeting him one day she inquired what he intended doing with the statue. He replied that he was going to have it packed up and sent to London. "Then," replied she, "England will possess one god the more, but one man the less." "How?" inquired our hero. "Why," replied the lady, "she will gain in possessing the statue, but her honour and yours will be sacrificed by this piece of Vandalism." The far-famed statue, however, was not sent to England.

Mr. and Mrs. Graham—their Soirées.—In the year 1816, a Mr. Graham and his wife, a pretty Sicilian lady, lived in Paris in a charming hotel in the Rue Taitbout. This gentleman, who belonged to an ancient Scotch family, went to Sicily during the continental war, where he met with his wife; and, by the good offices of Lord and Lady William Bentinck, the young people were introduced into the best society. Mrs. Graham's *réunions* were considered charming. The celebrated Prince Metternich, with his beautiful wife, Lady Oxford and her daughters, Mr. and Mrs. Cavendish Bradshaw, Mr. and Mrs. Hervey Aston, were her constant visitors; Pozzo di Borgo, the Russian ambassador, Baron Vincent, and Alava, the Austrian and Spanish representatives, also visited the Grahams frequently.

It is remarkable that all these diplomatists had accompanied the Duke of Wellington at Waterloo, and received wounds in that terrible battle. Metternich was considered by all who knew him to be one of the most astute and witty members of the *corps diplomatique;* but few are aware of the acuteness and sagacity evinced by Pozzo, who was the inveterate enemy of the first Napoleon. He was a Corsican by birth, and in his youth a constant playmate of the younger members of the Bonaparte family; but when the Revolution had caused nearly all the respectable families of Corsica to quit that island, Pozzo determined to try his fortune in Russia; where he succeeded in thwarting Napoleon's schemes in almost every instance. During the continental war he came to England, where, by his wise counsel, he prevailed upon our Cabinet to send subsidies to Russia and Germany. Napoleon ever afterwards entertained a most violent hatred against Pozzo; and on hearing his name mentioned, he would fly into a terrible rage, and exclaim, "The fellow is a traitor: he is ever in my way: he is like the erysipelas on the body. Whatever harm he can do me he does; and by him my brain is constantly disturbed, and my nervous system kept constantly on the rack." Pozzo was born in the same year in which Bonaparte, Wellington, and Metternich first saw the light. He died very rich, and his nephew, who married into one of the oldest families in France, succeeded to his property.

To return to the Grahams. The charming Mrs. Graham was courted by all who approached her; and such was the glow of health and cheerfulness in her countenance, that no one could be in her company long without being inspired with feelings stronger than those of friendship: yet not a word was heard against her honour. She had lived happily with her husband for forty years without being blessed with a child; but before her husband's death, to the amazement and astonishment of all her friends and of the family doctor, she bore a son, like Sarah of old. The heir-presumptive disputed the legitimacy of the little stranger, but evidence was forthcoming to prove that all was perfectly *en règle;* and the young Scottish chieftain, who will shortly attain his majority and inherit a splendid fortune, was acknowledged as the *bonâ fide* son of the aged couple.

MR. WILLIAM HOPE AND HIS MISTRESS.—This gentleman inherited on coming of age a fortune of £40,000 sterling a year from his reputed father, a Dutchman. He exhibited alternately extreme recklessness in expenditure and the stinginess of a miser. He would one day spend thousands of pounds on a ball or supper, and then keep his servants for days on cold meat and stale bread. His mistress, Mlle. Jenny Coulon, a charming actress, told me that Mr. Hope, suspecting her of infidelity, breakfasted with her at her lodgings as if nothing had occurred, and on leaving said, "Oh, my dear, I wish you would give me your diamonds, that I may have them newly set." Jenny, never imagining that her lover had the remotest idea of playing her false, readily gave them to him; and a fortnight afterwards he returned the ornaments, expressing a hope that she would be pleased with the setting. On the following day, what was Jenny's horror at receiving a visit from the jeweller, who called upon her with a bill "for taking out the diamonds and replacing them with paste." The enraged fair one applied to the police for redress, but found she had no remedy, having voluntarily relinquished all claim on the diamonds by giving them up to the donor. Yet this man has been known to portion the daughter of a lady of rank with £20,000.

How to get Invited to a Ball.—Mr. William Hope's large fortune enabled him to give the most splendid entertainments to the *beau monde* of Paris. At his balls and parties all the notables of the city were to be seen, and no expense was spared to make them the most sumptuous entertainments then given. It was his custom, when the invitations were issued, not to open any letters till the party was over; to save him the mortification of refusing those who had not been invited.

It happened that a certain Marquis, well known in Paris, who had married the sister of a prince, was desirous of being present at one of these assemblies, and accordingly wrote, requesting the favour of an invitation for himself, his wife, and his wife's sister, the Princess de C * * *. Receiving no answer, the Marquis called upon Mr. Hope, who received him with his usual courtesy. The Marquis began by expressing his surprise that his letter had remained unanswered, when Mr. Hope assured him that he had not received the letter in question; explaining the custom before alluded to. This explanation, however, did not satisfy the Marquis, who observed that such a proceeding was, to say the least of it, extraordinary, as letters were generally written in expectation of their receiving an answer with the least possible delay; and he added, "Mr. Hope, by your conduct you have not only insulted me, my wife, and sister-in-law, but several of my friends.

I must therefore tell you, that the first time I meet you in the Champs Elysées or the Bois de Boulogne, I will give orders to my coachman to drive against your carriage; which insult you will naturally resent." Mr. Hope replied, "I am not of your opinion as to the necessity of having my carriage injured through the awkwardness or stupidity of your coachman; and to avoid all further altercation, I will have the honour to send you as many cards of invitation to my next ball as you may wish for yourself and friends."

The Marquis swallowed the bait, returned to his wife, overcame the objections as to the manner in which the *entrée* was obtained, and appeared with her and her sister-in-law on the appointed evening. They were received with due honours, and when supper was announced, Mr. Hope advanced towards the Princess, and offering her his arm, conducted her to the place of honour at his right hand at the supper-table. The rank of the Marquis and his sister-in-law had probably more influence than his threat in procuring for him the invitation, as the vanity and ostentation of Mr. Hope were no less remarkable than his meanness and eccentricity.

MELANCHOLY RESULT OF A BALL.—At one of Mr. William Hope's balls, the crowd of visitors was so great that many persons were obliged, on leaving the saloons, to take shelter under an archway until the arrival of their carriages. The wind, a keen north-easter, was the cause of sore throat and fever to many of the fair visitors; and of those present, a General Didier and his wife, a remarkably handsome couple, were seized with quinsy, and in eight-and-forty hours afterwards they both died, and were carried to their last resting-place at Père la Chaise. This lamentable event created an unusual sensation in Paris at the time, and was the theme of conversation in every quarter. When it was mentioned to a friend of mine, he coolly observed that he pitied the lady, but not the General, for it was a glorious end for a soldier to be killed by a *ball*.

A ROLAND FOR AN OLIVER.—I recollect dining at the British Embassy at Paris when Lord Stuart was Ambassador. Among those invited were Long Wellesley and the elder Cornewall. The former of these gentlemen arrived very late, and was sarcastically asked by Cornewall if he would take some cheese. Mr. Wellesley replied in a good-natured manner, declining the offer, and commenced his dinner as if nothing had happened. When the finger-glasses were handed round, Mr. Cornewall made use of the water in his, as one does when dressing, with a tumbler and wash-hand basin; making, of course, an extraordinary noise with his mouth. Wellesley noticing this, leant over towards Cornewall, and quietly asked him if he should send one of the servants for a piece of soap, in order that he might complete his toilet.

SIR CHARLES SHAKERLEY.—This gentleman had a great horror of a dead body. On one occasion Henry Williams and some others were stopping at his house, when, some slight difference having arisen between him and Sir Charles, the latter spoke in rather an abrupt manner. The visitors, knowing their host's antipathy, determined to pay him off by a practical joke, and accordingly came down the next morning looking very grave, and informed him that Williams was seriously ill. Shakerley hastened upstairs, and found Williams lying in bed, foaming at the mouth and rolling his eyes wildly. Sir Charles, struck with the thought that his guest might die, became alarmed, and was about to send for a conveyance to remove him; but the "dying man" found it convenient to get better. When Sir Charles left the room, Williams took from his mouth a piece of soap, with which he had imitated the froth on the mouth of a man in a fit. Sir Charles was, however, so frightened, that he never said an unkind thing to the practical joker during the remainder of his visit.

"TAKING THE BULL BY THE HORNS."—The late Lord John Churchill, prior to his appointment as equerry to the lamented Duke of Sussex, commanded a frigate of H.M. Navy in the Mediterranean. The doctor of the ship, a man of great medical experience and decision, was one day expatiating to his Lordship on the efficacy of blisters, which, he stated, had cured all the sailors who had been attacked with fevers. Lord John replied, "All this may be quite true; but if ever you apply a blister to any part of my body, by God, doctor, I will order my ship's company to throw you overboard." "Be it so, my Lord; but you know I invariably take the bull by the horns," replied the medico: and the matter then dropped.

A short time afterwards, the noble captain was

seized with violent headache and fever, and his pulse was very high; the doctor therefore determined, "*coûte que coûte*," to apply his favourite remedy. Having prepared the blister, he contrived, while Lord J. slept, to place it on his chest without awakening him; he then retired to rest, but gave orders to be called if his presence was necessary. At an early hour the following morning, he was awoke by the captain's servant, who, looking more dead than alive, said that his Lordship was very violent, foaming with rage, and calling out with all his might, "Where's that damned doctor?" The terrified medico found his patient in a state of exasperation and excitement; but, upon feeling his pulse, ascertained that the fever had greatly abated. Lord J., though furious at the pain he was enduring, asked what the doctor had done to him, and quoting the *Corsair*, added,—

> "Prepare thee to reply
> Clearly and full; I love not mystery."

"In a word, sir, what does it all mean? I am suffering from blisters all over my body." The doctor, unconscious of what had occurred during the night, opened the captain's shirt collar to look at the effects of the blister; but the sufferer pushed him aside, saying, "No, doctor, it is not there; you will find it lower down." Lower down it certainly was, for it was discovered, like the one mentioned in *Tom Cringle's Log*, in a very awkward place. It had, no doubt, during the night, got rubbed off the chest and had slipped down to a very opposite part of the body, which was blistered severely. The doctor, to appease the captain's anger, explained:

"I found your Lordship last night in a violent fever, and had no alternative left but to take the bull by the horns: the blister was placed contrary to my orders, I confess; but 'all's well that ends well,' and I am happy to see your Lordship so much better."

Raggett, of White's Club.—Raggett, the well-known club proprietor of White's, and the Roxburgh Club in St. James's Square, was a notable character in his way. He began life as a poor man, and died extremely rich. It was his custom to wait upon the members of these clubs whenever play was going on. Upon one occasion, at the Roxburgh, the following gentlemen, Hervey Combe, Tippoo Smith, Ward (the Member for London), and Sir John Malcolm, played at high stakes at whist; they sat during that night, viz., Monday, the following day and night, and only separated on Wednesday morning at eleven o'clock; indeed, the party only broke up then owing to Hervey Combe being obliged to attend the funeral of one of his partners who was buried on that day. Hervey Combe, on looking over his card, found that he was a winner of thirty thousand pounds from Sir John Malcolm, and he jocularly said, "Well, Sir John, you shall have your revenge whenever you like." Sir John replied, "Thank you; another sitting of the kind will oblige me to return again to India." Hervey Combe, on settling with Raggett, pulled out of his pocket a handful of counters, which amounted to several hundred pounds, over and above the thirty thousand he had won of the baronet, and he gave them to Raggett, saying, "I give them to you for sitting so long with us, and providing us with all required." Raggett was overjoyed, and in mentioning what had occurred to one of his friends a few days afterwards, he added, "I make it a rule never to allow any of my servants to be present when gentlemen play at my clubs, for it is my invariable custom to sweep the carpet after the gambling is over, and I generally find on the floor a few counters, which pays me for the trouble of sitting up. By this means I have made a decent fortune."

The Café Tortoni.—About the commencement of the present century, Tortoni, the centre of pleasure, gallantry, and entertainment, was opened by a Neapolitan, who came to Paris to supply the Parisians with good ice. The founder of this celebrated *café* was by name Veloni, an Italian, whose father lived with Napoleon from the period he invaded Italy, when First Consul, down to his fall. Young Veloni brought with him his friend Tortoni, an industrious and intelligent man. Veloni died of an affection of the lungs, shortly after the *café* was opened, and left the business to Tortoni; who, by dint of care, economy, and perseverance, made his *café* renowned all over Europe. Towards the end of the first Empire, and during the return of the Bourbons, and Louis Philippe's reign, this establishment was so much in vogue that it was difficult to get an ice there; after the opera and theatres were over, the Boulevards were literally choked up by the carriages of the great people of the court and the Faubourg St. Germain bringing guests to Tortoni's.

In those days clubs did not exist in Paris, consequently the gay world met there. The Duchess of Berri, with her suite, came nearly every night *incognito;* the most beautiful women Paris could boast of, old maids, dowagers, and old and young men pouring out their sentimental twaddle, and holding up to scorn their betters, congregated here. In fact, Tortoni's became a sort of club for fashionable people; the saloons were completely monopolised by them, and became the rendezvous of all that was gay, and, I regret to add, immoral.

Gunter, the eldest son of the founder of the house in Berkeley Square, arrived in Paris about this period, to learn the art of making ice; for, prior to the peace, our London ices and creams were acknowledged, by the English as well as foreigners, to be detestable. In the early part of the day, Tortoni's became the rendezvous of duellists and retired officers, who congregated in great numbers to breakfast; which consisted of cold *pâtés*, game, fowl, fish, eggs, broiled kidneys, iced champagne, and liqueurs from every part of the globe.

Though Tortoni succeeded in amassing a large fortune, he suddenly became morose, and showed evident signs of insanity: in fact, he was the most unhappy man on earth. On going to bed one night, he said to the lady who superintended the management of his *café*, "It is time for me to have done with the world." The lady thought lightly of what he said, but upon quitting her apartment on the following morning, she was told by one of the waiters that Tortoni had hanged himself.

Among the prominent and singular personages who used daily to visit this *café* was the Russian Prince Tuffiakin, who was immensely rich, and perhaps the greatest epicure in Paris. When he attained the respectable age of seventy, he fell des-

THE CAFÉ FRASCATI IN ITS PALMY DAYS.

perately in love with a beautiful girl, named Anna Sinclair, who was born of Scotch parents. Upon one occasion, whilst sipping his ice, the old man observed his adored Anna ogling a young dandy, and a serious quarrel was the consequence; however, in course of time, a sort of truce was patched up between the lovers. The fair Scotch girl promised never more to ogle, and the old man proposed the following plan of reconciliation: they were both to meet at the church of Notre Dame de Lorette, and exchange rings at the altar, and afterwards to leave the church arm in arm. Though Tuffiakin was of a jealous disposition, he was nevertheless a great libertine, for he pretended to be in love with every pretty girl he met. He suddenly became enamoured of a well-known *danseuse*, who was living under the protection of an English nobleman. The Prince, well knowing the power of his money, boldly presented himself at the lady's house, and by the application of an immense bribe of money and jewels, he succeeded in obtaining the good graces of the inconstant daughter of Terpsichore. This old Russian *débauché* hastened his death by his excesses, and became an idiot.

Among the English persons of note who usually met at Tortoni's, I recollect Lords Brudenell Bruce, Bingham, and Chesterfield; also Lord Herbert, afterwards Earl of Pembroke, whom the French denominated *L'air bête:* not that the noble Lord was by any means deficient in intellect, but the envy and jealousy of the French were piqued; for he was extremely handsome, and his equipages were the finest in Paris. Sir Henry Milmay, with his beautiful and accomplished wife, created an immense sensation. Hall Standish, who spent fabulous sums upon pictures, dinners, and balls, was a *habitué* there; and you were sure to stumble upon the kind and excellent Tommy Garth, full of spirits and youth. Lord Stair, who was club-footed, and the most unpopular Englishman in Paris, might be seen sitting in his carriage, accompanied by two dogs, within hail of the waiters. I must not forget to mention Mr. Green, an epicure of the first water, who gave excellent dinners; and also poor Cuthbert, who died in Spain, much regretted by his old friends.

It was the custom for the great ladies who came to Tortoni's, to form their parties there; and I recollect, as if it had occurred yesterday, that upon one occasion, the Princess de Beauvau invited those who were assembled in the centre room to meet at her hotel at midnight to dance. On our arrival, we were agreeably surprised to find Musard, Colinet, and other musicians assembled, and ready to strike up a quadrille or a waltz. The charming daughters of the Princess, the Ladies Harley, with others whom I now forget, danced with all the grace of professional performers. In those days, the Minuet, Gavotte, and Monaco were the favourite dances, and if a gentleman could muster sufficient grace and agility for any of those fashionable dances, he was sure of receiving invitations from the best houses in the Faubourg St. Germain.

About the period I allude to, a young captain in one of the French regiments of hussars suddenly made his appearance at Tortoni's, the Count Walewski, a natural son of the great Napoleon. He was remarkable for his good looks; the ladies adored him; and it must be acknowledged he was one of the finest-looking men I ever saw. Not liking a military life, Walewski retired from the hussars and adopted politics ; in which sphere he soon evinced considerable talent. His friends the Ducs de Morny, and Mouchy, the Counts Antonin and Louis de Noailles, the Count Montguyon, and Lavalette, met here nearly every night. Upon one occasion, a strange scene took place between Lavalette and Montguyon, owing to a pretty girl, Mademoiselle D * * *, with whom it was said that they were both in love. Be this as it may, "the green-eyed monster" was aroused, and from high words, a duel was the consequence ; they fought with swords, and Montguyon received a wound in the arm, when the seconds interfered and put an end to the affair.

The Revolution of 1830 was a death-blow to Tortoni's. Persons in the best society, who had during many years been considered proud and exclusive, now began to keep entirely aloof, and studiously avoided going there, because of the new set which had been formed. This *café*, nevertheless, for some time continued to be in fashion, and the rendezvous of persons of celebrity. Victor Hugo, Lamartine, Sophie Gay, Alexandre Dumas, the bankers Rothschild, and the moneyed aristocracy, frequently met there. Clubs have, however, sprung up in Paris in every direction within a few years, and the consequence has been that Tortoni's has lost its *renommée ;* but, nevertheless, the ices here are still considered the best in Paris.

An Inveterate Gambler.—Mr. Lumsden, whose inveterate love of gambling eventually caused his ruin, was to be seen every day at Frascati's, the celebrated gambling-house kept by Mme. Dunan, where some of the most celebrated women of the *demi-monde* usually congregated. He was a martyr to the gout, and his hands and knuckles were a mass of chalk stones. He stuck to the *rouge et noir* table until everybody had left; and while playing would take from his pocket a small slate, upon which he would rub his chalk stones until blood flowed. Having on one occasion been placed near him at the *rouge et noir* table, I ventured to expostulate with him for rubbing his knuckles against his slate. He coolly answered, "I feel relieved when I see the blood ooze out."

Mr. Lumsden was remarkable for his courtly manners; but his absence of mind was astonishing, for he would frequently ask his neighbour where he was. Crowds of men and women would congregate behind his chair, to look at "the mad Englishman," as he was called; and his eccentricities used to amuse even the croupiers. After losing a large fortune at this den of iniquity, Mr. Lumsden encountered every evil of poverty, and died in a wretched lodging in the Rue St. Marc.

Colonel Sebright of the Guards.—This gentleman was well known in London, from the commencement of the present century down to 1820, as one of the most eccentric men of the age. He stuck to the old style of corduroy knee-breeches and top-boots to the day of his death. He never—that is to say, for many years before his death—left town; and his daily occupation was to walk from his house in Chapel Street, South Audley Street, to Hyde Park, accompanied by his wiry-haired terrier. Then he would stroll to the Guards' Club, finding fault with everything and everybody connected with the changes taking place in the dress, &c., of the army, and that of the English gentleman. From the windows of the Club he used to gaze at White's which was opposite, and abuse the dandies, especially Brummell and Alvanley, who were his especial aversions, ejaculating, "Damn those fellows; they are upstarts, and fit only for the society of tailors!"

I recollect on one occasion his dining, when on guard, with Colonel Archibald Macdonald (who was killed afterwards at Bergen-op-Zoom), when Brummell, Alvanley, and Pierrepoint were also of the party. These dandies were aware of the dislike he entertained for them, but nevertheless made a point of asking him to take wine. But to each invitation he replied gruffly, "Thank you; I have already had enough of this horrid stuff, and cannot drink more." His speeches were usually of this curt description.

When Sebright went to Spain with his battalion, he left directions to have the newspapers regularly forwarded to him, and on their arrival he desired his servant to damp them; then holding them to the fire, he would exclaim, "Why, my papers smell as if they were only printed last night." This operation was performed every day the mails arrived from England.

My gallant friend was a thorough John Bull, and an enemy to everything that was French, even to the dress of that nation. It was with difficulty that he bore the innovation of the black neckcloth, that had then just come into fashion. Upon one occasion, on entering the Guards' Club, he perceived Willoughby Cotton with a black cravat on, when he said, in a loud voice, "It is evident that the officers of the Guards are in debt to their washerwomen, or they would not wear dirty black cravats." Willoughby Cotton, feeling indignant, replied that he did not understand such impertinence. Sebright then jumped up from his chair, exclaiming, "I will not brook this language!" and left the room. Colonel Keate followed the irritable gentleman, and told him that he had brought it all on himself by his sarcastic observations; and, in short, so convinced him of his error as to cause him to shake hands with Cotton.

The Princess Charlotte of Wales.—A few months after the death of the lamented Princess Charlotte of Wales, Prince Leopold, now the King of the Belgians, went to Paris, where he lived at the Hotel des Princes, Rue Richelieu; but for a length of time he remained incognito. I was on one occasion dining in the company of his Royal Highness, who interrogated me about a shooting party at St. Germain, which had taken place a day or two before. When I mentioned the number of hares we had shot, the Prince observed, "I never intend again to shoot a hare, because at Claremont, one day, when walking with my beloved wife, we heard the cries of one that had been wounded by one of the shooting party; and so affected was she by its pitiful screams, that she begged I would not be the cause of pain to one of these animals in future."

The Duchess of Leeds used to tell an anecdote of her Royal Highness and her love of fishing. When engaged in this sport, on catching a fish the Princess used to tie a piece of ribbon round its tail and throw it back again into the water, noticing with delight that those which had not been caught attacked those decorated by her. Once, having been very successful in catching a great many, and having exhausted all her ribbon, she unpicked her bonnet and made use of its trimmings to decorate the fish she caught.

THE DUKE OF CLARENCE.—At the commencement of 1817, the Duke of Clarence, bent upon improving his pecuniary means, decided on marrying a rich heiress. The report was circulated all over England (where it produced the most intense sensation), that the Duke had, with the consent of his brother, the Prince Regent, actually proposed to Miss Wykeham, whose estates in Oxfordshire were large and of immense value. When the event was communicated to Queen Charlotte, his royal mother was outrageous; she flew into a violent rage, and with vehement asseverations (either in English or German), declared that her consent should never be given to the match. The law officers of the Crown were consulted, cabinet councils met daily, and after much discussion, ministers determined on opposing the Duke's project; notwithstanding the opinion of one of the best lawyers that "a prince of the blood-royal, being of age, and notifying his intended marriage previous to its taking place, was at liberty to marry without the consent of the King, unless the two Houses of Parliament should address the Crown against it."

The excitement among all classes was at its height, when the *Morning Post* informed the world one morning that the Duke's intended marriage was entirely "off;" H.R.H. having been prevailed upon by the Queen to forego his intentions. In this course Queen Charlotte was evidently supported by the rest of the royal family; and it was whispered that, as an inducement to the Prince to behave like a good boy, the Queen, the Prince Regent, and his royal sisters had subscribed a sufficient sum among themselves to pay off all H.R.H.'s debts, and to provide him with an increase of income for the future. Much amusement was caused at the clubs by a caricature of an old sailor, called "the love-sick youth."

The Duke of Clarence, together with his brothers, were in the habit of frequently dining at the table prepared for the officers who mount guard at St. James's, and it was the custom for their Royal Highnesses to send in their names when they intended to honour the Colonel with their presence. Although I was at the time very young, I recollect being present on several occasions when the Duke of Clarence honoured our mess with his presence, and the amusing anecdotes he used to relate. He astonished Colonel Archibald Macdonald one day at table by putting the following question to him: "Colonel, are you ever under the necessity of giving 'chocolate' to your young officers?" The Colonel (who was afterwards killed at Bergen-op-Zoom) replied that he did not understand what H.R.H. meant by "giving chocolate." The Duke replied, "Oh, I can see, Colonel, that you have not breakfasted with Sir David Dundas, for it was his invariable custom to ask such officers as had fallen under his displeasure for breaches of military discipline to breakfast with him, in order that during the repast, where some excellent chocolate invariably formed one of the comestibles, the culprit should be severely lectured, and sometimes recommended to leave the service." Ensign "Bacchus" Lascelles, who was present, a plain-spoken fellow, sang out from the end of the table, "Your Royal Highness, if the Colonel does not understand the meaning of 'chocolate' I do; for only this morning I received 'goose' from the adjutant for not having sufficient powder on my hair: it is quite immaterial whether a rowing be denominated 'chocolate' or 'goose,' for it is one and the same thing." The royal Duke laughed heartily at the *sang froid* of the young ensign, and ever after evinced great partiality for him.

Talking of military despotism, my old friend Upton, though an excellent man, was extremely rigorous in enforcing attention to military regulations. Having discovered that I shirked morning parade, he sent for me, intending to administer a due amount of "goose." On my arriving at the Queen's Lodge, where he lived as one of the equerries, and entering his apartments, I was horrified at finding this excellent fellow lying on the floor bleeding. It appeared that he had, in a temporary absence of mind, made use of a pair of razors to pull on his boots with! Fortunately, Dr. Heberden, who was on duty in attendance upon the King, was immediately sent for, and succeeded in stopping the hæmorrhage; but he at the same time expressed his fears that lock-jaw would ensue. Luckily, Upton's strong constitution carried him through the disaster, and in a few weeks he was able to resume command of the battalion : and ready to administer a plentiful allowance of "goose" to the first unlucky wight who fell under his displeasure.

The Origin of "Shocking Bad Hat." — At Newmarket, when the Duke of York, surrounded by the Dukes of Queensberry, Grafton, Rutland, Portland, and other noblemen and gentlemen, was busily engaged talking about and betting on a race which was about to be run, a little insignificant-looking man pushed his head into the ring, offering to bet a considerable sum against a horse in the race in question. The Duke of York's curiosity was aroused, and he asked his neighbour who it was that offered to lay the odds. Some one cried out, "Oh, it is Walpole." "Then the little man wears a shocking bad hat—a shocking bad hat," rejoined his Royal Highness. The late Lord Walpole and his father were both addicted to wearing hats with large brims and low crowns, which made the wearers appear anything but *comme il faut*.

Englishmen in Paris in 1817. — In the year 1817, Lord A * * *, his brother, and another friend, were staying in Paris. They had dined one day at Véry's, then the famous *restaurant* in the Palais Royal, and the conversation had turned upon the insults offered by the Parisians, particularly the military, to the English visitors. His Lordship was silent during this conversation, but took note of what had been said, while imbibing some potent Burgundy; and his indignation was none the weaker for having thus "bottled it up." On leaving the *restaurant* the first thing he did was to kick over a basket of toothpicks, which was presented to him for purchase; the next was to shove off the pavement a Frenchman, who proved to be an officer. Of course, there was a violent altercation; cards were exchanged, and each party went his way to make arrangements for the "pistols and coffee for four."

Our countrymen, when near home, picked up their friend Manners, who had been shut out of his lodgings, and promised to accommodate him with a sofa at their rooms. On their arrival, he partially uncased and wrapped himself up in a large Witney blanket and greatcoat, and then "turned in." At an early hour the next morning, two gentlemen called on our countrymen, and were ushered into the saloon. The first who presented himself to receive them was his Lordship, who had nothing on but a large pair of trousers, and a cotton night-cap full of holes: he being so particular about having it aired that it was constantly singed in the process. Not speaking French, he requested his servant to act as interpreter, and asked the strangers the object of their visit; the incidents of the preceding night having passed off from his memory with the fumes of the Chambertin. The discussion that ensued woke up Manners, who, wrapped in his blanket, rose from his couch, looking more like a white bear than anything else. It also drew from his dormitory Captain Meade, who made his appearance from a side door, clothed only in his night-shirt and a pair of expansive Russia duck trousers, whistling, as was his wont, and spitting occasionally through a hole that had been bored in one of his front teeth, in imitation of the stage-coachmen of the day. Lord A * * *'s brother next appeared on the scene, in a costume little more complete than those of the others.

The visitors, although astonished at the appearance of the group, proceeded to business. Manners conducted it on the part of his friends, who could not speak French; and, with a view of discharging his office more comfortably, drew aside the folds of his Witney blanket and placed his back against the mantelpiece, to enjoy the warmth of the glowing wood-ashes in the grate below. The Frenchmen were refused an apology by our friends, coupled with the observation, that with Englishmen the case would be different; but that it was impossible on the present occasion to arrange matters in that way. They therefore requested the other party to name their weapons. Manners coolly informed them that they had decided on using *fusils,* at twelve paces! This seemed rather to astonish the Frenchmen: they exchanged glances, and then cast their eyes round the room, and on the strange figures before them. Meade was whistling through his teeth; Lord A * * *, whose coppers were rather hot, had thrust his head out into the street through a pane of glass that had been smashed the night before; while the others were stalking about the room in their rather airy costumes. The gravity of the Frenchmen was overcome by the ludicrous aspect and *sang froid* of their opponents, and they burst out laughing. Lord A * * *, who was as full of fun as he was of pluck, stretching out his hand to the injured party, said, "Come, I see you are good fellows, so shake hands. I had taken rather too much wine last night." I need not say that the proffered hand was accepted, and the French officers retired. After their departure, Manners asked the servant what *fusil* really meant, as, when naming the weapon to be used, he supposed it to be a kind of pistol.

THE BOLD WIFE OF A RASH HUSBAND.—About thirty years back a bet was made in Paris by the Comte de Châteauvillard, that he would ride a horse which no groom would venture to mount because of its vicious propensities. The animal in question had been allowed to remain idle for several months, without having ever been touched by any one during all that time; for it was fed through a hole in a neighbouring stall, and watered and littered in a similar manner. As the time approached for the conditions of the bet to be carried out, great excitement prevailed in the clubs with regard to it, especially among those skilled in horsemanship, and a wager of 20,000 francs was jointly laid by several gentlemen against the Count. Information was, however, conveyed to the Count's wife, an Irish lady by birth, and foreseeing the danger her husband would inevitably incur, she armed herself with a brace of pistols, entered the stable, and placing one of them to the horse's head, fired. The animal reared and fell dead, the lady exclaiming, "Thank God, I have done my duty!"

A MISHAP AT ALMACK'S.—Among the many droll incidents which occurred at those elegant balls at Almack's I recollect one which created much amusement among those who witnessed it, at the expense of the person whose name I am about to mention. The late Lord Graves, who was extremely fat, but who danced well for his size, engaged the beautiful Lady Harriet Butler one evening as his partner in a quadrille. Her Ladyship had just arrived from Paris, where she had been brought up under the auspices of Joséphine, and having received lessons in dancing from the celebrated Vestris, she electrified the English with the graceful ease with which she made her *entrechats;* so much so, that a circle was generally formed to admire her dancing. Lord Graves, desirous of doing his utmost to please his fair partner, ventured on imitating the lady's *entrechat;* but in making the attempt, he unluckily fell heavily on the floor. Nothing daunted, however, he got on his legs again and finished the quadrille as well as he could; when his friends hastened to sympathise with him. But Sir John Burke, in a sarcastic manner, said, "What could have induced you, at your age and in your state, to make so great a fool of yourself as to attempt an *entrechat?*" Lord Graves, not relishing the manner in which the Baronet had addressed him, replied, "If you think I am too old to dance, I consider myself not too old to blow your brains out for your impertinence; so the sooner you find a second the better." Lord Sefton, who overheard the conversation, said, "Tut tut tut, man, the sooner you shake hands the better; for the fact is, the world will condemn you both if you fight on such slight grounds: and you, Graves, won't have a leg to stand on." This sensible remark led to the parties shaking hands, and thus the matter dropped.

Sir Astley Cooper.—I recollect meeting this celebrated surgeon in South Wales about thirty years back, when on a visit to some of his friends. I had only returned the day before from Paris, and Sir Astley was very inquisitive about everything I had seen there. He eulogised the French surgeons, but objected to the means employed after amputation; for instead of giving beefsteaks, port wine, and other stimulants, the French surgeons recommended lemonade and *tisanes*, whereby eight patients out of ten died, whereas by the English system only two succumbed out of ten. Nevertheless, he spoke of Dupuytren in the most enthusiastic terms, and acknowledged him to be the most skilful surgeon in Europe. I asked him his opinion of French cookery; he replied, "It suits the French; but it would never do in England; for our men require animal food twice a day, and porter; but the French, from their birth, live upon fruit and vegetables, and their meat is boiled down to rags; this is, however, congenial to their stomachs, and proves that digestion begins in the kitchen."

Our great surgeon, perceiving that I was fond of smoking, cautioned me against that habit, telling me it would sooner or later be the cause of my death. If Sir Astley were now alive he would find everybody with a cigar in his mouth: men smoke now-a-days whilst they are occupied in working or hunting, riding in carriages, or otherwise employed. During the experience of a long life, however, I never knew but one person of whom it was said that smoking was the cause of his death: he was the son of an Irish earl, and an *attaché* at our Embassy in Paris. But, alas, I have known thousands who have been carried off owing to their love of the bottle; ay, some of the noblest and famous men in our land, splendid in youth, strength, and agility. I regret to add, I have met with refined ladies, too, who never went to bed without a little brandy "to drive away the colic."

LADY HOLLAND AND "THE BRIDGE."—When Holland House was the rendezvous of all that was great and illustrious, a gentleman, well known on account of his literary attainments, requested permission from its noble hostess to introduce a friend of his, who had just written a novel which had been well received by the public. Lady Holland, ever happy to do a good-natured act, said, "You may bring him here to-night." The gentleman and his friend accordingly made their appearance that very evening, and were graciously received. On the following day, the introducer called on her ladyship to thank her for the honour she had conferred upon his friend, when she observed, "I can't say much for his good looks, for it was impossible for me to get over the bridge." "What bridge, my Lady?" "Why, the broken bridge of his nose, which has made him the ugliest man I ever saw." "Oh, madam, allow me to state that he was born with that unfortunate defect." "More's the pity, sir; and I conjure you never bring any more of your friends to Holland House who are not blessed with bridges to their noses."

THE BISHOP OF EXETER AND HIS SON.—The Bishop of Exeter, in the course of conversation at a dinner party, mentioned that many years since, while trout-fishing, he lost his watch and chain, which he supposed had been pulled from his pocket by the bough of a tree. Some time afterwards, when staying in the same neighbourhood, he took a stroll by the side of the river, and came to the secluded spot where he supposed he had lost his valuables, and there, to his surprise and delight, he found them under a bush. The anecdote, vouched for by the word of a bishop, astonished the company; but this was changed to amusement by his son's inquiring whether the watch, when found, was going. "No," replied the bishop; "the wonder was that it was not gone."

Lord Deerhurst (afterwards Lord Coventry).—Persons are still living who remember this nobleman hastening down Piccadilly after some pretty girl or other. Lord Deerhurst was distinguished for his good looks and manly bearing; but he always seemed in a hurry: his habits and appearance were in other respects singular, though they did not lessen the respect his rank and abilities deservedly commanded. His wit was proverbial: in short, such were his talents in society, that he was considered a match for Alvanley. Another good trait in his character was the attention he paid to Lord Coventry, who was blind.

His marriage proved a very unhappy one. After living some time with his wife on very bad terms, a separation ensued, which caused him great misery. I recollect, after this occurrence, seeing a letter dated from his father's place in Worcestershire, in which he said, "Here I am at leisure, free to indulge in my grief, and to correct those errors that have brought upon me so much mental suffering," He never completely recovered, and contrived to kill time by travelling from London to his seat in Worcestershire and back, once a week. Before his death poor Deerhurst became excessively irritable, and subsequently insane. He recovered his reason slightly, but died shortly after, attended only by a few trusty servants.

I recollect dining at Madame Vestris's pretty house in St. John's Wood, in company with him, Lords Alvanley and Foley, and Tom Duncombe. Deerhurst was the life and soul of the party; and although there was, of course, a little sparring between him and Alvanley, he was "cock of the walk." He was then in good health and spirits, and conversed easily, and without appearing conscious that he was delighting us all with his witty sayings. Of all the dinners I have been present at, I recollect this as being the most pleasant; it might be called a dinner of dandies, as most of those present belonged to White's, and led the *beau monde* at that period. Of Madame Vestris I can only say, that I never knew any lady more perfectly natural and agreeable in manner and conversation, and she did the honours of her house in admirable style.

MR. NEELD.—Lord Alvanley having been invited to dine in Grosvenor Square, at the house of Mr. Neeld, the heir to Mr. Rundell the wealthy goldsmith, was, previous to sitting down to table, shown some fine pictures which hung on the walls of the drawing-room, together with many articles of *virtù* that crowded the apartment; the host praising and describing each, and stating the cost, in by no means a well-bred manner. One would have thought that the infliction would have been discontinued on entering the dining-room; but, on the guests being seated, Mr. Neeld began excusing himself for not having a haunch of venison for dinner, and assured his guests that a very fine haunch of Welsh mutton had been prepared for them. He then returned to his favourite topic, and began praising the room in which they were dining, and the furniture; he had got to the gilding, which he assured his guests had been done by French artists at an enormous expense, when the mutton made its appearance. Lord Alvanley, who had been intensely bored, exclaimed, "I care not what your gilding cost; but, what is more to the purpose, I am most anxious to make a trial of your carving, Mr. Neeld, for I am excessively hungry, and should like to attack the representative of the haunch of venison."

The *nouveau riche*, though rather astonished by this remark, was obliged to let it pass without notice; his anxiety to form a circle of aristocratic acquaintances preventing his taking offence at anything said by such a person as his Lordship.

Mrs. Beaumont.—There are probably many persons who remember this lady. She was reported to have been of low origin, but inheriting vast estates in the north, and having married a colonel of militia, who became member for the county where her large estates lay, she became one of the leaders of the fashionable world in 1812. From that time to 1820, it was impossible, during the London season, to walk from St. James's Street to

Hyde Park at a certain hour in the afternoon, without seeing her and her daughters in her large yellow landau. Her style of living was most luxurious and full of ostentation. Her preference of a nobleman before a gentleman of no title was shown in a manner that was perfectly ridiculous, and evinced a great want of good sense and tact. Her *fêtes* were thronged with the *grand monde,* and her system of excluding all but persons of rank amused the fashionable world: even men of talent and good family rarely got the *entrée* of her saloons.

This recalls to my mind a rather ludicrous incident. Through the kindness of the Duchess of Marlborough, I was present at one of Mrs. Beaumont's balls, and this led to my being invited to the rest of them during the season. In fine, I became a constant visitor at her house in Portman Square, till one day I ventured to ask for an invitation for a friend of mine, a distinguished officer in the Guards, good-looking, and in every respect fit company for the best saloons. I was of course asked what was his rank; and on my replying that he was a captain in the regiment in which I had the honour to serve, Mrs. Beaumont exclaimed, "I want no more captains at my balls: you should consider yourself lucky in getting an invitation." I bowed and took my leave; and, reflecting on the injustice I had done Mrs. Beaumont in presuming to appear at her assemblies, I never again perpetrated the offence.

Mrs. Beaumont had three sons, two of whom died insane; the other sorely wounded her pride by marrying Miss Atkinson, the daughter of a hatter. When his mother died he succeeded to her large property, and this somewhat turned his head. Like all *parvenus*, he was ambitious of being raised to the peerage; but he threw away the only chance he had, by quarrelling with the only great man likely to forward his views—the celebrated Lord Grey. Mr. Wentworth Beaumont fought a duel with the late Lord Durham, and had to pay his second an annuity for life,—why or wherefore no one could tell. The issue of his marriage was a son, of whom he was very proud. Soon after the birth of his heir, poor Beaumont became in a measure insane; but there was method (or satire) in his madness, for in his last moments he ejaculated, "I cannot say that I have lived for nothing, for my son, besides inheriting my vast fortune, will become the 'Duc de Feltre.'"

In spite of all the anxiety and trouble Mrs. Beaumont had taken in bringing up her daughters, in the hope of their marrying men of exalted rank, she had the mortification of knowing that they had married men of low origin in Italy.

WINDSOR CASTLE IN 1819.—While on duty with my regiment at Windsor in the summer of 1819, I received an invitation to dine at the Equerries' table at the castle, or the "Queen's House," as it was then called, on which occasion I met Lord Liverpool, the Prime Minister, the Archbishop of York, Dr. Baillie, Sir H. Halford, Dr. Heberden, and the "mad Doctor" Willis. These personages had come from London, in virtue of their office, to inquire after the health of the King. I must confess to a feeling of aversion, and even horror, at being placed next the "mad Doctor" at table. He was sallow, ill-looking, and indeed had a most forbidding countenance. He was dressed in black, with silk breeches, white neckcloth, and frill. However, my feelings were soon calmed; for although he never spoke, he seemed to enjoy his dinner, eating and drinking as much as any two persons at table. Dr. Baillie was evidently a great favourite with the Prime Minister and the Archbishop. The equerries present were Generals Garth and Gwynne, both fine gentlemen of the old school, in powder and pigtails.

I once saw George III. walking with his favourite son, the Duke of York, with whom he talked incessantly, repeating his, "Yes, yes, yes, Frederick," in his usual loud voice. His beard was of unusual length, and he stooped very much. He wore the Windsor uniform, with a large cocked hat, something like that with which Frederick the Great is usually represented. The doctors walked behind the King, which seemed greatly to annoy him, as he was constantly looking round. It was said, and I believe with truth, that the poor King could not hear Dr. Willis's name spoken without shuddering. H.R.H. the Duke of Cumberland frequently visited his Royal parents, with his beautiful wife, whose figure at that time was such as few women could boast of.

I cannot pass by an event which caused some scandal at the time. The Duke of Cumberland, on his visits to Windsor, was generally accompanied by his aide-de-camp, Colonel Disney. One day, on the occasion of the Duke's recovery from the wounds received in resisting the murderous attack of his valet, H.R.H. arrived at the Castle to pay his respects to his Royal parents; when, finding that the Queen was walking on the terrace, he hastened to join her Majesty, desiring Colonel Disney to remain in waiting. The Colonel, who was a hare-brained, half-cracked sort of a fellow, finding waiting rather irksome, commenced making a tour through the apartments, and in his peregrinations entered her Majesty's bed-chamber, which was rightly held to be sacred ground. Curiosity led him to inspect the various toilet articles of the Queen, and still further to examine a golden vase, which he put to a use that cannot be named to ears polite. This breach of good manners was detected by the royal housekeeper, the Hon. Miss Townshend, who, with tears in her eyes, reported to the Duke of Cumberland the gross impropriety. His Royal Highness, a proud overbearing man, sought out Disney, and attempted to inflict summary chastisement for the insult he had perpetrated; however, the Colonel evaded the punishment so richly deserved, but he was almost immediately placed on the shelf, and died at his lodgings, in Bury Street, St. James's, heart-broken, on the second anniversary of his thoughtless freak.

A SHOULDER OF MUTTON À LA SOUBISE.—When George IV. passed through Carmarthenshire on his return from Ireland, he remained a day and night at Dynevor Castle, the seat of the nobleman of that name. His Lordship, desirous of entertaining his Majesty in a befitting manner, asked Sir Benjamin Bloomfield what particular dish the King preferred. Sir Benjamin replied, that his Majesty was very fond of a shoulder of mutton boiled with "*sauce soubise.*" Lord D. sent word to that effect to the cook, who, full of vanity and self-conceit, like the majority of Welshmen, did not deign to make the inquiry as to what a "*sauce soubise*" meant. The consequence was that Taffy got into a scrape, for when the shoulder appeared on the dinner-table, the King observing it, said that he had never seen a shoulder of mutton covered with currant-jelly, instead of onion sauce. The Welsh cook was called, and Lord Dynevor asked him what could have induced him to make such an egregious mistake. He replied, that he thought the gentleman (meaning the King) would prefer sweet sauce to that ordered by his Lordship.

ATTEMPT TO ASSASSINATE THE PRINCE REGENT.—An attempt was made to assassinate the Prince Regent when on his way home from the Houses of Parliament in 1819; but it happily failed. In the park, opposite Marlborough House, a bullet was fired from an air-gun by a man concealed in one of the trees, who escaped. This occurred when I was on duty at the Horse Guards, marching across the park with what was commonly called the "Tilt Guard," and I remember it was anything but pleasant to get through the mob of blackguards who were ripe for mischief. The Life Guards, who escorted the Prince Regent, evinced great want of energy on the occasion. The officer commanding the troop, when he saw the danger, should have commanded his men to charge and clear the way. Such was my opinion then; and I am persuaded, from all that I have witnessed abroad since, that the wisest plan upon such occasions, is to take the initiative and act promptly. The fact of this attempt having been made, was doubted at the time by the public at

THE ALLIED SOVEREIGNS ATTENDING A REVIEW IN HYDE PARK, 1814.

DUKE OF WELLINGTON — KING OF PRUSSIA. — PRINCE REGENT (GEORGE IV) — THE EMPEROR OF RUSSIA.

large, but I can speak from my personal knowledge that a shot was fired, and it was aimed at the royal carriage.

Coronation of George IV.—At this gorgeous solemnity it fell to my lot to be on guard on the platform along which the royal procession had to pass, in order to reach the Abbey. The crowd that had congregated in this locality exceeded anything I had ever before seen; struggling, fighting, shrieking, and laughing, were the order of the day among this motley assemblage. Little Townsend, the chief police officer of Bow Street, with his flaxen wig and broad-brimmed hat, was to be seen hurrying from one end of the platform to the other, assuming immense importance. On the approach of the *cortège* you heard this officious person, "dressed with a little brief authority," hallooing with all his might, "Gentlemen and ladies, take care of your pockets, for you are surrounded by thieves;" and hearty laughter responded to Mr. Townsend's salutary advice.

When the procession was seen to approach, and the royal canopy came in sight, those below the platform were straining with all their might to get a peep at the Sovereign, and the confusion at this moment can be better imagined than described. The pick-pockets, of course, had availed themselves of the confusion, and in the twinkling of an eye there were more watches and purses snatched from the pockets of his Majesty's loyal subjects than perhaps on any previous occasion.

Amidst the crowd a respectable gentleman from the Principality hallooed out in his provincial tongue,

"Mr. Townsend, Mr. Townsend, I have been robbed of my gold watch and purse, containing all my money. What am I to do? what am I to do to get home? I have come two hundred miles to see this sight, and instead of receiving satisfaction or hospitality, I am robbed by those cut-throats called 'the swell mob.'" This eloquent speech had a very different effect upon the mob than the poor Welshman had reason to expect; for all of a sudden the refrain of the song of "Sweet Home" was shouted by a thousand voices; and the mob bawled out, "Go back to your goats, my good fellow." The indignities that were heaped upon this unfortunate gentleman during the royal procession, and his appearance after the King had passed, created pity in the minds of all honest persons who witnessed this disgusting scene: his hat was beaten over his eyes, and his coat, neckcloth, &c., were torn off his body. For there were no police in those days; and with the exception of a few constables and some soldiers, there was no force to prevent the metropolis from being burnt to the ground, if it had pleased the mob to have set it on fire.

George IV. and Bishop Porteous. — Lord Brougham, the late lamented Thackeray, and others, have been very severe in their censures on the character of George IV. My readers will perhaps be interested in hearing the following:—Some few years before the death of the King, Dr. Porteous, then Bishop of London, having heard that his Majesty had appointed a review of the Household Troops to take place on a Sunday, ordered his carriage, though he was in a precarious state of health, and waited upon his Majesty at Carlton House. The Bishop was most graciously received, and proceeded to say, "I am come to warn your Majesty of the awful consequences of your breaking the Sabbath, by holding a review on that day which the Almighty has hallowed and set apart for Himself." The King upon this burst into tears, and fell on his knees before the Bishop, who bestowed upon his Majesty his blessing. The King then assured Dr. Porteous that no review should take place on the Sabbath during his life. Bishop Porteous then left the royal presence never more to return; for on arriving at his residence he took to his bed, and died shortly afterwards. The King was so deeply afflicted at the news that, on hearing it, he retired into his own apartments and was heard to sob as one in deep affliction.

LATTER DAYS OF GEORGE IV.—For some months prior to his death, the King abstained from eating animal food, and lived on vegetables and pastry, for which he had a great liking. His conduct, from being that of a sensual, greedy old man, became that of a spoilt child; and the way he spent his time was frivolous in the extreme. He was very fond of punch, made from a recipe by his *maître d'hôtel*, Mr. Maddison, and which he drank after dinner; this was the only time he was agreeable, and on these occasions he would sing songs, relate anecdotes of his youth, and play on the violoncello: afterwards going to bed in a "comfortable" state. But a nervous disorder which affected him prevented his sleeping well, and he invariably rose in the morning in the most unamiable of tempers. Poor man, he was greatly to be pitied; for he was surrounded by a set of harpies, only intent on what they could get out of him, among the most prominent of whom was Lady C * * *, the "English Pompadour." Sir Benjamin Bloomfield was not a favourite with this lady, and, at the first opportunity she found, she caused the King to give him his dismissal; replacing him by a tool of her own, Sir William Knighton.

DEATH AND FUNERAL OF THE DUKE OF YORK.—I perfectly recollect the sorrow felt in London at the death of the Duke of York, and the splendid funeral honours paid to him. The royal Duke died after three or four weeks' suffering from dropsy, in his sixty-fourth year. His administration at the Horse Guards will long be held in remembrance, as beneficial in the highest degree to the British soldier; and such was his popularity, that ministers, statesmen, and general officers followed his remains to the grave. I recollect my late lamented friend, John Scott, telling me that his father, Lord Eldon, spoilt a new hat by placing it on the ground and putting his feet into it to keep them warm; for it was intensely cold weather at the time, and the funeral took place at night. It is certain that a great many persons who took part in the procession caught severe colds from their not having sufficiently wrapped themselves up; and among them was Mr. Canning, who never entirely recovered: he died the same year, in the room at Chiswick where Charles James Fox breathed his last.

COLONEL THE HONOURABLE H. STANHOPE.—Next to the death of the Duke of York, there was no event which pained the Grenadier Guards so much as the untimely death of the Honourable Colonel Stanhope. He had seen much service; served as aide-de-camp to Sir John Moore and to Lord Lynedoch, and distinguished himself greatly at Waterloo. He was the only one of the staff accompanying the Duke of Wellington when the Duke took refuge in our square from the enemy's cavalry, as related in the previous volume.

The sensation the death of Colonel Stanhope created in the public mind was partly due to the melancholy circumstance of his suicide. He had never recovered from the effects of a gun-shot wound he had received at the siege of St. Sebastian, and under the combined influences of pain and nervous depression, he hanged himself in Caen Wood, the property of his father-in-law, the Earl of Mansfield. Besides his merits as a soldier, Colonel Stanhope was a most accomplished scholar and gentleman. In his youth he lived with his uncle, Mr. Pitt, the great minister, and he entered the army at the age of sixteen.

Sir Robert Peel's Hat.—A Welsh Baronet and M.P. entered the shop of Lock & Lincoln, in St. James's Street, to purchase a hat. The foreman could not find one sufficiently large for the Baronet's head, and stated that he only knew one person whose head was so large. "Who is that person?" asked the indignant Welshman. The foreman replied, "It is no other than the great minister, Sir Robert Peel." "Oh! oh!" exclaimed Taffy, "you make hats for that Radical, do you? Well, then, it shall never be said that you have sold me a hat. I have a horror of such men as your great ministers."

And the Baronet left the shop in dudgeon, much to the wonder and astonishment of the hatter.

AN IRISH WELCOME.—During Sir Robert Peel's administration, Lord St. Germains, who had been absent from his post on a visit to London, on returning to Dublin as Viceroy, was greeted at the railway station by some one in the crowd shouting, "'Tis glad we are to see your Honour back again amongst us!" This compliment having been gracefully acknowledged by a bow from his Lordship, the same voice was heard making the delicate inquiry, "But has your Honour taken a return ticket?"—a witty allusion to the instability of the ministry at the time, and a significant qualification of the original greeting.

THE PRINCE DE POIX.—During the reign of Charles X., the soldiers on duty at the garden gates of the Tuileries received strict orders to allow no one to enter. One day, however, a person of distinguished mien endeavoured to pass by one of the sentinels, who told him to go back, at the same time stating the orders that had been issued. "But," replied the intruder, "do you know who I am? I am the Prince de Poix, aide-de-camp to the King." "*Eh, sacre!*" was the answer of the soldier, "*quand vous seriez le roi des haricots vous ne passerez pas.*"

LADY NORMANBY'S BALL AT THE BRITISH EMBASSY, PARIS.—Lady Normanby once gave a brilliant *fête* in honour of the Duke and Duchess d'Aumale. In the entrance hall of the Embassy were ranged twelve footmen in splendid liveries; the landing was a *bosquet* of rose trees, flowers filled the drawing-rooms, and enormous *jardinières* were placed in every direction; the garden walks were covered with carpets, and furnished with sofas, and a gorgeous marquee for dancing was erected in the garden. The company was composed of the *élite* of society, and the most beautiful women England could boast of were present; much to the chagrin of the Parisians, whose admiration of the Englishwomen was intense, but mixed with envy. The supper was exquisite; and as there were not seats enough for all the company at once, it was arranged that none but ladies should sit, and consequently the men stood behind their partners during the repast. Notwithstanding this arrangement, our Ambassadress observed a noble marquis seated in conversation with a person with whom she was unacquainted. She asked somebody to inquire the stranger's name, &c., and the noble Lord replied, "I don't know him; but no doubt he is acquainted with Lady Normanby, or he would not be here." Her Ladyship having received this answer, stated that she had never seen him before, and requested the master of the ceremonies to demand his name. He accordingly accosted the intruder, who gave his card, on which was inscribed "The Baron Deldique." It was, however, subsequently discovered that this man was an impostor, and in the habit of attending balls without being known to either the host or any of the company.

LOUIS PHILIPPE'S SONS AT A MASKED BALL.—I witnessed a strange sight at one of the masked balls at the opera in Paris. A young man of herculean strength had intruded himself among a party of dancers in a quadrille, and laid violent hands on a young lady already engaged. The gentlemen of the party flew to the rescue, and for a few minutes all was confusion; but four or five of the secret police presently appeared on the scene, and arrested the cause of the disturbance. I was surprised to observe that none of the other persons engaged in the disturbance were molested, but allowed to dance as if nothing had occurred, and on quitting the ball I determined to unravel the secret. After some trouble, I found that the party was composed of the sons of Louis Philippe and some of their friends, who were completely metamorphosed by the aid of false wigs, &c.

On my mentioning the circumstance to a friend of mine, Count D * * *, he said that they often disguised themselves, and appeared thus in public; and that one day during the preceding summer, after dining with them at Chantilly, the Duke de Nemours proposed a stroll, and taking out of his pocket his false wig and whiskers, said, "You, sir, have no occasion to disguise yourself; but as it fell to my lot to be the son of a king, I am obliged to have recourse to disguise and strategy from morning till night."

Count Talleyrand Périgord's Private Theatricals.—Among the many ludicrous incidents that occurred during the reign of Louis XVIII., I recollect the following:—The Count Talleyrand Périgord having been appointed Ambassador—or, more properly speaking, minister—at Berne, determined to amuse his friends with theatrical representations; accordingly his dining-room was arranged with side-scenes, drop-scenes, and all the stage requisites, and he invited the dignitaries of Berne to witness the opening of his little theatre. The Count intended to have represented the part of a miller, and therefore ordered his *valet de chambre* to take off his coat, and to bring him some flour from the kitchen, with which to cover himself in a manner that would make the disguise appear natural. The valet obeyed his master's instructions to the letter, and, begging the Count to shut his eyes and remain motionless during the operation, the servant emptied the contents of a box of flour over his master's head. At that moment a courier arrived with the news that the Emperor Napoleon had disembarked at Fréjus. This intelligence excited the diplomate to that degree that he flew out of the house, with the intention of calling upon the English minister to know whether he had received any tidings of the kind. The strange appearance in the streets of the Count covered with flour, occasioned a commotion in the quiet town of Berne. Men, women, and children followed the French minister, crying out, "Take care of him, for he is mad." In a word, it was with difficulty he got back to his hotel, where he found the company assembled and waiting for the performance which had been promised; but, alas! the nerves of the Count were so terribly disturbed that he relinquished the idea of enacting the part of the miller.

PRINCE TALLEYRAND'S OPINION OF THE DUKE OF WELLINGTON.—There are some personages who seem to gain, and others who lose, dignity and importance, when the achievements by which they acquired honours and fame are recorded in biography. The name of Wellington, by universal consent, heads the list of military commanders: he is not more distinguished for his military genius than for his sagacity and judgment. The late Prince Talleyrand, being at a dinner in London, soon after the French Revolution in 1830, was asked his opinion of the Duke of Wellington. The Prince replied :—"First, I must tell you that when the Duke of Wellington came to Paris in 1814 as English Ambassador, I was then Minister of Foreign Affairs. The skill the Duke displayed as a diplomatist was astonishing. He never indulged in that parade of mystification which is generally employed by ambassadors: watchfulness, prudence, and experience of human nature, were the only means he employed; and it is not surprising that, by the use of these simple agencies, he acquired great influence over those with whom he was brought into contact.

"When the Emperor Napoleon returned from Elba, the Duke went to Vienna, where we (that is, the ambassadors and ministers of nearly every court of Europe) had been congregated for the last six months. On the Duke's arrival, his first question was, 'What have you done, gentlemen?' Prince Metternich replied, 'Nothing; absolutely nothing.' The Duke listened to what every one had to say, with his usual unassuming and nonchalant air; but it was evident that, while he seemed astounded at times at what he heard, he was exercising his great powers of observation and reflection. Determined not to lose a moment, he put his shoulders to the wheel, and the machinery, which had before moved so slowly, was at once put in rapid motion: in the incredibly short period of three days everything was arranged and finished, to the wonder and satisfaction of all his colleagues.

"After the battle of Waterloo, the illustrious Duke returned to Paris, where he had frequent opportunities of communicating with me, and, on the return of the King, I occupied my old post, that of Minister for Foreign Affairs. I was then more than ever convinced that the man who had fathomed the designs of all the cabinets of Europe was an extraordinary statesman. I discovered that, while others found everything impracticable which was proposed to them, Wellington appeared never to discover a difficulty. In a word, gentlemen, if we consider him in all his relations, public and private, it can safely be said that the Duke of Wellington is the greatest man that England, or any other country, ever produced."

MOTS OF TALLEYRAND.—General Count de Girardin had a most ugly squint and was extremely inquisitive. Upon one occasion, he asked Talleyrand, "*Comment vont les affaires, Prince?*" "*Comme vous voyez, Général; tout de travers.*"

Fontaine, the architect, who built the triumphal arch in the Carrousel, placed upon it an empty car, drawn by the famous bronze Venetian horses. Talleyrand asked him, "*Qui avez vous l'intention de mettre dans le char?*" The answer was, "*L'Empereur Napoléon, comme de raison,*" upon which Talleyrand said, "*Le char l'attend.*"

General Flahault, who when young was bald,

had received an invitation to dine with the Prince de Talleyrand. In the course of conversation, he expressed to the Prince a desire to present something rare to a great lady as a mark of his esteem. Talleyrand replied, "Then present her with a lock of your hair."

THE EMPEROR NICHOLAS AT THE HAGUE.—On the occasion of the late Emperor of Russia's last visit to England, he returned home *viâ* The Hague, for the purpose of paying a visit to his relative the King of Holland. During the few days the Czar remained there, a levee was held by the King, in order that his Imperial Majesty might have an opportunity of seeing the flower of the Dutch aristocracy. Among those present, the Emperor singled out a remarkably tall but well-built man, who was considered the handsomest fellow in Holland, the Baron Capellen, whose right arm had been amputated, owing to a wound received in a duel. The Emperor, little imagining how the limb had been lost, approached the Baron, and inquired in what battle he had had the misfortune of losing his arm. "I lost it in a duel, your Majesty," was the cool reply. The Emperor, without a word, turned upon his heel, and said afterwards to one of his friends, "It is a pity so fine a fellow should have been sacrificed: he had better have been killed in battle."

THE PRINCE DE LIGNE.—I had the honour of being invited by the Prince de Ligne to his country seat, Bel' Œil, one of the most magnificent mansions I ever saw. In looking over the old portraits of this princely family, the Prince jocularly observed,

SOUVENIRS OF THE ARMY OF OCCUPATION IN PARIS, 1815.

ENGLISH UNIFORMS FROM A FRENCH POINT OF VIEW.

"You have few old families in England: in other words, your nobility are mostly of modern date; but no one will contest that you have no Lords, for they are created by every minister who holds the helm."

Speaking of the manners we English indulge in towards foreigners, the Prince told me the following anecdote:—"I was sent by the King of the Belgians to London, as Ambassador Extraordinary, to congratulate your Queen on her accession to the throne. During the period of my sojourn at your Court, diplomatic dinners were given daily. It happened that upon one occasion I was asked a question as to the state of the Belgian army, when a noble Lord, a *ci-devant* ambassador, without the slightest provocation, made a very offensive remark to me. I instantly left the dinner-table to consult a friend as to what steps ought to be taken to resent the insult offered; but, after thinking the matter over, it was considered the act of a madman, and therefore, to prevent scandal, and the creation of a bad feeling between the English and the Belgians, the affair was allowed to drop."

It is much to be regretted that we English are even now in the habit of regarding all foreigners in an unfavourable light. The vulgar brag that any John Bull is a match for three Frenchmen, and other extravagances of a similar description, are becoming obsolete; but English tourists are still apt to disparage foreigners, and entertain the notion that when we set foot on the Continent, a system of cheating and extortion commences. These and similar prejudices, arising from ignorance of the language and usages of foreign nations, naturally create a bad feeling towards England and Englishmen. Foreigners say, and not without justice, that we are pre-eminently self-conceited, boastful, and proud.

Pride of a Spanish Grandee.—The Marquis of St. Jago, a young Grandee of Spain, was at one time the theme of conversation in Paris, owing to his eccentric habits and the dissolute manner in which he lived. Although well born, and sufficiently educated to be selected to accompany the Spanish Ambassador to England on the occasion of our gracious Queen's Coronation, he possessed an unparalleled fondness for dissipation, and an extensive acquaintance with the class of flatterers. Moreover, an absurd idea as to his pretensions to rank induced him to wear the ribbon of the French Cross of the Legion of Honour, and although "chaffed" about it, he continued to do so; until one day, at the Jockey Club, some one present flatly told him that he had no right whatever to the decoration then in his buttonhole: which was true. This public rebuke proved such a stunning blow to the pride of St. Jago, that he returned to Madrid broken-hearted, and died there at the early age of thirty.

The Emperor's Extra Equerry.—Some persons will have perceived with surprise that an Englishman, moving in good society, should have consented to receive the appointment of extra equerry to the Emperor of the French. The occasion of his being installed into that office was as follows:—The gentleman in question had, when at Rome, shown some civility to Prince Louis Napoléon. The gossip of the day ran, that on the Prince's elevation to the purple, some one meeting our countryman coming out of the imperial stables, recommended him to ask for General Fleury's post, as he was better qualified for an equerry than that gallant General. Our countryman, taking the hint, promptly solicited an audience of the Emperor, which being granted, he coolly made the surprising application that had been suggested to him. The Emperor endeavoured blandly to silence the aspirant to stable honours, by reminding him that he was an Englishman; but added, "If, sir, you are really in earnest, I will name you one of my extra equerries." And this offer was gratefully accepted by the gentleman in question. *Tempora mutantur!*

THE DUKE OF WELLINGTON AND LORD STRANGFORD.—Not long before the death of the Duke of Wellington, the late Lord Strangford, on his return from Paris, was invited by the Duke to pass a few days at Walmer Castle. His Grace inquired whether, during his sojourn in the French capital, he had seen Lord Hertford; upon which Lord Strangford replied he belonged to the same club, where they frequently met. "Ah!" added the Duke, "Lord Hertford is a man of extraordinary talents. He deserves to be classed among those men who possess transcendent abilities. What a pity it is that he does not live more in England, and occupy his place in the House of Lords. It was only the other day," added the Duke, "that Sir Robert Peel observed, when speaking of Hertford, that he was a man of great comprehension; not only versed in the sciences, but able to animate his mass of knowledge by a bright and active imagination. In a word, if he had lived in London, instead of frittering away his time in Paris, he would have no doubt become Prime Minister of England."

Marshal Magnan's Opinion of British Soldiers.—Soon after the *Coup d'État*, it fell to my lot to hear Marshal Magnan state, in the presence of several persons who expressed a doubt of the efficiency of the British army, that he had been in the Peninsula in 1813 and 1814, and in eleven battles, but never saw the back of the British soldier. This announcement, on the part of a Frenchman high in command, who had seen real service, completely silenced his garrulous countrymen.

Marshal Canrobert Reviewing the British Army.—At Compiègne, some two or three years back, Marshal Canrobert related a fact which redounded to his credit. At a review of the British army in the Crimea, the Duke of Cambridge, who was to have inspected the troops, observing the French Marshal approaching with his staff, requested him to assist, and to take the right; whereupon the Marshal acquiesced. When they came to the drooping of the colours, Canrobert's blood thrilled in his veins at seeing the names of several of our victories over the French; however, having undertaken the task of reviewing our troops, he accomplished the arduous and painful duty imposed upon him, and went down the line without evincing the slightest emotion. When he related this incident there were several general officers present, some of whom ventured to expostulate. The Marshal said, "There is no use in expostulating and endeavouring to conceal the fact; but those victories inscribed upon the colours were won by the British troops against us."

A Ready Retort.—C. de M * * *, one of the most fashionable, at the same time one of the cleverest, young men of the Restoration, had the singular taste of being in love with two ladies each old enough to be his mother—the one a duchess, the other a celebrated actress. When the Duchesse de Berri asked him whether it was really true that his taste was for old women, he replied, "*Oui, Madame, je suis l'homme du siècle.*"

An Act of Charity.—Not many years back, on a cold winter's day, an eccentric Baronet was in the shop of Mr. Mitchell in Bond Street, where a few friends of his used to congregate to pick up the news of the day. On this occasion, the Baronet was boasting of his munificence, when in came Colonel de B * * * of the Guards, and addressing him said, "My dear S * * *, I have just left our poor friend, Jack S * * *, in a spunging-house without a shilling in his pocket to pay for a mutton chop." "Is it possible?" exclaimed our eccentric friend. "I will go and order something for the poor fellow which shall make his heart glad." And saying this he jumped into his cab, which was waiting at the door. Colonel de B * * * lost no time in calling on the poor debtor, and told him he was in luck, as S * * * had promised to do something for him. In a short time our charitable Baronet arrived at the spunging-house, bringing—not the good things that a man needs in such a predicament—but a pottle of strawberries, which he boasted he had given two sovereigns for!

MADAME ALBONI.—About twelve years ago the inimitable Alboni, having finished her engagement at the Théâtre des Italiens, Paris, entered into one with the manager of the Opera at Nantes, to sing there and at the watering-places adjacent. She left Paris dressed, as usual, in male attire, accompanied by a lady who passed as the wife. During the first week after their arrival at Nantes, they lived in furnished lodgings on the Place Royale, and thought of nothing but the piano and their scales; the incomparable singer attracting the other occupants of the house to the landing-place, ever and anon, by the power of her splendid voice. One day, something occurred which created a misunderstanding between Alboni and her friend: from high and violent words they came to blows, and a neat "backhander" of Alboni's on the other's nose caused blood to flow. The injured lady ran downstairs, and implored the porter to go for a surgeon; but the man, alarmed for the respectability of the house, instead of obeying, went to the police and informed them what had occurred. On his returning with two policemen, Alboni and her friend were found in hysterics; nevertheless, they were hurried off, more dead than alive, to the police office.

When the Commissary began to interrogate the lady with the bloody nose as to the origin of their quarrel and other particulars, Alboni stepped forward, and addressing the man in authority, explained that they began to quarrel about a note in a song in "La Gazza Ladra," which opera was to be given that evening. The Commissary, wondering what it all meant, asked their names, which were given by the ladies, and Alboni implored him to release them with as little delay as possible, as she had scarcely time left to dress for the theatre. The Commissary took the ladies by the hand, and conducted them to the door, saying that he was extremely sorry that his agents had acted in so precipitate a manner as to bring through the public streets two ladies of such standing, without first ascertaining that there were good reasons for their being arrested. Alboni bowed, and said she hoped to see the officer that night on the stage. The invitation was readily accepted; and when the vocalist perceived him at the conclusion of the opera, she flung her arms round his neck, to the astonishment of all present.

THE DERBY OF 1865 AND FRENCH RACING.—The victory gained on the 31st May 1865, on Epsom Downs, by what is technically known as the "French stable," is a proof what good blood, careful training, and good living, under the superintendence of English trainers and stable-boys and a "captain" like Grimshaw, can do for such a specimen of horseflesh as "Gladiateur;" whose pretensions to being French consist in just this, that his sire was born in France, together with his dam: but their pedigrees run through the very purest blood of English racehorses. His owner, the Comte de Lagrange, well deserves the success which has crowned his perseverance in turf matters.

Unfortunately, the French will not understand

what sport really is, in the generally received acceptation of the term in England. At a French race, nine-tenths of the men go there merely because it is fashionable, and because it is a more exciting way of killing time than sitting in a club reading the newspapers; and as for the women, it is an opportunity for showing off a "fast," but, be it confessed, a becoming toilet, and thus it becomes an attraction irresistible to a Frenchwoman. Of the true spirit of the affair the French comprehend not one iota.

Since the introduction of racing into France by Sir Charles Smith,—when the races run in the Champ de Mars were more often won by the mounted police, who accompanied the horses from the start to the finish, than by the beautiful specimens of "thoroughbreds" that were then imported,—the breeding of "blood stock" has occupied the attention of many Frenchmen, and has been attended with no small success; for not only have our neighbours procured from us our purest bred stallions and mares, but they have secured the services of English trainers and jockeys: upon whom they will have to depend for many, many years to come.

INDEX.

THE END.

LIST OF SUBSCRIBERS UP TO 15th JULY 1985

Michael J. Abberton
J.S. Abbott
Robin Addison
Major J.W. Aggleton MBE
J.A. Allen
J.H. Allen
James Allen
J.R. Allt
Mrs. M.R. Ambrose
Miss Diane Andrews
G.F. Arnold
Lt. Col. R.M. Arnold
D.A. Ashley
P.R. Ashley
Mrs. M. Atkinson

D.F. Bailey
W.G. Baister
Mrs. R.W.S. Baker
Col. & Mrs. Glenn O. Baker
H.A.S. Bancroft
John Barker
Lt. Col. B.A.S Barnes
F.J. Barratt
A.G.S. Barstow
H.R. Barton
Paul Bass
W.G. Bate
Anwer Bati
J.R. Beaumont JP DL
Walter Bee
Diana Lady Beith
Nicholas John Belcher
William Bell
J.B. Bell
J. Bellchamber RMPA
F.G. Bendell
Mrs. G. De V. Beveridge
J.R. Bickford Smith
Major K.R. Mck Biggs
R.J. Bird
Drayton Bird
Dr. Bernard Black
The Rev. F.A. Black
His Hon. Judge Blackett-Ord
Peter Blacklock
G.H. Blair
A.H. Boddy
James T. Bowie
L.F. Bowyer
Dr. O.B. Brears OBE
R.P. Brett
J.A. Brew
Mrs. Richard Bridges
Major J.L. Bridges
Dr. D.A. Brigg
D.C. Bright
Frank Brightman
G.C.V. Brittain
Sir Ronald Brockman
C.K. Brown
J.F. Brown
Mrs. P.M. Brown
N.S.F. Browne
The Hon. James Bruce
Nigel W. Buchanan
John S. Burgess
T.F.J. Burland
Lieut. A.G. Burns RN
Dermot S.L. Butler
K.F. Butler

A.O.F. Caddick
G.A. Calver
L.R. Campfield
R.J. Canning
Major J.S. Carter
Mrs. Roger Cass
Mrs. E.L. Catto
Mrs. Eileen Cawkwell
Lord Charles Cecil
D.J. Challen
Michael Charles
Mrs. B. Chetwynd-Stapylton
J.R. Clack
D.L. Clarke
B.R.D. Clarke
F. Clegg
H.L. Coatalen
M.A. Coates
Mrs. V.E. Coates
A.C.T. Cochrane
The Hon. R.H.V. Cochrane DL
J.W.G. Cocke
Robert Coggins
C.J. Collingwood
Richard A. Collinssplatt
Mrs. S.P. Conan-Davies
Capt. I.S.M. Condie
Prof. Carl B. Cone
M.L. Congdon
F.A. Connelly
J.C. Conner
Terence Cooke
W.H. Cooper
Anthony Cooper
Michael F. Corbett
M.D. Corke
M.H. Couchman
B.R. Couzens
T.J.L. Cox
H.P. Craig
J. Creek
Miss G.E. Cresswell
M.G. Cripps
Miss M. Crookes
J.P.O. Crowe
C.C. Cumming
G. Cuttle

T.L.A. Daintith
J.C.P. Dalton
John H. Daniels
Major D.C. Darley
Mrs. J.A. Davis
Simon Daw

J. Dawkes
Elizabeth Janet Dawkes
Lt. Col. C.P. Dawnay CBE MVO
Mrs. H.L.R. Day
C.V.W. De Falbe
Max De Trense
Mrs. A.D. Deacon
Martyn J. Dearden
E. Dearing
Rowland P. Dell
Simon Dell
Lord Denham
John Devaux
Matthew Dobbs
Dr. William Dodd
Flt. Lt. R.C.T. Dorsett
Viscount Downe
P.J. Downs
J.E.S. Driver
H.I. Duck
P.G. Durrans
Daniel J. Dwyer

Major F.M. Edwards
P.S.A. Edwards
Frank Ellis
M.G. Esther
M.R. Etherton
J.H. Etherton
Commander Raymond Evans RN
L.J.C. Evans
J.M. Evans

Dr. J. Hamilton Fairley
J.C. Fareham
T.C. Farmbrough
Miss C.A. Farnon
Major A. Farrant
J.E. Farrer
R.W. Fielding
R.A.J. Finn
J.M. Fison
G.J. Fletcher
Mrs. S. Ford-Hunter
Dr. C.A. Foster
Mrs. D.J. Foster
Charles Fox
K.M. Fox
Miss M.M. Fraser-Roberts
Mrs. R. Fremantle
J.C. Fuller

R. De V. Gaisford
A.F. Garnett
N.A. Gatrell
N. George
Mrs. R.I. Gilchrist
His Hon. Judge S.S. Gill
Richard Gilman MD FACS
Leslie Gobey
Anthony Goddard
Captain W.E.B. Godsal RN
Lt. Col. D.H. Godsal
C.A. Gold
Mrs. H.B. Goldsmid
J.G. Goldsworth
G.B. Graham
Mrs. Allen J. Greenough
Robin E. Greenwood
Capt. J.S. Greenwood
G.S. Griffiths
His Hon. Judge B. Griffiths QC
John D. Grossart
A.D. Gunner
Brig. C.R.L. Guthrie MVO OBE
P.L. Guy MH

Darby Haddon
Mrs. P.R. Hadfield
J. Hafok
A.D.A.S. Hall
Mrs. A.B. Hall
J.R. Hall
The Hon. Mrs. E.A. Hamilton
Cecil Hamilton-Miller
G.W. Hamlyn CBE
Daniel Hanbury
C.D. Hankes-Drielsma
J.I. Hardwick
Mrs. Rita F. Harris
C.E. Harrison
Lt. Col. J.A. Harrison
Major General L.A.D. Harrod
Dr. Nicholas Hart
Charles Harvey
Count J. Havenaar Kazimirski
Joseph Hawes
P.W. Hawkes
Derek Hayes
Sir Claude Hayes KCMG
I.S. Haynes MFH
Jiro Hazama
Sir Francis Head BT
John Heald
S/Leader N.V.O.P. Healey
John E. Heath
T.R.W. Heneage
A. Herriott
E.C. Hicks
P.M. Hicks
S. De Premorel Higgons
C.J. Highton
Peter Hiley
F.B. Hill
G.E.D. Hiller
J.R. Hinchliffe
Miss J. Hirschfeld
M.R. Hoare
Lady Christina Hoare

A.R.A. Hobson
T. Hodson
Mrs. C.W. Holden
W. Holt
John Hope
Mr. & Mrs. R.W.J. Hopkins
G.W Hopkinson
Mrs. S. Horgan
Mrs. G.R. Horsfall
W. & A. Houben Booksellers
Capt. M.A. Houghton
Gordon Howard
D. Howcroft
F.G. Howell
Miss Wendy Howes
P.B. Hunter
I.W.M. Hurst MFH
T.F. Hutchinson
G. Hyland

Col. F.J. Ingham
G.W. Iredell
H.B. Ismay Cheape

Mrs. J.M. Jachim
L.A. Jackson
D.M. Jarvis
David Jeffcoat
C.P. Jenner MH
Mrs. P.A. Jerram
N.M. Johns
Simon Johnson
B.J. Johnson
Colonel J.F.J. Johnston
J.P. Johnson
H. Thompson Jones

L.S. Kale
Mrs. E.C.W. Kaye
Michael Leo Keane
J.E. Kelly
Francis Kelly
Dr. A.J.I. Kelynack
J. Kenneth
F.C. Kent
Dr. D.F. Kerr
Alistair W.J. Kerr
T.W. Killick
Andrew Kirby
Dr. Mary Ellen Kitler
D.A. Knight
Michael Knight
Martin Kochanski
J.M. Kolbert
H.P. Kos
Miss T. Kynaston-Jones

L.P.F. L'Estrange OBE
E.A.S. La Croix
R.E. Lambert
Miss I.M. Lamont
R.J.O. Lascelles
Arvin Law
Clare Le Vay
M.S. Ledger MOH
His Hon. Judge C.N. Lees
G.C.M. Leggett
Frank Lehmann
J.W.P. Lewis
H.M. Liddell
G.M. Lilly
Sir Anthony Lincoln KCMG CVO
Dr. Charles Lipp
William Lister
John Lockie
G.A. Longbottom
T. Longuet-Higgins
John Lonnen
The Hon. Mrs. Anthony Luard
P.M. Luttman-Johnson
R.J. Lyle

His Hon. Judge G. Macdonald
A.M. Macewan
Lt. Col. C.H.T. Macfetridge
The Rev. Hugh Mackay
S.C.R. Mackean
J.H.M. Mackenzie
J.A.H.M. Mackenzie
Capt. M.J. Mackinlay Macleod
B.E. Maclean-Eltham
Mrs. Macleod
Miss S. Macmillan
J.J. Macnamara
R.N. Alington Maguire
Miss J.M. Mahony
Stephen Mahony
Capt. Dugald Malcolm
Mrs Ann Mansel
William G. Martin
Major H.D.G. Martindale
Dr. Martyn-Johns
Peter I. Maslen
R.J. Mason
T.S. Matthews
H. Maynard
John McCaig
Denis J. McCarthy
Dr. Ewen McEwen
Dr. D.J. McGlynn
Brian McGregor
W.A. McIntosh
Mrs. Sheila McKinley
M.A. Meacham
Paul Mellon
The Lord Middleton
Col. D.A.N.C. Miers
A.P. Millen
C.H. Millin
D. Mitchell
E.G.H. Moody
Mrs. J.D. Moore

David Jonas Morgan
I.J. Morgan
G.E. Morris
Maxwell Morris
H.E. Morten
Sir William Mount BT
Mrs. A.M. Mumford

Mrs. S.J. Nash
David Negus FRCS
D.E.A. Neville
C.S.W. Newbury
Brian Newton
M.T. Nicholson
R. Le N. Noble
J.N.F. Norman
A.H.W.P. Norton

Edward O'Doherty
Roseanne O'Reilly
D. O'Halloran

Col. N.H. Pakenham Mahon
Anthony V. Parker
H.M. Parker
John Gordon Parker
Mrs. C.H. Parlby
Jonathan R.H. Pearson
Mervyn R.C. Peckham
R.S.L. Penn
His Hon. Judge David Pennant
R.W. Perceval
D.J. Peters JP MA
Mrs. V.M. Pettifer
Dr. A.J.B. Phillips MB BS
A.O. Piggott
Frank Pitt
The Hon. R.W. Pomeroy
Mrs. Pooley
Dr. Vincent Powell-Smith

Col. R.F. Preston
Lt. Col. J.C. Preston
Dr. H. Preston-Thomas
J. Maurice Price QC
A.T. Prince
Mrs. A.J. Prior-Willeard
Timothy Proctor

Dr. T.J. Quaite

Maj. Gen. Sir Digby Raeburn
J.H. Ratcliff
Peter Read
P.F. Rednall
P.J.D. Regester
Dr. Robert Reid
N.J. Reid
W.F. Rendall
Dr. R.E. Rewell
W.S.C. Richards
Sir Charles Richmond Brown
Andrew W.G. Rickett
Capt. N.J. Ridout
T.J. Roberts
J.C. Robertson CBE
Wg/Cdr. S. Robinson RAF (rtd)
B.E. Robinson
E.P.S. Rogers
D.R. Rosevear
C.M. Ross
The Lord Rothermere
Pamela Rowe
Ronald A. Russell
J.F. Rutherford

Captain R.P.A. Sale
John N. Savory
Capt. O.N.G. Scholte
Lt. Col. S.R.G. Scott
Dr. J.P. Scrivener
J.C. Sedgwick
Antony Sefi
J.A. Seymour-Jones FRCS
M.M. Shannon
M.E. Sharp
Dr. J.C.H. Shaw
A.J. Shears
N.E.C. Sherwood
Mrs. F.R. Short
Stuart Sillars
E.G. Silvester
C.A.G. Simkins
P.F.J. Simms
M.K.O. Simpson-Orlebar
A. Singer
Douglas A. Sloan MFH
Michael J. Smith
N.L.H. Smith
Bombadier M.B. Smith
S.T. Smyth
Mrs. I.J. Barclay Sole
Sir John Sparrow
Major B.L. Speegle
J.D. Spicer
Mrs. P. Spiller
Mrs. A.B. Spiro
The Hon. Mrs. Stacey
Mrs. M.D. Stacy-Marks
Mrs. Stainow
H.J.A. Stanford
J.G. Stanford
E.W. Stearn
T.F.G. Stevens
Charles Walter Stewart
J.R. Strong FRCS
Dr. F.S. Stych
P.A. Surtees
Dr. R.N.P. Sutton
Susan Swantek

Sir Ronald Swayne
Mrs. Annette Syder
A. Symonds

Elizabeth Talbot-Rice
Alec I. Taylor
E. Hugh Thomas
P.C.F. Thomas
Edward Thompson
Ray Thompson
R.D. Thomson
Miss D.G. Thomson
Brig. M.C. Thursby Pelham
Eric A. Tidy
E.H. Tindall
Maj. Gen. D.A.H. Toler
H.W. Townsend
J.J. Trapp
D.W. Tudor-Pole
T.S. Turnbull
S.J.E. Turner
C.H. Tutton
R.C. Tyrrell

D.B. Vale
S. Van Praet D'Amerloo
William Von Raab

Michael Wace
T. Wainwright
J.H. Walker
Mrs. Owen Walker
Major P.J.R. Waller MBE DL
B.J. Wallis
W.J.F. Ward
David W. Wates MFH
R.K. Watson
I.H. Wear
The Rev. W.P. Webb
G. Westall
Col. L.H.M. Westropp
E. Davan Wetton CBE
George A. Wheatley
Edmund H. White
Rupert White
A.P. Whitehead
J.C.A. Whitworth
K.V. Wickes
J.G.S. Wilkinson
John Williams
Lt. Col. G.T.G. Williams
A.F.F. Williamson
John Winch
K.R. Wing
Mrs. Wolrige-Gordon of Esslemont
Harry Wolton QC
Douglas J. Wood
F.A. Woods
J.H.G. Woollcombe
Mrs. David Wright
W.D. Wright
Dr. R.F. Wyatt
C.P. Wykeham-Martin
Rhydain Wynn-Williams

John H. Yarroll

IN MR. KNOX'S COUNTRY

by E. Œ. Somerville and Martin Ross

In the last of the *Irish R.M.* trilogy, whose title commemorates Mr. Flurry Knox M.F.H., Major Sinclair Yeates R.M. continues to recount his experiences. They are as laughable as ever, although in one or two the possibility of tragedy arises. The authors' skill in the construction of plots is at its peak. *In Mr. Knox's Country* was their last book before the death of Martin Ross.

The R.S. Surtees Society's edition is a facsimile of the first (1915) edition of *In Mr. Knox's Country*. Its format is similar to, though not exactly the same as, *Some Experiences* and *Further Experiences of an Irish R.M.* It includes the 8 full-page black and white illustrations by **Miss Somerville** which appeared in the first edition.

Molly Keane, who wrote the best-seller *Good Behaviour* and has lived most of her life in Southern Ireland, has written an Introduction.

Price **£7.00,** including packing and postage, until 1st December, 1985. Thereafter **£7.95.**

SOME EXPERIENCES and FURTHER EXPERIENCES OF AN IRISH R.M.

by E. Œ. Somerville and Martin Ross

Some Experiences and *Further Experiences* each contain twelve episodes in which Major Sinclair Yeates recounts, with sober dignity, humour and tolerance, his social, sporting and professional discomfitures as a Resident Magistrate in South-West Ireland at the turn of the century. The rhetoric and deceit of the natives provide the wit and drama. Circumstances make Major Yeates a connoisseur of whole-hearted insincerity.

The R.S. Surtees Society's editions of *Some Experiences* and *Further Experiences* are as nearly as practicable facsimilies of the first editions, of 1899 and 1908 respectively. They include the black and white illustrations by **Miss Somerville** from the first editions (30 in *Some Experiences* and 35 in *Further Experiences*).

Price **£7.95,** in each case, packing and postage included.

SET OF THREE

The price of a set of *In Mr. Knox's Country, Some Experiences* and *Further Experiences of an Irish R.M.* is **£21,** including packing and postage.

Ordering

Send your order to The Hon. Mrs. Robert Pomeroy, Rockfield House, Nunney, nr. Frome, Somerset. Your cheque should be made payable to "The R.S. Surtees Society".